MW00331317

CITATION

CITATION

In a Class by Himself

PHIL GEORGEFF

FOREWORD BY	INTRODUCTION BY
TOMMY TROTTER	ELMER POLZIN

TAYLOR TRADE PUBLISHING

LANHAM • NEW YORK • OXFORD

Published by Taylor Trade Publishing
A Member of the Rowman & Littlefield Publishing Group
4501 Forbes Boulevard, Suite 200
Lanham, Maryland 20706

Distributed by National Book Network

Library of Congress Cataloging-in-Publication Data

Georgeff, Phil.
    Citation : in a class by himself / Phil Georgeff.
        p. cm.
Includes bibliographical references (p.   ).
    ISBN 0-87833-292-8 (cloth : alk. paper)
    1. Citation (Race horse) 2. Race horses—United States—Biography.
I. Title.
    SF355 .C58 G46 2003
    798 .4'0092'9—dc21

                                                             2002015052

™ The paper used in this publication meets the minimum requirements
of American National Standard for Information Sciences—Permanence of Paper for
Printed Library Materials, ANSI/NISO Z39.48–1992.
Manufactured in the United States of America.

Contents

Foreword

Citation Story Captures Those Glorious Racing Days of Yore

Tommy Trotter

*I*t was the best of times for American thoroughbred racing—the 1940s and 1950s when Calumet Farm, under trainers Ben and Jimmy Jones, moved with wonderful abandon about the country. Kentucky, Illinois, Florida, Maryland, New York, and New Jersey headed up their busy schedule, later California in the 1950s with Citation as a "comeback" five-year-old.

Though the thoroughbred world abounded with many prominent stables—it read like a "Who's Who in Racing"—without question mighty Calumet Farm was the most diversified in all age and sex categories, having horses for almost every condition and distance, speed, power, and class wherever one looked.

For those around at the time, an impressive, unforgettable sight to admiring viewers and horsemen as well, was to watch the morning workouts as Calumet paraded out in sets of eight to ten horses over a given period of time. With well-groomed horses, and a special gleam to each, and one horse looking better than the next, each was assigned an exercise rider wearing tan wool cap, sweater of the Calumet devil's red and blue, breeches, and polished boots. What a sight! Upon entering the track, a pause at the gap, they then were allowed to enter a trot, with Ben and Jimmy Jones following astride their familiar ponies.

It's always great to reminisce about those special times in thoroughbred racing, and being privileged to be around during the Calumet Farm years, Phil Georgeff's excellent book on Citation brings back many wonderful memories.

It was at Washington Park in 1954 that I first met Phil. He was a track publicist at the time, working for the late Harry Sheer. I was with the racing department, both of us employed by Benjamin F. Lindheimer and his daughter, Marjorie Webb Everett.

Phil was a most knowledgeable and tireless staff member. He could be found at any time, at any area of the race track, whether it be the jockeys' room, press box, backstretch, or racing office, taking notes on the daily activities. With all his mounting duties, somehow he was still able to assist in the promotion of the Illinois Breeders program, publicizing the state-breds.

Phil was a young man of many talents. I wasn't a bit surprised when he stepped into the job as Arlington-Washington track announcer in the late 1950s.

Then and today, you don't have to be around Phil too long before the conversation leads to his admiration for the greatness of Citation. His being an eyewitness to Citation's career, plus his years of research, Phil makes a strong case for Citation as the greatest thoroughbred who ever lived, especially when the colt was a two- and three-year-old, after which most everybody agrees he should have been retired for good.

And Phil's admiration for Citation persists even though he had the great fortune in his career to "call" such bona fide greats as Secretariat, Kelso, Spectacular Bid, John Henry, Dr. Fager, Buckpasser, Tom Rolfe, Round Table, Candy Spots, Meadowlake, and Alydar, among others. His, therefore, is a meaningful conviction.

Phil strikes home when he writes of Citation's rare courage against older horses in his three-year-old 1948 season, an unheard of feat; how this great animal whipped the best sprinters and stayers of his time with only short periods of rest between races, racing long, then short, then long again—and still unbeatable!

It's all here in this remarkable story of a true champion and genuine racing legend, and why Phil Georgeff will not allow this great thoroughbred to fall unnoticed between the cracks.

Preface

Love at First Sight

$\mathcal{I}$ was a sixteen-year-old jockey wanna-be in 1947 the day I first laid eyes on Citation. He was a fine, upright two-year-old; I had journeyed to Washington Park race track on Chicago's South Side expressly to see Calumet Farm's unbeaten two-year-old filly, Bewitch. Instead, I saw Citation. Instinctively, I sensed thoroughbred greatness in the making. Happily, I was right.

From 1941—the year I saw Whirlaway at Arlington Park—until 1953, my first year as a race track publicity department employee, and until I called my first race May 18, 1959, until retirement in 1992 with a world-record 96,131 "calls" under my belt, I devoted countless hours discussing, recalling, reviewing, and reliving Citation's grand career with everybody I met and knew. And I mean *everybody*.

That included the owners of Calumet Farm, Warren and Lucille Wright, trainers Ben and Jimmy Jones; race track executives Ben Lindheimer, Tommy Trotter, and Bob Henderson; Calumet Farm general manager Paul Ebelhardt and farm secretary Margaret Glass; jockeys Eddie Arcaro, Steve Brooks, Doug Dodson, and N. L. Pierson. I really never got to know jockey Albert Snider before his tragic death in March 1948, but I did get to "know" him by way of lengthy conversations with Arcaro and Brooks.

My race track tenure, particularly my early years as track publicist, put me in regular contact with sports writers Arch Ward, John P. Carmichael, Joe Palmer, Red Smith, Dave Feldman, Warren Brown, Joe Agrella, and

Elmer Polzin. I exhaustively raided their brains to augment my love and interest in Citation, his personality, and his career.

I called such greats as Secretariat, Spectacular Bid, Kelso, Dr. Fager, Candy Spots, Tom Rolfe, Buckpasser, Meadowlake, John Henry, Round Table, and Alydar. And I familiarized myself with such prior heroes as Man o'War, Exterminator, Twenty Grand, Sun Beau, Seabiscuit, Equipoise, Colin, Sysonby, Count Fleet, and Phar Lap.

There was only one Citation!

Acknowledgments

With Fairness to All

GREAT (adj.): distinguished, famous, of noble rank, skillful; first rate; someone who has achieved importance or distinction in his field.—SYN: Immense, prominent, grand, absolute, titanic, herculean.

$\mathcal{W}$e prefer not to indiscriminately dust off the adjective "great" to describe people, places, or horses. However, applying greatness to Citation was so easy, we feel the reader deserves a full explanation.

For starters, this book in no way aimed at minimizing the talents, feats, or personalities of a crackerjack roster of thoroughbred *greats* before and after Citation.

There's absolutely no intention to downplay the careers and impact of such outstanding predecessors as Man o'War, Phar Lap, Gallant Fox, Colin, Sysonby, Seabiscuit, Equipoise, Armed, Twilight Tear, Busher, Assault, Whirlaway, and Count Fleet. Their greatness is unquestioned, their stories the stuff of which legends are made.

Nor does this work attempt to diminish those greats who followed in his hoofprints—Secretariat, Kelso, Nashua, Swaps, Real Delight, Round Table, Bold Ruler, Tom Rolfe, Ruffian, Spectacular Bid, Seattle Slew, Affirmed, Alydar, John Henry, and Cigar. Their places are assured among racing's star galaxy.

Debate, however, could easily prove endless, also futile, should we upgrade the conditional "great" to the comparative "greater." Comparisons would cause inevitable contention. Therefore, our story will, for the most part, skip over that conjecture.

Rather, with humble, but implicit, conviction, we dedicate this opus to *why* and *how* Citation achieved, and genuinely deserves, the lofty accolade as "The *Greatest* Thoroughbred Who Ever Lived!"

Ours is that of wide-eyed innocence and unadulterated joy in inviting you to join us in a return to those wonderful days of yesteryear. If only we could have his time again.

We shall indeed try.

Introduction

Phil Knows of What He Speaks

Elmer Polzin

$\mathcal{I}$t was a spring day in the year 1946, and the scene was a well-trodden paddock on the twelve hundred acres of Calumet Farm, located just a hop, skip, and jump from Lexington, Kentucky, where breeding champion race horses was the name of the game.

It was on that special sunny morning fifty-seven years ago that my wife, Patricia Polzin, and I came face-to-face with a handsome, freewheeling youngster who was to become a champion of champions, surely the greatest three-year-old ever to race, an equine performer who would bring American thoroughbred racing to new heights of public acclaim.

His name was Citation.

Ironically, that same crop of royally bred yearlings represented perhaps the finest batch of babies ever produced by a single breeder in a single year. For along with Citation came Coaltown, 1949's Handicap Horse of the Year; Bewitch, the champion juvenile filly of 1947 and one of racing's grandest ladies; as well as winners Free America, Beau Dandy, and Whirl Some.

Phil Georgeff and I became lifelong friends after he joined the Arlington Park publicity department in 1953. As a racing correspondent and public handicapper for the William Randolph Hearst paper in Chicago and later the Chicago *Tribune*, I joined the Phil Georgeff fan club in 1959 when he became the Arlington-Washington Parks track announcer, the job that ultimately propelled him to the championship level of his profession.

We could become bitter rivals when it came time to vote for each year's equine hero, but our friendship was bound with a common adhesive, the superglue that had fiery eyes and a heart as big as a melon. That glue was Citation.

Georgeff is unsurpassed as Citation's most ardent fan and now with this book certainly his staunchest personal biographer. His probing search into those tragic years when "our hero" suffered the pains and anguish brought on by human error is unmatched in the world of horse racing.

Listen to Eddie Arcaro, surely one of the finest jockeys ever, explain, sometimes with sadness, the highs and lows of his experience with Citation. How touching to hear Steve Brooks, one of jockeydom's hardest hitters, tell of his part in the Citation saga. How he stayed with the ailing heroic racer until together they climbed the ultimate peak.

In this wonderful, emotional tale of a horse and the "family" around him, including Hall of Fame trainers Ben and Jimmy Jones and owner Warren Wright, Phil's words come alive in his description about an animal that was sometimes "half human and half horse." And why not? After all, to some that's what horse racing is all about.

Dramatis Personae

Cast of Leading Characters

Citation	America's Greatest Thoroughbred
Calumet Farm	Legendary Owner of Citation
Warren and Lucille Wright	Owners of Calumet Farm in Kentucky
Ben and Jimmy Jones	Father-Son Training Twosome
Bull Lea	Famed Sire (Father) of Citation
Hydroplane II	Dam (Mother) of Citation
Kentucky Derby, Preakness, Belmont	Racing's Fabled Triple Crown
Eddie Arcaro	America's Premier Jockey
Al Snider	Citation's First Jockey
Doug Dodson	Calumet Contract Jockey
Steve Brooks, N. L. Pierson, Jackie Westrope, Conn McCreary	Other Noted Calumet Farm Riders
Paul Ebelhardt	Calumet Farm General Manager
Bill Raetzman	Calumet Farm Breeding Manager
Margaret Glass	Calumet Farm Secretary
Freeman McMillan	Calumet Groom and Citation's Exercise Rider
Ben Lindheimer	Chicago Tracks Executive Director
Bob Henderson	Chicago Tracks Business Executive
Tommy Trotter	Distinguished Racing Official

"Sunny" Jim Fitzsimmons	Renowned Thoroughbred Trainer
"Canny" Max Hirsch	Hall of Fame Trainer
Bewitch, Coaltown,	
Free America	Citation's Two-Year-Old Stablemates
Armed	Calumet's 1947 Horse of the Year
Whirlaway	Calumet's First Champion 1941
Ponder, Fervent, Pensive,	
Faultless, Twilight Tear,	
Twosy, Two Lea	Other Calumet Farm Equine Stars

SOME PROMINENT HORSES CITATION BEAT

Phalanx, Coaltown, My Request, Billings, Better Self, Escadru, Bolero, Bewitch, Ponder, Bovard, Eagle Look, Salmagundi, Noor, Roman In, Fervent, Faultless, Delegate, Vulcan's Forge, Two Lea, Stepfather, Be Fleet, On Trust, Papa Redbird, Volcanic, Piet, Eternal Reward, Spy Song.

MEDIA (PLAYED BY THEMSELVES)

Arch Ward (*Chicago Tribune*); Warren Brown, Dave Feldman, Elmer Polzin (*Chicago Herald-American*); John P. Carmichael (*Chicago Daily News*); Joe Kelly and Bill Boniface (*Baltimore Sun*); Eastern columnists Joe Palmer and Red Smith; Billy Reed and William Nack (*Sports Illustrated*); Charles Hatton, Joe Hirsch Jr., J. J. Murphy, John McEvoy (*Daily Racing Form*); race historians William H. P. Robertson and Tom Gilcoyne; Ed Schuyler, Associated Press; radio commentators Clem McCarthy, Bill Stern, and Jack Drees.

Chapter One

Baby Steps

*N*ot until you saw him on race day dressed for equine warfare—neck proudly arched and head regally bowed in that personal trademark canter of his own creation, then exploding full tilt from the gate with a magisterial will-to-win dynamism borne of innate nobility—only then did Citation begin to suggest what he truly was: "The Greatest Thoroughbred Who Ever Lived!"

Actually, from his mother's womb to his grave twenty-five years later, Citation in personal appearance hardly impressed observers as uncommon or unique. You'd never find his picture under "cynosure" in Webster's. Not that he was an ugly duckling—actually his face was downright handsome—but he never drew raves as strikingly individualistic, surely not pretty; and though cleanly coupled, neatly put together, he was neither eye-catchingly muscular nor exceptionally tall.

There was no shimmer to his coat or color. No showy gray as with Native Dancer, Spectacular Bid, or Monarchos. None of the flashy chestnut glitter of Man o'War and Secretariat. No long tail like Whirlaway. Certainly none of the blatant physicality of Forego, Point Given, and the legendary Phar Lap.

If he were a matinee movie idol he'd be Harrison Ford as opposed to Clark Gable. For pure beefcake, he'd be Bruce Lee, not Arnold Schwarzenegger. As a boxer—Rocky Marciano rather than Muhammad Ali. In football, he'd fit somewhere between Jim Brown and Gayle Sayers.

"If it wasn't that he was so downright intelligent, you'd probably never give him a second look," was the way his trainer "Plain" Ben Jones put it during the summer of 1948 when Citation ruled the world. Ben's son, Jimmy, who enjoyed a more intimate kinship once the colt was race-worthy, often praised Citation: "He had the smarts, no doubt about it, and—you couldn't help but see it in his face—it was his intelligence that helped make him one in a million."

Citation was born, or foaled, on April 11, 1945, at Warren Wright's fabled Calumet Farm near Lexington, Kentucky. As a baby, however, he was just another spindly-legged toddler, unmarked and dark bay in color, sprightly and eager, yes; but virtually faceless amongst a spate of Calumet Farm homebreds, most of them paternal half brothers and half sisters fathered, or sired, by the greatest thoroughbred progenitor of his time, the immortal Bull Lea.

Immortal as a sire, anyway. As a racehorse, Bull Lea was so-so, mostly a disappointment. He ran out of gas early in the 1938 Kentucky Derby. Speed was his forte, ample in supply to win ten of twenty-seven starts, earning $94,825. No cartwheels there; just another racehorse.

Incidentally, the colt who beat Bull Lea on Derby Day—the total coincidence here is awesome—was Lawrin, trained by pre-Calumet Ben Jones, with son Jimmy at his side; with a young, grinning, big-nosed twenty-two-year-old jockey named Eddie Arcaro in the saddle. All three—Arcaro and the Jones boys—would play pivotal roles in Citation's life and career.

By 1945 Calumet Farm was racing's reigning dynasty, stable name of a smallish, seemingly modest man, Warren Wright, who earlier launched a meteoric business career as an office boy at age fifteen for the Calumet Baking Powder Company. Before he turned twenty-five, that unassuming young man had climbed the summit first as president, then owner, of the Calumet Baking empire. He was smartly attuned to success; in 1931 he reportedly sold Calumet Baking to General Foods for $40 million—big money even back then. Now he had the lucre to conquer new worlds.

This time, Wright—whose slight stature belied, besides a genius for business, a perfectionist ego and a snappish temper if crossed—parlayed his obsession for capitalism into "new-vista" success, taking over Calumet Farm, a small parcel of Lexington pasture land his father had previously owned and operated to raise trotting horses.

Wright didn't cotton to "them jugheads." Out they went; in came the thoroughbreds, whom he admired—and history was made.

But not immediately. Success didn't come overnight for Wright, though his lovely wife, Lucille, stood by dutifully, supporting his dream of creating his own thoroughbred empire.

What everybody knew—though no one dared tell Wright—was that the self-made millionaire, despite being a confessed slave to racing's analeptic spell, was sorely bereft of breeding acumen, lacked a working knowledge of horseflesh, and was simply unqualified, perhaps incapable, of transferring his fervid passion for racing as a sport to an equally fiery desire of creating from scratch a quality stable all his own. The challenge seemed insuperable.

The farm treaded water for several years. What Wright needed was another instinctive genius like himself—but one who knew the huge difference between baking soda and thoroughbred horseflesh.

That man would be Ben Jones. The decade of the 1940s was approaching. "Plain Ben," as Jones was known throughout the racing fraternity, already was bigger than life, his potential for greatness tapped since 1922. He came as "savior" for Wright and brought son Jimmy with him. Two for the price of one. Calumet Farm's date with destiny, though delayed somewhat, had arrived.

Bull Lea, in hindsight a bargain fourteen-thousand-dollar yearling purchased by Wright in 1936, retired after three mediocre racing seasons. His immense fame as a sire was still a few years away. Nobody sensed his greatness.

Meanwhile, Calumet was poised to unleash its first great warrior upon racing. No, not a son of Bull Lea; not yet was the latter set to make his ubiquity felt. Rather, an offspring of the English import Blenheim II; the newcomer's mommy was Dustwhirl; his name: Whirlaway, wonderfully dubbed by no less a student of the game than Wright himself. Give the man credit; he and wife were peerless when it came to naming horses.

Whirlaway was foaled in 1938, the year Bull Lea flopped in the Derby, a year before the Jones boys would be officially hired to oversee the fortunes of Wright's struggling kingdom.

Thus, the Jones boys in 1940 busied themselves with an erratic but charismatic Whirlaway. Unbeknownst to them, Bull Lea's first of twenty-four crops—he sired a grand total of 377 babies—was set for launching.

Bull Lea was a well-named son of the sire Bull Dog out of the mare Rose Leaves, and he was an immediate hit at stud. His vibrant blood and potent sperm resonated throughout the realm of thoroughbred racing and breeding. Bull Lea instantly and thoroughly captivated the game, at the same time revitalizing Wright's faith in his dream to rule the Sport of Kings.

By the time baby Citation first saw the light of day in April of 1945, Bull Lea had already generously treated racing to awesome stakes stars Durazna, Twilight Tear, and Armed, the latter pair eventually crowned as 1944 and 1947 Horse of the Year, respectively. And that was just for starters; from his very first crop, too!

Yes, Bull Lea was just beginning, saving his best, not for last—he'd continue to dominate breeding until his death in 1964 at the fine old age of twenty-nine—but for his 1945 crop, when he'd bequeath the cherished silver spoon to his finest son, baby Citation.

Lest some forget, some credit is also due Citation's mother, Hydroplane II. As Wright did with Whirlaway's daddy, Blenheim II, he imported her from England. She arrived on American soil following a tense sea journey, braving dangerous waters and German submarines, a bold, circuitous crossing to keep her heavy date with Bull Lea. The year was 1942, shortly after the start of World War II.

Curiously, Citation's mama was an even bigger race track bust than his papa. Hydroplane II started seven times in homeland England, failed to win a single race, earning a paltry, actually embarrassing, sum of $81. For some reason, Wright, who surrounded himself with sundry breeding experts and advisers, believed Hydroplane could cut the mustard as broodmare, her track failure notwithstanding.

Citation was her third of eight foals, and her first son. Her first two babies—Fly Off and Mermaid, foaled in 1943 and 1944—were fillies, both race track duds.

Thus, the mating of Bull Lea and Hydroplane II was of no particular import, at least as far as the dam's contribution went, though she was a daughter of Hyperion. Bull Lea was on autopilot, turning out champions right and left, virtually at the drop of every foal. So Hydroplane's newest baby, a male, arrived amid customary high hopes and expectations despite her record. All that really mattered was that the newborn was sired by the great one himself.

Bull Lea's 1945 crop was big and beautiful in quantity and quality. The Wrights spent days and hours pouring over pedigrees, cleverly combining names of sires and dams, searching for names à la such prior striking monikers as Whirlaway, Twilight Tear, Pensive, Twosy, and Armed. Whether a conscious notion, the Wrights increasingly were choosing one-word names for their color-bearers, a young tradition they'd champion for years. Other stables followed suit, lending vitality to name-giving, just another facet of racing's exciting "glory days."

"We all suggested names," said Freeman McMillan, a longtime Calumet farm employee. He wanted to be a jockey, was denied that dream by weight, and later worked as groom and exercise rider. He and Citation would become inseparable companions by 1947.

"Most of the good names, though," McMillan ceded, "came from the Wrights themselves. They'd glow when they hit on a good one, like Armed, Pensive, Fervent, or Faultless. They thought Whirlaway the best named of 'em all. But then he was our first top one, a real favorite."

The Wrights outdid themselves in 1945. By then the stable was in deep clover; every Bull Lea son or daughter was viewed as a potential stakes star. So they studiously devoted themselves to naming that crop.

There were colts galore among Bull Lea's boy babies. One they named Coaltown; for Hydroplane's newborn, they chose Citation. And Bull Lea also had several spanking-new fillies; one comely one was named Bewitch. And Calumet had other fancy-named youngsters by other sires among that 1945 contingent, including Free America and Whirl Some, the Wrights deigning to use two-word names where fitting.

There were several ways one might be privy to the private goings-on at Calumet. Among sources, Mr. Wright was probably the least informed. Sure, he was the boss, and a hard-nosed one at that. Irascible, autocratic, and short-tempered—sometimes all at the same time—he was also clever enough to compensate those unsavory traits by surrounding himself with experts of all shapes and sizes. And, yes, there were the usual minions to keep him happy and assured that all was well in Calumet heaven. Winners and results were the bottom line.

Wright, learning from the experience of his wild climb to success as a baking powder magnate, saw the wisdom in delegating authority, relying heavily not only on the proven expertise of the Jones boys, but also the savvy of general farm manager J. Paul Ebelhardt and faithful farm secretary Margaret Glass. They kept the farm humming.

The media romanced all of the above with unabashed fervor. Calumet was racing's answer to the New York Yankees. Actually, Wright was the media's least-sought target. The "old man" was no more than superficial spokesman, a kind of carousel barker.

"Talk to Mr. Wright about Calumet and his champions," proffered the late Arch Ward, who was *Chicago Tribune* sports editor during the 1940s and 1950s, "and all you'd get was how 'smart and clever' he was, that he wanted nothing else but to win the Kentucky Derby, possibly the Triple Crown, as many times as possible, and, of course, the next rich stakes to tap. Oh, yes, he'd love to tell you how he created this great thing called Calumet Farm almost all by his lonesome."

Or you could be a close friend of *Chicago Herald-American* sports scribes Warren Brown and Elmer Polzin, or *Chicago Daily News* columnist John P. Carmichael. Close proximity to either Joe Palmer or Red Smith was another channel of inside communication.

It was rare that Wright was approached or interviewed for his opinion anywhere but at the track, where the dapper little man regularly held court every time his stable's famous devil's red and blue colors would be flying in a race.

Others "in the know" would include officials at Chicago race tracks, particularly Arlington and Washington Parks, which were exclusive home base to Team Calumet. Several officials enjoyed privileged insight into activities back at the farm. One such person was Bob Henderson, before and after he became general manager for the Arlington-Washington combine owned by ingenious impresario Ben Lindheimer.

Lindheimer regularly hobnobbed with racing royalty; among his favorites were Mr. and Mrs. Warren Wright. Lindheimer left oversight of the tracks to Henderson, a jovial, gregarious track official, perfectly suited to the task. Both tracks purred under his direction.

Henderson, however, didn't socialize with the Wrights; he preferred the company of farm manager Paul Ebelhardt and later successor Melvin Cinnamon during their Calumet stay; they were close buddies, in the trenches, so to speak. Henderson and his family spent many a weekend visiting Calumet. Fact is, he was there the very week Citation was born.

Not that baby Citation's arrival caused any stir. To the contrary, he was just another progeny of the redoubtable Bull Lea. In fact, he was still unnamed, though the Wrights had already concocted the names Citation, Coaltown, Free America, and Bewitch for those they considered elite among the farm's newest baby crop.

Much of Bob Henderson's time was spent in and around the breeding sheds which Bull Lea and his equine harem called home. He was in Hydroplane's stall the day after she gave birth to baby Citation. He saw nothing special in the youngster. Said Henderson: "Heck, there were new foals all over the place. The season was in high gear. Ebelhardt and his crew, including breeding manager Bill Raetzman, figured each new one better than the other. They'd been around thoroughbred royalty so long, no one birth, unless complicated, drew any special attention."

No one—not Ebelhardt, neither Ben nor Jimmy Jones, nor the Wrights—saw anything unique in baby Cy, though word had it, it was Lucille Wright who chose "Citation" as the newborn's name.

Wright that spring was more concerned about winning the Kentucky Derby a third time in four years. His appetite for success—the Derby was racing's most cherished prize—was now insatiable. He tasted its sweetness when Whirlaway rolled from far back to score a resounding eight-length victory in the 1941 Derby in track record time.

Pensive won both the Derby and Preakness for Wright in 1944; the long-winded colt, blessed with much of the same kind of late kick that made Whirlaway a living legend, failed, however, to capture the Triple Crown, losing the Belmont Stakes by a half-length to Bounding Home after appearing home free in the final sixteenth of the race.

The Jones boys had another outstanding colt cranked up for the 1945 Derby. Fetchingly named Pot o'Luck, a stretch-rusher in the tradition of Whirlaway and Pensive—he and jockey Doug Dodson, then first-string rider for the Jones boys, went off as Derby favorites.

"Wright died that day," Henderson recalled. "He thought he had it in the bag. Pot o'Luck tried mightily, came in second, but six lengths behind a speedster named Hoop Jr., who was giving jockey Eddie Arcaro his third Derby win, tying him with Earl Sande and Isaac Murphy."

Thus began Wright's love-hate relationship with jockey great Arcaro. The owner of Calumet usually left choice of jockey to Ben and Jimmy and was pleased with Arcaro's Triple Crown victory ride on "Mr. Longtail," Whirlaway's popular nickname in honor of his long, flowing chestnut tail that all but touched the ground when standing.

Conn McCreary was aboard Pensive in 1944. Did fine, too. Wright sought to get Arcaro back to ride Pot o'Luck, but Eddie had agreed to ride Fred W. Hooper's fast colt, Hoop Jr. Then Arcaro had the gall to beat Wright and Pot o'Luck for top dollar in the 1945 Derby.

Wright shared the Jones boys' opinion that Arcaro was America's number one jockey; because of that lofty and deserved ranking, the rider could pick and choose mounts. Wright wanted Arcaro full-time; the latter preferred to freelance. Wright struck back by hiring Doug Dodson as the stable's contract jockey.

Arcaro didn't exactly rue his decision to ride freelance, accepting his choice amidst mixed emotions following some frank soul-searching.

Ultimately honored as "The Master" in his profession, in most minds the greatest jockey of the twentieth century, Eddie later candidly examined and explained his decision: "If I wasn't riding freelance I wouldn't have won with Hoop Jr. in 1945. Pot o'Luck was a nice colt, but no way could he have beaten Hoop Jr. that day.

"Yes, I would have had both Armed and Citation, also Ponder, when he won the 1949 Derby, fourth Derby of the 1940s decade for Ben and Jimmy. But had I stayed with Calumet, I may never have had the opportunity to ride horses like Shut Out, Devil Diver, Hill Prince, Nashua, Olympia, Bold Ruler, Assault, Battlefield, Native Dancer, or Kelso. Then, in retrospect, if I could do it all over again, maybe I'd have strung along with Calumet. But we did manage to get together for two great full-time years in 1952 and 1953, but that was after Mr. Wright had passed away a couple of years earlier.

"It all boils down to speculations," Arcaro shrugged. "At any rate I got to ride the greatest horse of all time [Citation] even though I wasn't Calumet's first-call rider. What a grand privilege, though the tragedy that made it possible broke my heart."

Meanwhile, back on the farm, Citation, Coaltown, Free America, Bewitch, and a host of blue blood sucklings, most of them sons or daughters of patriarchal Bull Lea, were frolicking with their dams, enjoying "the good life" befitting equine aristocracy.

Charlie Critchfield, former rider turned exercise boy, finally serving as superintendent of stalls at Arlington and Washington in the 1950s, recalls a short stint served at Calumet Farm in the mid-1940s: "I was around when Citation, Bewitch, and the others were weaned. Calumet was up to their ears in young bloodstock. Most of 'em were bays, and I remember Mr. Ebelhardt pointing 'em out to us.

"Not once was anything special made of Citation. I certainly never saw nothing unusual. He ran with the other weanlings. I'm sure he missed his mother. Only thing I remember—Bewitch seemed the fastest, and Coaltown appeared a mite taller. But they were so young, still growing, and havin' the time of their life."

While baby Cy was getting accustomed to life minus his mother, the latter was back making love, this time to a sire named Sun Again. She'd make him a proud papa of a brand-new baby girl in 1946; the filly would be named Sunny Flight, not the soundest of Calumeters. Sunny Flight would start only five times in her career. She'd fail to win a race. Just another Hydroplane dullard.

Fact is, Hydroplane was mated with the enigmatic Whirlaway in 1947. That colt, On Wings, also Citation's half brother, left much to be desired, managing only eight wins from eighty-eight trips postward during a hollow four-year career on the track. At least he held together physically.

It wasn't until 1949—Hydroplane was barren in 1948—that the Wrights, by then riding cloud nine what with Citation an undisputed giant among thoroughbred greats, that they bred Cy's dam back to Bull Lea, hoping lightning would strike twice! They aptly, and hopefully, named that colt—a *full* brother (same sire and dam) to Citation— "Unbelievable."

Unbelievable was "unbelievably" mediocre, managing three wins in nine starts before being shelved permanently by injury.

Twice more before her death, Hydroplane was sent to Bull Lea in an effort to recapture lightning in a jar. Neither a 1952 filly foal named Siena Way, nor a 1953 colt called St. Crispin, even made it to the races. Bloodline pundits remain mystified as to the vagaries involved in the daring, at times inscrutable, challenge to reproduce greatness in the thoroughbred realm.

Baby Citation was a "freak," in the finest, most complimentary sense of the word. And no one knew it, not even as he romped and pranced as a just-turned yearling on January 1, 1946.

Young Cy continued to grow, continued to "play" with his peers. Before his yearling season would close, about late summer, he and his friends had begun training in earnest as 1947 fast approached, which would be their two-year-old racing year and their introduction to the world of horse racing.

Long before that, however, the inborn competitive instinct was awakened in Cy and his soul mates. What once was just carefree fun and games, including mindless running and jumping—"tag" and "catch me" sort of stuff—suddenly blossomed into ego and speed not even Calumet's spacious pastures could contain forever.

Still, nothing of note about young Cy stood out.

"Hey, at that time Ebelhardt told me," explained Henderson, "hopes ran high for each and every foal, especially among Bull Lea's offspring. Everything he threw was a champ, or star, or contender. It wasn't like we were searching for a needle in the haystack. He just figured they'd all be good ones.

"And since at that stage of their lives they all looked like the runners they were bred to be," Ebelhardt told Henderson, "no one individual took center stage. There was no reason for special treatment. Heck, if Bewitch, Coaltown, Free America, or Whirl Some were poorly-bred bums or anything like that—which they weren't—little Citation would have stood out like a sore thumb. But they all had that special look in their eye."

Therefore, January 1, 1947, came and went without extraordinary celebration. January 1, of course, is the universal birthday of all thoroughbreds, and the pressing business at hand had arrived—that of becoming a wage-earning racehorse.

Citation was ready. He stood proud and erect. Maybe he wasn't as fast as Bewitch then, nor as husky as Free America, nor as tall as Coaltown; but his superior brain was starting to take charge. He was born to race; he'd do it with uncommon verve and dedication.

Cy's brainy approach to work, coupled with his upbeat spirit and an early turn to maturity, suited the Jones boys just fine. They didn't believe in coddling their horses. They believed the horses, young and old alike, were there to earn their keep. They were bred to race, and race they would.

Not that the Jones boys ever mistreated their charges. They asked no more of their standard bearers than they did of themselves or of Calumet's loyal human backstretch personnel, which included a proud battalion of veterinarians, grooms, handlers, and exercise boys. Calumet had no trouble finding good help. Charlie Critchfield remembered: "Calumet meant 'class.' Everybody who worked farms in those days would die to work for Mr. Wright and Ben Jones. An employee walked proud in the farm's devil's red and blue. It was *the* uniform—one of distinction."

So the 1947 two-year-old crop had its work cut out. There would be first, meticulous grooming; second, obedience classes; third, energetic gallops and time trials; fourth, schooling from the starting gate; fifth, periodical health checkups; finally, all of the above, plus hands-on training and plain old hard work. But all the colts and fillies supped and slept well. They earned it.

Thus, Citation metamorphosed into a gifted, young athlete. No more baby steps. From now on, he'd be making giant hoofprints so grand, so unprecedented, no thoroughbred racehorse—past, present, or future—would ever truly duplicate him.

Chapter Two

Taking Care of Business

$\mathcal{W}$arren Brown, one of the nation's most respected sports writers of his day—and a thoroughbred junkie like so many of his associates back then—visited with his friend Ben Jones in early March 1947 at Calumet in Kentucky, the pair taking an hour or so to inspect the stable's most promising two-year-old crop ever.

"They're all good ones, or so they look," Jones said with his usual droll, stroking the brim of his omnipresent white hat, "but I kinda like that bay over there. I think, yes, his name's Citation. He could be a runner. And he knows it, too."

"Got brains, huh?" Brown replied, the latter as slim and tall as Jones was husky and robust.

Both Jones and Brown knew that most animal behaviorists took a dim view of a horse's intelligence, particularly thoroughbreds; that the equine was chiefly a product of raw instinct refined only by repetitive training; therefore, virtually devoid of reasoning ability.

Jones agreed to a point that the ape, possibly the pig, maybe even the dog, were smarter than thoroughbreds. "But that doesn't make racehorses dummies, or stupid, nothing like that. They're bred with instinct, or common sense—I suppose that's where 'horse sense' comes from—and some, like Citation, have a real savvy, an understanding, a know-how, more than the others.

"Now that doesn't mean the intelligent ones can automatically run faster," Jones told Brown, "but good old common horse sense is important for a horse, especially if the bugger can also run a bit."

Brown wasn't the only media person with whom the Jones boys freely shared their high opinion of young Cy. Son Jimmy complimented Citation's brainy ways when asked by Baltimore *Sun* sports writer Joe Kelly to assess that year's crop of juveniles. But then both Ben and Jimmy also liked Free America a bit.

For that matter, Wright himself took a shine to Coaltown, while Mrs. Wright, being a woman, favored Bewitch.

Moreover, there were debates and disagreements aplenty among the youngsters' various grooms and exercise riders as to their steeds' comparative skills and talents. Groom–exercise rider Freeman McMillan encapsulated the stable's general opinion and mood: "They were all, each and every one of the two-year-olds, something special. Sure, each had his or her own personality. But they were all runners, bred in the purple, and packed with speed and class. Most of them were still playful, except maybe Citation. Oh, he enjoyed himself, but of 'em all, he was the most businesslike. Kinda more serious-minded, I'd say."

One thing Ben Jones noted: whereas Bewitch and Coaltown would often pulverize some other lesser-regarded training partner with eye-popping speed and exuberance in work sprints, Citation would be content to run as slow or as fast as his partner, even when pitted in tandem with Bewitch or Coaltown or Free America.

Neither Bewitch nor Coaltown nor Free America ever "burned" Cy in morning trials. Fact is, no one ever really beat him at all, as Jones recalled. As the two-year-olds matured and advanced in conditioning, they'd often work and train in pairs. They'd turn for home in three- or four-furlong drills heads apart and still be that close at the wire, but Cy's head would always be a nostril or so in front. Or so observers recalled. Exercise boys on either horse never asked for their mount's best; there was no reason to prove anything.

Even then, though, Citation hated, actually refused, to lose; but since neither rider was actually trying to beat his opponent, Cy's defiant attitude and behavior wasn't seen as extraordinary, at least never taken that seriously. It all seemed part of the learning process.

Most people, including the Wrights and the Joneses, were saving their final assessment for when the youngsters would hit the track in actual competition. That was the test of fire.

Because Wright was accustomed to success, winning as many of the blue ribbon stakes as possible became an overpowering obsession. Thus, the Jones boys were attuned to assembly-lining stars and superstars in each and every racing age-sex division.

Whirlaway was their first, though not a progeny of Bull Lea. But Mr. Longtail not only swept the 1941 Triple Crown for Wright's Calumet, heralding the stable's arrival among the nation's elite, but nailed down consecutive Horse of the Year titles (1941–42).

Wright didn't seem fazed when Eddie Arcaro was "set down" by New York stewards, or judges, for flagrant rough riding in the fall of 1942. As much as he admired "Banana Nose," as Eddie was known especially among New York racing cognoscenti, Wright seemed satisfied with jockey Conn McCreary's handling of Pensive in winning both the 1944 Derby and Preakness; but he was aghast when denied another Triple Crown hero—Pensive getting beat in the Belmont Stakes by long shot Bounding Home was bitter wine.

Arcaro's "vacation" extended a full year, after which it took the chastened rider a short while to reconnect with horsemen.

Wright did find solace that year, however, when his stout-hearted filly, Twilight Tear, actually the first of Bull Lea's great ones—she was foaled in 1941, the year of Whirlaway's Triple Crown—grabbed the baton from Pensive, embarking on a win spree that tickled her greedy owner Wright down to his little toe.

Twilight Tear also made her sire proud, piling up eleven straight victories, many against males, strutting her wares in New York, Florida, Maryland, and Illinois. She conquered all in the Pimlico Oaks, Belmont's Acorn and Coaching Club American Oaks, also the Princess Doreen at Washington Park.

Most of those wins were registered with Conn McCreary in the saddle. Whatever the reason, Wright and Ben Jones soon turned her over to Lee Haas, a comparatively unknown jockey. McCreary was retained in a lesser capacity, usually riding Pensive, who had been in a tailspin since his Belmont debacle.

While Twilight Tear dominated the sport as no filly before, Pensive's career was on the wane. He started as Twilight Tear's entrymate in the 1944 Arlington Classic, in those days almost as prestigious a race as the Kentucky Derby. Big question: could Twilight Tear humble "the boys" with all the big money on the line?

Bull Lea's finest daughter annihilated her field, which included Old Kentuck, who finished second, and Challenge Me, who wound up fourth. Poor, weary Pensive saved third—he'd start a few more times that season without winning—and was retired to stud, his record somewhat tarnished, one of few Calumeters to bow out ingloriously.

Through all this public hullabaloo, Citation was no more than a gleam in Bull Lea's eye. The latter courted Hydroplane in May of 1944, about the time Pensive was winning both the Derby and Preakness. Cy's unheralded birth was still eleven months in the future.

Twilight Tear's brilliance, however, did not go unsung. For all her achievement, including a victory that fall at Laurel in which she was ridden by another new rider, Doug Dodson—he'd play a strange role in Citation's life three years hence—Twilight Tear was unanimously acclaimed "1944 Horse of the Year," becoming the first filly so honored.

Calumet was aglow; Wright became richer and prouder; for Ben Jones, who rarely broke the phlegmatic mode, it was another banner season. No one expected less; few, however, realized the best was yet to come.

Pensive, incidentally, expiated his dismal late racing career by becoming a sire of worth. One of his finest sons, beautifully named Ponder—an even more powerful late-finisher than his daddy—who would explode incredibly from off the pace to capture the 1949 Kentucky Derby, later would back up Citation during Cy's comeback in 1950.

Parenthetically, Ponder was ridden in all his big races by a jockey famed for his "heavy whip"—Steve Brooks. The plot surrounding the life and times of Citation continues to thicken. Brooks, much like the aforementioned Doug Dodson, not to forget the fiery Eddie Arcaro, also would play an integral part in Cy's career.

It was 1945—the year of Citation's regal crop—and coincidences mounted. Another son of Bull Lea, out of the mare Armful, was making waves, standing at the threshold of greatness. Like Twilight Tear, this son of Bull Lea also was foaled in 1941, and like most Calumet babies would boast a snappy name—he was named Armed, and he, too, would become a buddy, albeit an older paternal half brother, to Citation.

Citation influenced his age like none before or since. Never would one horse be so closely associated with such a wide array of jockeys, also great or near-great thoroughbreds; he'd climax, at the same time bring to a close the greatest dynasty period, one that embraced twelve matchless years—1941 through 1952—that any thoroughbred breeding or racing establishment could ever enjoy, let alone imagine, in the history of the game.

Armed eventually displaced Phar Lap as the top money-winning gelding of all time. Curiously, Armed as a budding 1943 two-year-old was ordered castrated by Jones because of his ribald, unruly ways. Robust and brown in color, Armed was all but discarded as potential racing material even after losing his manhood. For weeks Armed was shunted to the lowly job of "lead pony," embarrassingly forced to escort legitimate Calumet runners to the starting gate, all but totally forgotten as an athlete, that occupation for which he was bred.

But Jones gave Armed "one more chance" to prove his worth. The gelding was three when he faced the barrier for the first time. He didn't turn too many heads, winning three of seven, but no stakes. He even flopped in his four-year-old debut, the year Citation was born. Suddenly the reluctant gelding magically "caught fire," blasting into unbelievable orbit for the next three years, 1945–47, capping his career as American Horse of the Year in 1947, Cy's two-year-old season.

And the coincidence as to future happenings in what would prove to be "the Citation saga" weren't finished yet. There was still another exceptional Calumet combatant who'd get to know, test, and taste Cy's brilliance. His name: Faultless.

Faultless also had Fervent—both magnificently named Calumet colts—as running mate from his 1944 crop. Faultless lost the 1947 Kentucky Derby in a searing three-way photo finish to Maine Chance Farm's frontrunning Jet Pilot and C. V. Whitney's stretch-charging Phalanx.

A few days later Faultless jumped to the top of the nation's three-year-old division with an authoritative victory in the Preakness. By then, late spring of 1947—Cy had already been unleashed as a two-year-old—Doug Dodson had graduated to the rank of first-string rider for Calumet.

Dodson, who was quiet and unassuming to the eye—he also owned a sharp nose though not as prominent as Arcaro's—was a sad, smoldering, insecure young man inside. For a while, some observers felt he fooled himself into thinking his rising preeminence among riders was due to his own skills, rather than the remarkable array of steeds presented him on a daily basis by Wright and the Jones boys.

Dodson also was regular rider of the late-developing Fervent, who picked up the slack when Faultless faltered a bit in early summer. Among Fervent's major scores were the American Derby and the Pimlico Special. Dodson felt he was king of the world; he was, too.

Dodson had Horse of the Year Armed, three-year-old stalwarts Faultless and Fervent, plus his pick of the amazing 1947 two-year-old crop that included, in addition to Citation, such whiz kids as Bewitch, Coaltown, and Free America. Most riders would kill for such a privilege.

Ben's son Jimmy by then was Calumet trainer of record, though Ben's wizardry kept the stable machine well-oiled and purring like a big cat curled before a warm fireplace. Jimmy had learned his job well, but Master Ben was always close by, still the brains behind it all.

Dodson was about to make the biggest blunder of his or any athletic career, one from which he'd never fully recover. Only true crystal ball-gazing, better still, diving foreknowledge, could have told him that Citation was about to become "the thoroughbred for the ages."

Calumet not only was loaded with thoroughbred blue bloods, but also a gang of top jockeys—great ones like Arcaro and McCreary; riders they helped make, such as Wendell Eads, Alfred Shelhamer, Alfred Robertson, and, of course, Dodson; also up'n'coming stars Al Snider, Steve Brooks, and Newbold L. Pierson.

The Jones boys preferred to enlist their own special jockey colony, including one top rider always eager, willing, and available. Because they had so many fine horses, there was constant need for back-up riders they could count on. That's why Snider, Brooks, and Pierson were recruited. Dodson was suspicious, hated their presence; but he was always number one. He had pick of the litter. If he were more wise and grateful, he would have had no complaints.

How it all came together was truly amazing; for a fact unpredictable. Each person had a job to do: Wright, Ben and Jimmy Jones, Dodson, Snider, Pierson, Brooks, Bewitch, Free America, Armed, Ponder, Coaltown, Faultless, and, of course, young Citation; and in one way or another each would play an important role in young Cy's rise to stardom and racing immortality.

In fairness to all concerned, there was no one sure omen pointing up Citation's extraordinariness. Thus, as his career unfolded from his initial race on April 22, 1947, not unless one was a proven soothsayer could one have acted or done differently. Sadly, there was tragic time and unforeseen circumstance—what most would call "bad luck"—that also dealt some a lousy hand.

Fact is, nobody was really looking for one thoroughbred world-beater. The stable brimmed with quality champs and near-champs. Calumet looked for and expected greatness all around. They weren't searching for that one elusive needle in the haystack. They expected to find twenty needles, each one better than the next.

And they were right; they had quality horseflesh galore. Such plenty, however, blinded them—but only until soundly awakened to the reality— that they had found that "one in a million!"

Before that discovery, however, Calumet was so well-heeled in thoroughbred horseflesh that the Joneses smartly took a veritable shotgun approach as to where and when they'd fire their fastest bullets. That meant dividing the stable, sending powerhouse divisions around the country to prey upon lucrative stakes opportunities. Often that meant their two-year-olds would be separated—some to Florida, some to California, others to Maryland, or to Ohio, and, eventually, all to converge on Chicago, which was the stable's summer home base.

As a result, Calumet riders also rode the coattails of the youngsters with whom they were paired. Dodson got first choice, but once a rapport was established with a young colt or filly, that relationship would be maintained, unless exigent or emergency circumstances arose.

Dodson reportedly saw nothing wrong with the arrangement. In early April, Calumet's two-year-old "big gun" appeared to be Coaltown, a towering son of Bull Lea out of the Blenheim II mare, Easy Lass. "That Coaltown has wings for heels," was Dodson's first impression.

Only trouble was that Coaltown for all his precocious physicality suffered a chronic throat disorder, a pesky ailment which would sideline him for his entire 1947 juvenile year.

No matter. Dodson had also fallen "in love" with Bewitch, a high-spirited brown daughter of Bull Lea whose physical advancement preceded that of male counterparts Citation and Free America. Of the 1945 crop, Bewitch was crowned "the fastest, overflowing with energy, zip, and pizzazz," if backstretch gossip were to be taken seriously.

Except for Coaltown, Calumet's other members of that 1945 harvest were all sound of both mind and limb. Riders Dodson, Robertson, Brooks, and Snider took turns working the youngsters, sharing their opinions and beliefs, boiling down to one inescapable conclusion: each youngster was special in his or her own way; not one stood out; actual competition on the track would be the final denominator.

Therefore, when Bewitch capitalized upon her precocity as the first ready to race, Doug Dodson stepped front and center.

Bewitch was shipped to nearby Keeneland with others in care to Ben. Son Jimmy took another division, including Citation, to Maryland. Dodson stayed with the elder Jones; Al Snider accompanied Jimmy to Maryland and a small race track named Havre de Grace. Thus, princess Bewitch was separated from her princely paternal half brother Citation—and the twain wouldn't meet again until midsummer in Chicago.

Both Bewitch and Citation went about their chosen profession with aplomb and dispatch.

Bewitch was the first to face the starting gate—April 10 at Keeneland at the odd distance of a special course called Headley, some forty feet shy of a half mile. She spun like a top from the gate to spread-eagle a maiden field by six commanding lengths in :46⅕, just a fifth off the track record. A star was born. The first of the 1945 Bull Lea babies had graduated in sensational style, a good omen indeed!

Bewitch was unstoppable. She hammered all comers, including colts, in her very next start, a race called the Thoroughbred Dinner Purse, in which she sparkled with a run that matched the track record. If she feared not the boys—and she'd continue to dominate males with éclat—she very well may have rated consideration as the nation's best two-year-old, sex notwithstanding.

Less than two weeks after Bewitch's spectacular debut, it was Citation's turn, April 22 at Havre de Grace, at 4½ furlongs, but over a track converted into a sea of slop by morning rains. Cy broke alertly, allowed Al Snider to drop back to third until midstretch, then with but a cluck from his rider's lips swept by the leaders for a going-away three-parts-of-a-length victory in :54⅖, excellent time considering the sloppy going.

Cy's victory waltz impressed Snider in two ways: one, Cy proved he could handle "off" going, so he didn't need a fast track to show his stuff; two, he rated kindly, flashed not only speed, which was vital for a two-year-old, also demonstrated an ability to come from behind to run down speedy rivals—the sign of a superb, tractable athlete.

Already evident was the contrasting modus operandi of Citation and Bewitch. The filly was all at once grandiloquent, vainly ostentatious; a saucy showboat, the possessor of lightning-quick speed. "Flash" or "pizzazz" was her middle name. You had to love her brass.

Citation, on the other hand, simply did his job, which was to win; excel, yes; but "winning" was the real name of his game. Bewitch would dazzle opponents with showy footwork, heartlessly plunging them into despair and defeat, an overpowering "no prisoners" superiority, a youthful contempt for challengers, made all the more imperious by her obvious disdain for the boys.

Citation entertained no such flamboyance. He was methodical as he was governable. He'd knock out his foe; but he'd not beat him to death just to please or entertain a crowd. Besides, he was doing his thing "on the road," so to speak, while Bewitch was starring in blue grass country where she and Calumet were the object of affections.

And star she did. Following her two thumping scores at Keeneland, she danced home an eight-length winner in the Debutante Stakes at Churchill Downs in Louisville before catching a van to Chicago where she again on June 16 vanquished colts in the Hyde Park Stakes, a ridiculously easy eight-length tally. She deigned to restrict her quick feet to fillies in her next two Chicago outings, annexing both the Pollyanna and Arlington Lassie, always with lengths to spare, and with a jaunt that suggested blatant invincibility.

Citation kept pace in Maryland, but not with Bewitch's flourish. He changed tactics in winning his second start at Pimlico, scoring easily in front-running fashion by 3½ lengths. That was May 3; less than three weeks later, May 21, he recorded another win, this time in a five-furlongs Maryland baby race, resolutely rolling from three lengths off the leader turning for home, reporting under the wire by nearly two lengths in snappy time over a "good" strip. Yes, again he won; again he conquered a track other than "fast"; and again he had Al Snider at the controls.

Snider, younger than Dodson but considerably more genial and confident of life, was also a shrewd judge of horseflesh. He saw Cy's potential, loved their relationship, but rarely sang his praises to anyone but Jimmy Jones. Al was aware of Dodson's "top gun" persona, didn't want to lose Cy once they got to Chicago.

His fears were justified. Dodson had kept abreast of Cy's Maryland feats; he wanted to see this youngster for himself. So he exercised contractual privilege, leaping aboard Cy for an ordinary five-furlongs dash at Arlington Park on July 24. Again in midpack early, Citation roared from fourth to notch a narrow but resourceful half-length tally in track record time of fifty-eight seconds flat!

Dodson liked what he saw and felt. He tasted Cy's developing skills a second straight time less than a week later, July 30, at Washington Park, in what would be the colt's first stakes try, the Elementary Stakes at the longer six furlongs, which was as far as two-year-olds were asked to go in those days before early fall.

Once again versatile Cy broke smartly from the gate, wrested command before the opening quarter, and, setting all his own pace, scooted home two lengths before Salmagundi and Billings. His time also was crisp—1:10 ⅗; and he wasn't even breathing hard. More important, and it didn't escape either

Dodson or Jimmy Jones, Cy carried twelve pounds more than the weight assigned to Salmagundi's jockey, an indication the colt could not only handle the extra distance, but could pack weight without batting an eye.

Doug "liked" Cy, but for obvious reasons continued to "love" Bewitch. He was impressed by her high octane speed and her gusto in dispatching opposition, particularly her mastery over colts, and, doubly important, her growing celebrity. Doug could read, and Bewitch was preceded everywhere by her press notices. Veteran horsemen everywhere were freely hailing her as America's champion two-year-old.

Therefore, as the rich Futurity at Washington Park on Chicago's bustling south side approached, Doug never thought twice—he strung along with lightninglike Bewitch.

Doug at this point ruled the Calumet roost, certainly as far as jockey assignments went. He consistently rode stable heroes Armed, Fervent, and Faultless in all their endeavors. He and Bewitch were unconquerable, sweeping all seven of their starts, including two wins over males. Taking on the boys again in the six-furlongs Washington Part Futurity was like taking candy from a baby.

However, another of Calumet's two-year-olds, Free America, was making waves that summer, not tidal in scope, but sufficient to warrant respect among juveniles. Free America was a slow-starter as well as a late-bloomer. He lacked Bewitch's exuberance and vivacity. He couldn't match Cy's determination or dedication.

"Free America can run all day," the elder Jones told Chicago Tribune sports editor Arch Ward, "the only trouble is that it seems to take him all day to get into high gear. He's a runner, no doubt about it. Just doesn't seem to have the attitude the others have."

Free America started his juvenile season slow but was finishing fast, as was his wont. By mid-August as the Futurity loomed, he had won three of four, including the George Woolf Memorial Stakes. So what once was Calumet's fearsome 1-2 punch of Bewitch and Citation was now an awesome 1-2-3 knockout fist capable of flooring any rivals.

Dodson liked things simple. If Faultless was the stable's number one three-year-old, so be it; Doug would ride him. No fuss, no debate. And if Armed was Calumet's top older star, he belonged to Doug, no questions asked. Same for the stable's older filly and mare division.

But now there was uninvited debate and consternation caused by a plethora of potential two-year-old stars. True, Doug had first refusal, which he needed and wanted, a form of carte blanche, a necessary panacea for his throbbing insecurities.

Nevertheless, he was confident he did right sticking with unbeaten Bewitch for the rich Futurity despite the stable's decision to also start Citation and Free America—the most formidable three-ply entry in American stakes history to that time.

A sidebar question: What was Eddie Arcaro up to while all this was going on?

The renowned reinsman was in New York, plying his trade with typical success. His on-again-off-again affair with Calumet was in the "off" mode. Back in 1941, when Ben Jones tapped Eddie to ride Whirlaway to Triple Crown glory, Arcaro was a contract rider for Helen Payne Whitney's Greentree Stable. The latter's trainer, John Gaver, graciously "loaned" Arcaro to Jones and Calumet for the 1941 Triple.

Eddie had since been riding freelance, winning his third Kentucky Derby in 1945, the spring Cy was born, astride Hoop Jr.; a year later he joined forces with Assault following the colt's Triple Crown triumph under Warren Mehrtens. Assault unaccountably was in a tailspin, losing six straight; Eddie was summoned from the jockey bull pen to help restore Assault's greatness. The King Ranch champion earned acclaim as 1946 Horse of the Year.

And when Faultless and Dodson finished a powerhouse third to Jet Pilot in the 1947 Kentucky Derby, splitting them, beaten a scant head for it all on the wire, was Phalanx and Master Arcaro.

Eddie was totally committed to summer action in the East; he was geographically out of step with Calumet's summer doings. He busied himself with New York two-year-olds, among whom My Request, Better Self, and Relic figured most prominently. Unfortunately for Eddie, they weren't in the same league as Team Calumet. All Arcaro knew of Citation was what he read in the *Daily Racing Form*.

Back in Chicago, news that Ben and Jimmy Jones would seek a 1-2-3 sweep of the Washington Park Futurity resonated throughout the turf world. Their quest, though unprecedented, was realistically attainable, so compelling were the credentials of Bewitch, Citation, and Free America.

Bewitch was unbeaten in seven starts, Citation untouched in five, and late-comer Free America was riding a string of three straight wins following a narrow defeat in his racing bow.

Dodson, as indicated, winced not one whit choosing Bewitch over both Citation and Free America. Moreover, both Ben and Jimmy thought her unbeatable. For that matter, Ben may have even favored Free America a bit over Citation. Jimmy, however, maintained his respect for the maturing Cy, simply wondering if the colt could cope with Bewitch's speed at this early stage. She was for real; she curtsied to no one's horse, including males.

Snider would have gleefully back-flipped in Dodson's choice. But Al had run afoul of the stewards, was suspended, and was sadly unavailable to ride Citation. So the Joneses called on energetic, hard-hitting Steve Brooks as Cy's third different rider in six starts; for Free America they hired the cagey veteran Jackie Westrope.

Racing was aglow on Futurity day. Mr. and Mrs. Wright as usual drank and dined with racing mogul Ben Lindheimer. Calumet Farm manager Paul Ebelhardt drove from Lexington for the occasion, hung out with general manager Bob Henderson. Sports writers packed the Washington Park press box, including Arch Ward, Warren Brown, John P. Carmichael, Dave Feldman, Joe Agrella, and Elmer Polzin, many of whom had closely tracked the classy trio since their birth two years earlier.

If ever there was a festive family affair, it was Calumet on Futurity day. To allay the stable's only real concern—that there could *only* be one first-place finisher among their three starters—all three jockeys agreed to split their riding fees, so no one rider might be tempted to upstage the other.

Jimmy Jones also gave this stern order: "Whoever's in front in the stretch should be allowed to win the whole thing." Plain and simple. Not too much later, Jimmy confessed had he truly sensed Cy's upcoming date with destiny, he would never have issued such a "stupid" command.

Chapter Three

A Flash of Greatness

*W*hat nobody suspected as the August 16, 1947, Futurity field was loaded into the starting gate was that a major brouhaha was afoot, primed to escalate into a nationwide storm.

No other race—except perhaps for Upset's titanic "upset" score over otherwise insuperable Man o'War at Saratoga on August 19, 1919— would create such a stir among race aficionados as this one event.

For those who attach importance to such things, Sam Riddle's Man o'War, "Big Red" himself and the absolute against whom future stars were judged, died at the grand old age of thirty in November 1947. To sentimentalists who honor such coincidences, it seemed providential that Citation be the one to inherit Man o'War's mantle of greatness.

"I loved that Citation from the moment I saw him," said his Futurity rider Steve Brooks, who was aboard the frisky bay for the first time in live competition, deputizing for a grieving Al Snider. The latter would have given his right arm to ride Cy that day.

"Once Jimmy Jones told me I had the mount," Brooks recalled, "I asked Freeman [Freeman McMillan was Citation's regular exercise rider] if I could gallop or breeze him before the race, just so the two of us could get acquainted. Right then and there, I told myself Cy was not of this world, the kinda super horse you see every hundred years or so."

One question deeply bothered Brooks prior to the Futurity. Why would Jimmy assign Citation to a guy with Steve Brooks's reputation for whipping and kickin' and a no-holds-barred approach to race-riding, and then issue the order that "whoever's in front in the stretch gets to win the whole damn thing"?

"I was just hoping Bewitch would be impossible to catch," Steve shrugged, "otherwise, Cy and I could be in big trouble."

Though innately suspicious, woefully insecure, and jealously protective of his domain, Dodson rarely bragged; so it surprised both Steve Brooks and Jack Westrope, riders of Citation and Free America, when Doug declared while walking to the paddock where their Futurity charges were being saddled: "You guys can try all you want today—you won't know which way my filly went. I'm telling you now—she's that good."

It was as if Dodson was intentionally tempering Jimmy's command to "let the filly win" only because she'd naturally be in front in the stretch, given her blistering early speed. He was telling Brooks and Westrope that Bewitch didn't need their cooperation to notch the victory; she could do it all by herself.

What some hadn't factored in was the length of Washington Park's towering homestretch—1,531 feet, nearly a sixteenth of a mile longer than the lanes at either Churchill Downs, home of the Derby, or Chicago neighbor Hawthorne Race Course, whose elongated mile oval mimicked Churchill Downs.

By comparison, Arlington Park, like sister track Washington a sprawling 1⅛ miles oval, sported a comparatively short stretch—1,049 feet. This meant that Bewitch—for all her class, speed, and unblemished record—would have to take one huge, deep breath when she'd stare down the track's alpine home straightaway.

"Washington Park's homestretch was humongous," Brooks confirmed. "The turns were a bit sharp and narrow, which favored speed. But that long home lane was the great equalizer—chocolate cake for late-runners."

Bewitch, however, also was sitting on greatness. She was bred to be special; her speed was genuine, nothing cheap; she had murdered her opponents mercilessly in seven straight starts; in two of those she clobbered males; and she was never asked for her best. Dodson felt her bank of reserve was bottomless.

He was confident she'd win. And she did, too.

But not without a little help from her friends. That "help" was in the form of cooperative restraint by both Citation and Free America during the final furlong of the Futurity's six furlongs ultimately clocked in 1:10⅖, fastest in the stakes' history to that time.

Once released from the gate, the field of ten—only seven others dared test the Calumet trio—went on its merry way, Bewitch assuming her usual role as pacemaker. Dodson moved not one muscle as the powerful filly "left" her pursuers, lancing to a three-length lead as they swung around the far turn.

Brooks sat conspicuously uneasy aboard Cy in fourth, about four or five lengths off the flying leader. He glanced back—Free America was another three or four lengths back among the trailers.

Bewitch was a house afire turning for home, blasting away by five open lengths. Cy was still fourth, noticeably losing ground, now seven or eight lengths away, but striding fluidly, probably wondering why Brooks still had him under tons of restraint.

From the quarter pole in upper stretch to the furlong marker, an eighth of a mile from home, Bewitch widened her victory margin. Cy had moved up a notch at midstretch, now a distant third, some six lengths off the high-flying Bewitch.

Steve craned again, spotted Free America closing boldly outside rivals. It was time to let Citation run "a bit" if they were to achieve the historic 1-2-3 Futurity finish Calumet Farm sought.

"I never touched Citation," Brooks swore, his word confirmed by the film patrol account of the race. "But there was this tremendous explosion under me. It was as if Cy were asleep—and I woke him up! I just chirped to him, let loose the reins ever so slightly, and he came alive like a wild horse. He scared the hell out of me! He started picking up Bewitch with every stride. Remember, I was not supposed to beat her. That was our deal."

Bewitch was still five lengths ahead of Cy inside the furlong pole, and Dodson sensed the closing presence of his two friends.

Anyone familiar with Steve Brooks and his hard-hitting riding style knew the "fix" was in. Nothing so nefarious as in a so-called fixed race; rather, Brooks was not really letting Cy run. For that matter, Jack Westrope was also in on the "fix," so to speak. He was also limiting Free America as the trio hurled to the wire.

Officially, Bewitch was under a steady hand-ride from Doug Dodson, scoring "ridden out," as the *Daily Racing Form* chart of the race put it. It meant that she hadn't been strapped by her rider, or put to a full-out effort under any larruping. Simply translated: Bewitch could have shown more were she asked.

What was a five-length bulge in midstretch was slashed to a one-length winning margin at wire's end. Citation was a flying second, a scant head in front of Free America who had stormed from last to complete the memorable 1-2-3 finish that made racing history!

That's how the race formally turned out. What followed, though, was an uproar, an upheaval of assumption, a peppery exchange of opinion and conjecture—a source of debate to this day. Apparently, everyone in attendance that day, including Calumet Farm and its people and friends, saw the race differently.

Dodson explained: "Bewitch won the race with such authority, she could've won by any margin I wanted. She was just coasting at the end. She's still the best two-year-old in the land."

Brooks begged to differ: "I was strangling Cy, had my feet on the dash board, his head cranked back, else he would have swallowed her up in the final thirty yards."

Westrope proffered: "Free America would have caught the both of 'em in a few more strides. Heck, he had just started to run when it was all over with. But we did our job, didn't we? One-two-three, just like we were supposed to. But we were still fastest at the end."

Many years later, Brooks would explain why Cy, in finishing second to Bewitch, was just a dwindling head before Free America when the trio hit the wire: "Westrope and I discussed the race many times, and, thanks to hindsight, after Cy later had proved he could beat Free America anytime he wanted, I think I know why there was so much fuss after the race.

"Doug and Bewitch were doing their level best, as I see it. Me and Cy were the first to charge at her from out of the pack. I was all but throwing him down the final eighth to keep him from running all over her. I know he didn't understand what was happening. He was a born winner, but I wasn't letting him do the job. So Cy was in a sorta 'stall,' so to speak, in the final run to the finish.

"Meanwhile, Westrope was on a roll with Free America. He realized he had no chance of catching Bewitch, nor did he want to—remember that was our game plan—so he tried to gun us down for second. Cy caught 'em flying out of the corner of his eye, and was reaccelerating when the wire came, almost pulling my arms out of their sockets. Bad enough I didn't let him win like he should, but he'd never allow another horse catch him from behind."

Both Brooks and Westrope, however, were forced to applaud the filly. Bewitch shouldered top weight of 119 pounds, one more actual pound than the 118 hauled by both Cy and Free America. And she was a filly, entitled to a three-pound concession on the scale for that time of the year. Here was an Atlantean performance—a gal beating the boys for the third time in eight flawless outings.

Brooks, despite being an unwilling partner to ending Cy's five-race win streak, did allow the proud colt to assume his stately head-bowed canter back to the winner's circle where Calumet's remarkable Three Musketeers were allowed to share the unprecedented glory of that historic moment.

"Snider told me how he loved to cock his head, as if he were bowing to the throng," Brooks reminisced, "galloping that way to and from the gate, especially in front of the stands. You can get most horses to assume that dignified gait if you work at it. Cy, however, did it on his own. He seemed to know he was 'the greatest.'"

Not everybody agreed with Brooks' assessment. Sports announcer par excellence Jack Drees called the Futurity on local radio. Admittedly a Bewitch fan, he saw her victory as "another extraordinary display of speed and class . . . she could have won by fifteen lengths if Dodson let her. . . ."

The Wrights gave no thought to assigning merits or demerits to their three standard-bearers. They basked in national acclaim. The Jones boys likewise took pride in the achievement, although Jimmy expressed some guilt in not allowing Citation the luxury of victory. Had he known what greatness awaited Cy in less than a year, he'd have given Brooks the "go" sign without a second's hesitation.

There was fallout everywhere. Bewitch fans predicted she'd go unbeaten as a two-year-old, might prove to be only the second filly in history 'til then—Regret was the first in 1915—to conquer males in the 1948 Kentucky Derby.

Brooks and Westrope continued to rave about their colts, careful, however, to stop short of incurring Calumet's displeasure or anger. Sports media had no such governor; most, not all, opined either Citation or Free America would have collared Bewitch had they been given free rein. Some felt Bewitch had just reached her peak; a few doubted she'd ever beat Citation again.

One happy camper for sure was jockey Al Snider. If he played his cards right, he'd be back on Cy. Once he was assured that Dodson "wouldn't give up Bewitch on a bet," Snider launched what he considered a friendly, ongoing verbal tug of war between the two riders should Cy and the filly ever match strides again.

Snider may have overstepped his relationship with Doug a time or two, but he was convinced nothing could change Dodson's mind or faith in the unbeaten Bewitch. There was no way Doug could switch mounts, not as long as Bewitch continued to excel. He let Dodson know, however, that Cy would always be there should Bewitch "ever come up short." Dodson, of course, grimaced as only he could those days.

What should have been nothing more than teasing banter between two pro athletes might really have turned into something ugly were it not for the fact that Doug Dodson had fast emerged as America's top jockey in money and stakes won, thanks to Calumet's all-star stable—which meant he could afford to be cordial. By year's end, Doug would set a record $1,426,949 as money-earning champ, most of which enriched the coffers of Mr. and Mrs. Warren Wright. As if they needed more.

Doug was an excellent jockey with or without Calumet's starry runners; the devil's red and blue merely helped ensure his place in the sun. He had no viable reason to begrudge the successes of any other jock, Arcaro, Johnny Longden, Teddy Atkinson, and Al Snider included.

Fact is, 1947 was Armed's greatest season, unanimously exalted to Horse of the Year grandeur. If Doug valued any other mount than Bewitch that summer, it had to be the grand old gelding Armed, the latter piling up stake tallies as if there were no tomorrow.

For starters, Doug and Armed won the Stars & Stripes on July 4, also swept both the Arlington and Washington Park Handicaps. In between, Doug also piloted Fervent to victory in the time-honored American Derby for three-year-olds. All this and Bewitch, too.

Later that fall, in New York, he was aboard Armed when the gelding took the measure of Assault in a special match race, which totally clinched Horse of the Year. No prior jockey ever enjoyed such financial success—and Dodson's pockets jingle-jangled a merry winning tune.

When Washington Park closed on Labor Day, 1947, unbeaten Bewitch and once-beaten Citation were shipped to Belmont Park in New York. Easterners never cheered that much for Chicago luminaries; even the most provincial, however, admitted to Calumet's greatness in general, to the brilliance of Bewitch and Citation regardless of who got top billing.

The Belmont Futurity was their big target. By then, Jimmy Jones suspected he had the makings of a potential superstar in Citation, the latter rebounding from his controversial Chicago defeat much like boxer Sugar Ray Robinson might shrug off a glancing blow.

Bewitch and Dodson suffered a major setback of sorts shortly after the stable arrived at Belmont. The filly was her own sure-footed self, exuding class but probably too much bravura in hauling down the top prize in Belmont's Matron for two-year-old fillies. Mostly because of Doug's carelessness, Bewitch flagrantly impeded a filly name Ghost Run during the Matron, was disqualified, and placed last. Dodson drew the stewards' ire and was suspended for ten days.

This guaranteed Al Snider would ride Citation in the Belmont Futurity Trial on September 30. Six weeks had passed since Cy finished an unwilling second to Bewitch in Chicago. He had licked his wounds with a vengeance, also had put on fifty pounds or so of pure muscle. His chest was filling out; his handsome bay face wore a frown of sorts, more resolute than stern. And he galloped postward with that familiar bowed head. It was still business, but now more meaningful.

His "look" said it all: There'd be no more cowering, no more holding back, and, significantly, no more concessions. Finishing second meant being second-best. No more such foolishness.

Not surprisingly—New Yorkers always favored their own—the Eastern colt My Request was sent off as favorite over Citation in the Trial. The purse was an underwhelming $10,000. Didn't matter.

By this time Cy had demonstrated he could sprint or close with the best of 'em; he loved a fast track, he loved an "off" track—good, sloppy, or muddy—equally well. Apparently, there was no chink in his armor.

However—what if—what if he broke tardily, perhaps in a tangle, not fully prepared for the starter's gong? Could he overcome that obstacle? That became his acid test in the Belmont Futurity Trial.

Ninth leaving the gate in the six furlongs dash, Snider and Cy calmly bided their time as the field bunched up in the first three furlongs. Favored My Request was doing his best, as were Up Beat and Gasparilla. The field tightly waded (or "bunched up") a furlong out. Cy was sixth, but within hailing distance of the embattled leaders.

"I wish I were still riding him," Steve Brooks would reply back in Chicago when told what Cy did that fall afternoon in New York. Actually only two years away from becoming Calumet Farm's newest contract rider, Brooks wouldn't have that privilege again, not for three years when Citation "Part Two" would be released.

What Citation did in the Futurity Trial was incredible. From ninth at the start, seventh at the half, and sixth at an eighth of a mile from home, he effortlessly vaulted to the fore to register a "going-away" one-length triumph over Gasparilla and Up Beat—My Request was on his way to the showers.

Snider was ecstatic but hid his zeal; he didn't want Dodson either upset or envious. He needn't worry that day; Dodson was still sitting out his suspension, knowing he'd soon be reunited with Bewitch, but not in time for the Futurity. Jackie Westrope would deputize for Doug, though the latter was predicting, "she'll win the Futurity big!"

Belmont's rich Belmont Futurity was presented less than a week later, the distance stretching 6½ furlongs down the Widener straightaway, a genuine test of a young two-year-old's fortitude and intrinsic class.

Eddie Arcaro had a bird's-eye view of Citation that fall: "I really just saw him from afar, in his two starts. He won me over as probably the best two-year-old in the land, but I reserved any real judgment until the Futurity itself. But I've been around two-year-old champs before. I can't say he looked any better than the others. But then, I wasn't riding him. Snider was; and Al wasn't saying too much in those days."

The hint of greatness Cy dropped in finishing a closing second to Bewitch in Chicago seven weeks earlier ignited into a single flash of brilliance on Belmont Futurity day. By now, even New Yorkers realized they were privy to a legend in the making.

Remember, Snider had kidded Dodson that he and Cy would be there should Bewitch "ever come up short." That dramatic prophecy was fulfilled for all to see at Belmont Park on October 4.

Even with her Matron miscue, Bewitch could still boast that no horse had ever finished in front of her. She was determined to keep it that way, but this time Jimmy gave no command that she had to win; it was every horse for himself—and Citation was crying for satisfaction.

Free America, incidentally, had been sidelined by injury; he watched from afar as Citation and Bewitch again paraded postward side by side— king and queen of American two-year-old racing. Westrope may have thought Bewitch capable of winning it all, but Snider was convinced not even Man o'War incarnate could beat his colt, then or ever.

Bewitch, to her credit, tried mightily. She was neither stale nor tailing off. She vied with the first flight from the start, wrested command with her usual authority; but—she had to face it—the males were getting tougher and stronger. And when Whirling Fox grabbed her by the throat-latch, she and Westrope were in deep trouble; her tank was empty. She sent out an SOS loud and clear.

It was Citation to the rescue! The moment for which he was bred and raised. Fourth early, then third as they approached the final quarter mile, Mighty Cy cut loose! No gentlemanly scrapes and bows. No more of that chivalrous Sir Walter Raleigh nonsense. Just raw power. And no need for the whip. Snider merely said: "Go!" And it was over before it started.

Cy inhaled Whirling Fox and Bewitch like they were standing still, and, with his ears pricking against the crowd's roar, swept on by to win the Futurity by three lengths—and he was just starting to run.

Snider's chest swelled with a heart that throbbed with uncontrollable joy. He could only imagine how Citation felt. It was as if God had created a super equine machine, fitted it with a heart and soul, then commanded: "Go, proceed and conquer, and do so with power, style, and dignity!"

Citation realized his destiny that day. But like the great warrior who had just begun to fight, Cy had greater glories to achieve, and a reputation for promised greatness to defend.

It might have been a semi-happy ending for all, if only Dodson had accepted Bewitch's disappointment graciously. Doug would insanely make another major career faux pas because he couldn't control his steaming insecurities and his penchant for pettiness.

Dodson sat atop the world of thoroughbred racing. He had it all, would continue to have it all, too—but he also wanted Citation again, at least for the moment, to salve his out-of-control ego.

Snider had not finished savoring Cy's Futurity triumph, and Doug was already pulling rank. Al later told Arcaro he was flabbergasted by Doug's greed and small-mindedness: "I would have knocked him on his ass, I was so mad. But I didn't want to blow my relationship with Ben and Jimmy. But I did tell Doug he 'should be ashamed of himself.' He was one selfish bastard."

Dodson never batted an eye. Jimmy was inclined to let Snider keep Cy, at least for the balance of the two-year-old campaign. But Ben didn't want to rock the boat. Mr. Wright, who honestly couldn't tell one end of the horse from the other, also seemed satisfied with Dodson's work. So the Jones boys reluctantly turned Citation over to Dodson for the colt's final 1947 appearance in the Pimlico Futurity at the "classic" distance for juveniles—1 1/16 miles, their longest journey to date. Bewitch had called it quits for the year.

It was around this time that Calumet was breaking in a comparative unknown to its jockey colony—Newbold L. Pierson, or N. L. Pierson as his name would be carried in the track program. He was a mediocre but savvy saddlesmith. His lack of track popularity and success made him a Calumet hanger-on. But the association rubbed off; it paid his bills. Astonishingly, in less than a year his name would be bandied about in the same breath as Citation, Arcaro, and Coaltown. For the time being, however, Pierson was satisfied to be around guys like Dodson and Snider, horses like Armed, Citation, and Bewitch, and even ride a race or two when the first team wanted a break.

Pimlico's Futurity, which was scheduled for November 8, would mark Cy's ninth outing as a two-year-old over nearly a seven-month span. Bull Lea's finest son had tackled the best juveniles in America, and in eight prior starts, in distances from four to six furlongs, had finished worse than first only once, that excusable second to Bewitch in the Washington Park Futurity, a defeat that should never have been.

He atoned for that single season blemish by whipping Whirling Fox and Bewitch at Belmont on October 4. There was no Breeders' Cup in those days, so the Pimlico Futurity was the last world to conquer if Cy were to achieve national landslide election as two-year-old kingpin.

Snider was relegated to the stands. Returning Cy's reins to Dodson was a bitter pill to swallow. Al privately shared his chagrin with both Arcaro and Steve Brooks, both of whom had suffered similar disappointment. Eddie reminded Snider of his blunder in choosing Devil Diver over Shut Out in the 1942 Kentucky Derby, one year after he and Whirlaway won the Triple Crown. Shut Out won the Derby, Devil Diver faded to sixth. Shut Out went awry in the Preakness won by Alsab, but was reunited with Arcaro to win the Belmont Stakes.

"It always seems to work out, you'll see," Eddie mollified.

Brooks shared Snider's high regard for Citation, particularly Steve's unwilling role in "getting Cy beat" at Washington Park. "No matter how much I tell Ben and Jimmy how great this colt is, they seem to take it all in stride," Steve said. "Calumet has so many good ones, they sorta take Cy for granted. I'll never get to ride him again, but don't you give up, Al."

"Don't give up, Al," became Snider's secret war cry. He loved Cy dearly, yet a shameful part of Al's psyche was hoping the colt and Dodson might lose at Pimlico, as if that defeat would have a negative impact on Doug come Cy's 1948 three-year-old season. Glamour, riches, celebrity, also possible racing immortality awaited Citation's three-year-old campaign just around the corner. Hardly seemed likely Dodson would ever give Cy back to Al.

Dodson surprisingly was visibly concerned about the heavy rains the night before race day at Pimlico. The slop had turned to deep mud by post time. Doug's only two victory rides atop Cy had taken place over fast tracks in July at Arlington and Washington.

Snider, however, feared not. He had won twice before aboard Cy in "off" going. In fact, Cy won in the slop in his very first outing at Havre de Grace on April 22, relishing the goo like a kid elbow-deep in chocolate cake.

"Cy can run on glass, if need be," Snider would later confide in Arcaro.

Two things may have combined to cloud Dodson's objective assessment of Citation's true worth at that time. First, Doug was fresh off Armed's New York match race triumph over arch rival Assault, which cinched Horse of the Year for Calumet's golden gelding. Doug had only sincere affection for Armed's class, gameness, and consistency. Second, unraced Coaltown back on the farm had shaken off the throat ailment that sidelined him all of his 1947 two-year-old season. Farm rumor had it that once in gear Coaltown would prove superior to all teammates, including Citation, Bewitch, and Free America. He was that fast.

Therefore, Dodson may not have had his heart in it when he expropriated Citation for the colt's final two-year-old start. He simply wanted the whole pie for himself. The muddy strip also concerned Dodson as Cy and his then most formidable two-year-old opponent, Better Self, lined up on Pimlico Futurity day, first time these young thoroughbreds would have to run 1 1/16 miles, and around two turns.

By now, Cy was truly a pushbutton colt. He had Bewitch's speed and Free America's endurance, but, more importantly, he possessed the versatility they lacked to employ either weapon whenever called upon. Plus, he owned the intelligence, and, now, an ego to match. He knew how good he was; how great he'd soon be. Cy could outrun any foe around; he could catch any opponent, at any time, just for the asking.

Young Citation put it all together that day. He flashed needed speed early; dutifully stepped back when rated; churned effortlessly through the thick mud; then uncorked an electrifying late surge when called upon—defying opponent, distance, and running surface—reporting "home free" by 1 1/2 lengths over a game but outrun Better Self. A weary Ace Admiral salvaged third.

"He toyed with them that day," Jimmy Jones smiled. "We had ourselves a genuine champ," Jones would reflect, "but just how great we really didn't know. But then we've had a lot of great ones before, like Whirlaway, Twilight Tear, Pensive, Twosy, and Armed.

"Cy was just getting started as our newest top horse," Jimmy continued, "and nailing down the two-year-old title was enough for us at the moment. Remember, we also had Bewitch and Armed that year, and when Bewitch was injured, Whirl Some ably replaced her." What Jimmy meant was that in some ways Cy was simply Calumet's newest champion.

At year's end (1947), Armed ruled thoroughbred racing as Horse of the Year; Bewitch wore the crown as champion two-year-old filly; and Citation was unanimous choice as America's top juvenile colt. Moneywise, Bewitch would have broken Top Flight's two-year-old money record had she not lost the Matron in New York via disqualification—she still banked $213,675.

Citation was the top money-winning colt with $155,680. Calumet surpassed a million in earnings with a record $1,402,436, more than doubling its own all-time previous high. Bull Lea naturally topped the roster as champion money-winning sire ($1,259,718), and trainer Jimmy Jones saddled winners of top dollar ($1,334,408), easily eclipsing, more than doubling, the previous mark. And Dodson, of course, set a new record for jockeys in money won with $1,429,949.

Dodson ceded Citation's genuineness. But he was still smarting over the revenge Cy wreaked on Bewitch after he—Dodson—had boldly, and prematurely, proclaimed the filly queen over all she surveyed.

Moreover, Doug truly valued Armed over Citation; he was Armed's regular pilot. He unequivocally declared Armed his "greatest mount," and his resolve to stick by that choice, as forthright and commendable as it was, ultimately would prove his undoing.

Jimmy Jones did his best to keep peace behind the scenes at Calumet, though he, too, was tiring of Dodson's temper tantrums and the rider's insatiable desire to have it all. But Jimmy felt—correctly too—that the stable had more than its share of talented horseflesh to go around. He pacified Snider with the tempting lure that Coaltown was being cranked up as a 1948 three-year-old, that Citation's paternal half brother also had the makings of a wonder horse.

Snider couldn't care less. He wanted no part of Coaltown; his heart belonged to Cy despite reports from exercise riders, including Freeman McMillan, that Coaltown was "a born runner!"

Nonetheless, Snider lost valuable sleep the entire winter in Kentucky and Florida, worrying himself sick whether he'd ever get to ride Citation again. Dodson continued riding high, calling the shots, unconcerned that the high and mighty have been known to fall.

Unlike today, when Breeders' Cup two-year-old winners rarely amount to a hill of beans as three-year-olds—Fusaichi Pagasus in 2000 was the first favorite to win the Kentucky Derby since Spectacular Bid in 1979—in Cy's day juvenile title-holders, also Derby favorites, were held in high esteem. Previous two-year-old luminaries as Man o'War, Equipoise, Twenty Grand, Bimelech, Whirlaway, Alsab, and Count Fleet followed up excellent two-year-old campaigns with equally superb efforts as three-year-olds.

Same for two-year-old stars who immediately followed Citation—Hill Prince, Hill Gail, Battlefield, Tom Fool, Native Dancer, Hasty Road, Nashua, and Needles, among others.

Citation thus became the winter book favorite—probably long before such a proviso existed—for the 1948 Kentucky Derby when such an honor really meant something.

Chapter Four

"And I Saw Man o'War . . ."

"*Citation* just may be the thoroughbred we've been waiting for all these years since Man o'War."

Those words, actually hopes, were chorused by two of Chicago's most enlightened sports entrepreneurs—*Chicago Tribune* sports editor Arch Ward and Arlington-Washington major domo Ben Lindheimer, whose combined efforts to hype local sports helped belie Chicago's dubious "Second City" status.

Ward was a sports promoter nonpareil, whose work with all-star football and baseball games would become legendary. His private love, however, was thoroughbred racing, a passion fed by close personal ties with the Lindheimer family and its expanding racing kingdom.

In 1940 it was Lindheimer, then director of Chicago's south side race emporium Washington Park, who purchased north side Arlington Park in partnership with John D. Allen, vice president of Brinks & Co. Not long afterward, Lindheimer assumed sole control, combining Arlington's thirty-six-day meeting with Washington Park's thirty-one-day season into a coordinated summer festival extravaganza, to which he proudly, and accurately, attached the label, "America's Finest Summer Racing."

Fact that Lindheimer and Warren Wright were drinking buddies helped persuade Calumet to embrace Chicago as the stable's annual "summer home base." That distinction alone helped exalt Chicago as the undisputed summer mecca of thoroughbred racing. Also, Calumet's fabulous dynasty almost single-handedly was responsible for converting racing's time-honored cachet as the Sport of Kings into the King of Sports. For years horse racing would reign as America's number one spectator sport, if the stats distributed in those days were trustworthy.

Ward and Lindheimer weren't the only ones who applauded Cy's heroics as a two-year-old. There were others equally as vocal, including sports scribes Joe Palmer, John P. Carmichael, Joe Kelly, Bill Boniface, Warren Brown, Elmer Polzin, and racing historian Tom Gilcoyne. Most of them, however, while ceding Citation's great capability, were holding off using the adjective "great" for the time being.

Cy certainly crashed turf headlines with impact rivaling Man o'War, who won nine of his ten starts as a two-year-old (1919); after his sole defeat by Upset in his seventh outing as a juvenile, Big Red rolled to fourteen straight wins to wrap up an unprecedented record of twenty wins in twenty-one starts, retiring after his unbeaten three-year-old season of 1920.

Other thoroughbred greats, including the Australian icon Phar Lap and the American sensation Seabiscuit, both of whom dazzled in the 1930s (though Phar Lap also sparkled down under in the late 1920s as perhaps the world's all-time great gelding), accomplished little of note as two-year-olds, awaiting later seasons to lay claim to fame. Equipoise, another standout in the 1930s, also saved his best for his three- and four-year-old seasons.

That Cy was off to a rousing start as a two-year-old no one could deny. Several things, however, worked to his disservice. Being a Calumeter and a son of Bull Lea helped classify him as "expected royalty," just another of Calumet's pack of blue bloods.

Truthfully, his biggest drawback—though hardly a fault—was his lack of panache and sparkle. If he weren't flamboyant, then he was expected to have at least an idiosyncrasy or two; if not a quirky nature, surely a long tail like Whirlaway, a flaming coat like Man o'War, or a club foot like racing's most recent Triple Crown hero Assault (1946). He had none of the above.

For that matter, nor was Cy an "incredible hulk" physically, nothing to catch the eye, certainly nothing worth mentioning. And his handsome face and well-known intelligence apparently weren't enough to capture and sustain media attention or imagination.

Furthermore, Jimmy Jones's reluctance to extol was because the young trainer was immersed in a plethora of champs and contenders. Free

America was slowly on the mend, and the unraced but ebullient Coaltown was back in light training, still an unknown quality. Jimmy knew Cy was special, but not *how* special.

Al Snider knew. But he wasn't talking. For sure not for media consumption. Certainly not within earshot of Doug Dodson. He'd utter nary a word lest he dissuade Dodson from his love for both Armed and Bewitch. And they'd be ready for action in the not too distant future. Al's lips were sealed.

As Calumet turned the corner into 1948, its starry lineup loomed even more formidable than the year before, especially among those horses who just turned three years old on January 1. Like MGM, the stable had more stars than there were in the heavens. Calumet took a brief respite in Lexington before journeying to Florida and what was then a prestige-laden Hialeah winter season.

Bewitch was back on the farm convalescing from a popped osselet, a hard, bony growth usually found on either the inner side of the knee or the outer side of the fetlock just above the hoof. It was a painful ailment, but the filly, now three, was recovering nicely, obviously enjoying the time off for good behavior.

Citation was as healthy as, well, a horse! He didn't have a pimple anywhere; his muscular frame was just about perfect. No strains, no sprains, no fuss. He ate heartily, a "good doer," to hear his handler tell it.

Cy had been unwinding slowly since his November 8 Pimlico Futurity romp, evidently relishing the regimen of rest and relaxation that racing allowed thoroughbreds of his caliber. He was taken for daily walks and gallops. Nothing strenuous or challenging, just enough to keep him limber. He was actually anxious to return to the racing wars, but was willing to wait for the official call to arms.

Al Snider and Eddie Arcaro were more than just friendly riding rivals; they were fervid golfing buddies as well. Whenever possible, even if it meant catching a plane, they'd often connect on racing "dark" days for what surely was Arcaro's primary recreational hobby—next to gambling, drinking, and womanizing, all of which he juggled adroitly—namely, a competitive game of golf. Eventually, Eddie would list golf as, if not his true, at least his first, love.

Arcaro later admitted to a tang of envy as far as Snider was concerned. "Al was sitting on a ton of gold with Calumet," Eddie recalled, "but either he didn't know it, or he didn't appreciate it. He was insecure, not as bad as Dodson, but then Al was in a queer position, what with Doug do-ing all the dictating.

"Al cracked to me that Citation was something special. I was flattered he trusted me. I would've loved the colt, especially if he was half as good as Al claimed. But I did the right thing. I listened, and—what's the word?—I 'commiserated' with him. I told him just wait, and 'you'll get what you want in the end.'"

Snider figured that crunch time as far as Citation was concerned wouldn't come until sometime early February—the colt's number one tar-get was the February 28 Flamingo Stakes, then a major springboard to the Kentucky Derby, first leg of the Triple Crown.

Arcaro advised Snider to "get as close as possible to both Ben and Jimmy Jones." By endearing himself to the Jones boys, especially Ben, whose experience and maturity made him the ideal "father figure," Al might gain some inside leverage by the time mount assignments came due. By this time, Snider wholeheartedly concurred with Arcaro's public confession "that the jock's only as good as his horse." Dodson's phenom-enal 1947 success had indeed ratified Arcaro's pronouncement.

Snider played his cards just as Eddie suggested, but his "ace in the hole" came about not as a fruit of own doing, rather as an inadvertent gift from, of all people, Doug Dodson himself!

But that's jumping ahead of the story and the events which would have a direct bearing as to which jockey would have Citation as the 1948 three-year-old season approached in all its glamour and glory.

January 1948 had arrived in Florida; Citation was merely galloping and stretching his limbs in light daily exercises. However, there was another Hialeah-based stakes-winning, newly turned sophomore named Relic—owned by successful horseman Eddie Moore—a speedy sort who gained a measure of fame as a two-year-old by winning New York's Hopeful Stakes, no mean feat.

As a 1947 two-year-old, Cy had already thoroughly vanquished Ben Whitaker's multiple stakes hero My Request—winner of the Juvenile, National Stallion, Grand Union, and Cowdin, among others—and King Ranch's brilliant Better Self, who had won the East View Stakes and Saratoga Special before dropping the Pimlico Futurity to Calumet's won-der colt. And Cy had finished ahead of Arlington Futurity winner Piet in Bewitch's controversial Washington Park Futurity.

He had never faced Relic, however, and the latter's contentious owner, a drinking buddy of Warren Wright, entertained grandiose ideas for his nimble-footed three-year-old. Every owner reportedly falls in love with his "good" horse. And Moore fell hardest of all.

Plus, Moore enjoyed a considerable jump on Wright and Citation when his Relic won the Hibiscus in January at Hialeah in a snappy 1:10 flat for six furlongs over an off track, only two-fifths of a second off the track record. The victory was authentic; Eddie Moore was hopelessly intoxicated by the thrill of victory, to the exclusion of common sense.

Apparently all it took were a few drinks between two wealthy egoistic men, Moore ultimately challenging Wright to "a match race between Relic and Citation." A match race at that time was impractical, but Moore still bragged that his Relic would dump Citation "on his ass" the next time, or anytime, the two colts would meet. Wright fell for the dare hook, line, and sinker.

Jimmy Jones found himself squarely in the middle. "Mr. Wright was fuming. He had a low flash point, and it didn't take much to set him off. Besides, I think he and Mr. Moore were backing their talk with wagers."

Jones said Wright "told me he wanted to shove Relic right down Moore's throat, that he'd like to run Cy against Relic as soon as possible to settle this damn thing. 'But I don't want Citation beat,' he told me, as nicely as the man could when his temper was hot.

"Now I was young then, didn't know too much, so I kinda took what he said as an order. So I figured I better get the horse cranked up else face the consequences."

Jimmy's father, Ben, probably would have nixed the idea and stuck to Cy's original schedule—the Everglades on February 18 and the Flamingo ten days later, both races restricted to three-year-olds.

Thus Jimmy "cranked up" Citation earlier than he wanted. But Cy was in excellent shape despite the layoff; he responded instantly to Jimmy's accelerated training regimen. The colt smoothly segued from gallops to serious works and time trials. His mien was workmanlike, his attitude upbeat and positive, intelligently sensing the urgency of the situation.

Now all Jimmy had to do was find a race for Cy. "I looked all over, tried all conditions. Naturally I wanted as soft a spot as possible to tighten him up to meet Relic, whenever that'd be. So I was looking for a sprint, just an overnight allowance dash, to get him race-worthy, even if it meant going against older horses."

Jimmy found what he considered the "perfect spot," a six furlongs overnight dash on February 2 for a $5,000 purse; and, yes, against older horses. The "spot" was so good Jimmy also entered Horse of the Year

Armed as entrymate. Armed also was being primed for another banner season.

Dodson spied the entry; he chose Armed in what he considered a no-brainer. Armed was America's best. Dodson was pleased with his choice. So was Snider; he'd be back aboard Cy.

Jimmy was shocked to see all the others who also found the February 2 dash "a soft spot." Armed, of course, was forced to tote top weight of 130 because of the race's allowance conditions. Citation as a just-turned three-year-old got in with 113, which on paper didn't seem that heavy.

According to racing's weight scale at that time, Cy's 113 pounds was equal to 128 on a four-year-old, equivalent to 130 on an equine older than that. In effect, then, Citation was sharing top weight of 130 with stablemate Armed; but the latter wasn't Cy's only worry as Snider guided the colt postward that afternoon.

"Kitchen Police was a quick one, was five at the time," Jimmy recalled, "and got in with only 110, which meant we were giving an older horse three pounds. Say Blue also was in the race, and she had earned some $100,000, so she had some class then—and she got in with only 107. Then there was a four-year-old named Tavistock, also a winner of $100,000, not to forget Rampart, a grand old mare who was six that year when she won the Black Helen and Gulfstream Park Handicaps, and she got in with only 113 pounds."

Jimmy didn't have to tell Dodson how to ride Armed—they were the perfect twosome. But he did warn Snider not to "kill" Cy with "needless pressure . . . we just want to tighten him up, that's all."

Snider nodded, smiling inwardly, gently patting the powder keg he knew so well. "Don't worry, boss," Al agreed, "everything will be okay, I promise."

"Okay" was an understatement. Cy leapt from the gate as if shot from a cannon. Al reached down, took a solid hold, and allowed Kitchen Police to take control for the first half mile. Cy was coolly breezing right at Kitchen Police's neck as they hit the top of the homestretch. Jimmy saw it this way: "Citation blew by Kitchen Police at mid-stretch and won by a length without any trouble at all." Say Blue grabbed third; Rampart and Horse of the Year Armed were nowhere.

Cy was no slowpoke either, streaking six furlongs in 1:10⅗. But running "time" would never play that mighty a weapon in Cy's growing arsenal. He'd run only as fast as needed to get the job done. He'd run as fast as the fastest foe if need be; or he could be rated right off the pace; and he was relentless when in pursuit; yet was easily content to stalk, then collar, when so instructed; he'd put away his adversary like blowing out a candle, always well within his self-contained power.

Jimmy saw no despair in Armed's failure. The vaunted gelding was making his first start, obviously needed the race, perhaps was not that formidable at the sprinting distance. Jimmy didn't need Al Snider to remind him that Citation also was making his first start of the season, and though he had won seven of his eight in sprints as a two-year-old, he also was coming off the middle distance of $1\frac{1}{16}$ miles of the Pimlico Futurity. He, too, was coming back to the sprint.

What Jimmy failed to factor into Citation's effort was that the colt was razor-sharp despite his abbreviated training program following a brilliant juvenile year. He not only possessed speed to stay with the likes of Kitchen Police, but he left 'em all when asked in late stretch.

Dodson brooded a bit, but the veteran felt his standing with Wright, Calumet, and the Joneses inviolate. There'd be ample time for vindication. Besides, he could have Citation any time he wanted. Plus, he was hearing Coaltown's pounding hoofbeats yet in the future.

Jimmy felt Cy was ready for Relic. Two days after Cy's sprint triumph, however, Relic scored his second straight stakes triumph, running off with the Bahamas. That disturbed Jimmy. Was Citation ready for Relic off that one victory, as impressive it was over older steeds? No, Jimmy reasoned, the colt would need one more tightener.

"Well," said Jimmy "there was nothing in the condition book for us except the Seminole Handicap nine days later. It was at a longer distance—seven furlongs—but again against older horses. So I figured, we have to go for it, but I wasn't taking any chances, so I entered both Armed and Faultless along with Cy."

Jimmy wasn't broadcasting it, but he secretly craved another 1-2-3 stakes finish, this time expecting a herculean effort from Armed. And he didn't discount hard-hitting Faultless, who just the year before scored handsomely in the Preakness Stakes after failing by two scant heads in third behind Jet Pilot and Phalanx in the Kentucky Derby.

But to pull it off the trio had to face a truly classy field. Four-year-old Delegate, fresh off victory in the Hialeah Inaugural and heir apparent to honors as America's champion sprinter, was poised to rumble, as was the speed-minded six-year-old Buzfuz. Also lined up against

Calumet was the five-year-old Round View, no slouch here. Other older challengers included Wide Wing, Tavistock, and Gestapo. The race was legitimately what the industry today would call a bona fide Grade I event.

Armed dropped two pounds to 128, while Citation was given 112, top impost ("top weight") on the scale. Fleet-footed Delegate got in with 123. On paper, Cy would have to be one top thoroughbred to even get close.

Jimmy was no dummy. He could read and appreciate that the Seminole was no "walk in the park." Because of imposing lineup of elders, he seriously considered, then decided against, scratching Citation. So what if he gets beat; at least he'll be ready for Relic.

Jimmy did command, however, that Snider was not to rush, hurry, or unduly ask the impossible of the three-year-old bay, who despite officially celebrating his third birthday weeks earlier on January 1, was still really a two-year-old, having been foaled on April 11, 1945, exactly two months to the day shy of chronological three-year-old status on this February 11, 1948!

Cy's uniqueness in taking on older horses so early in life did not go unnoticed by rival horsemen, particularly heralded trainers "Sunny" Jim Fitzsimmons and "Canny" Max Hirsch, two of the most respected men of their profession.

Sunny Jim already was revered as the sport's only two-time Triple Crown trainer—Gallant Fox (1930) and Omaha (1935).

Hirsch also was Hall of Fame bound. He saddled Bold Venture to capture both the 1936 Kentucky Derby and Preakness. A bowed tendon prevented Bold Venture from coveting the Belmont. Hirsch did win the Triple Crown ten years later with Bold Venture's son Assault.

Sunny Jim Fitzsimmons trained for the Belair Stud, Canny Max Hirsch for King Ranch. Along with Calumet's Ben and Jimmy Jones, with notable assists from Greentree's John Gaver and public trainers Hirsch Jacobs and Bill Molter, Fitzsimmons and Hirsch ruled the turf world. And that turf world valued their opinion.

Sunny Jim and Canny Max especially had been watching Citation's development. Fact that Cy didn't limit his feats to Chicago—his last four starts, three as a two-year-old, were outside Illinois—exposed him to Eastern and Southern observers. He had won both the Trial and Belmont Futurity in New York, followed that up with victory in the Pimlico Futurity in Maryland, and capped it with his Hialeah triumph in Florida.

Therefore, expert eyes focused on Citation in the February 11 Seminole. The dynamic Bull Lea bay was the *only* youngster in the field, technically a just-turned three-year-old but literally still a two-year-old with high ambitions. He faced a spate of stakes stars, again locking horns with America's undisputed champion, seasoned seven-year-old Armed, equipped with a confident and unforgiving Doug Dodson.

Jimmy was stunned at what he saw once the field was dispatched. Cy started alertly, and, with no urging from Snider, ding-donged it stride for stride with fleet merchant Delegate as if out for a leisurely stroll. The early fractions were lively—Delegate under stress to establish the rapid pace, Citation right at his neck, unhurried. Snider followed orders to a T, no pressure, no whip, no extra encouragement.

"Wow," Jimmy exhaled, "Cy was just playing with some of the fastest, best horses in the country, and Armed was trying, for that matter they were all trying. Cy was merely toying with 'em, taking control in mid-stretch, then whipping Delegate easily by a length, with Armed, full out, another length back in third!"

It finally dawned on Jimmy; he didn't have to have a house fall on him, not this time. Citation had just conquered a bonny band of older horses with virtually no effort at all. He stopped the timer in 1:23 flat, which would turn out to be the fastest seven furlongs clocking for the year at Hialeah. Heaven knows he could have run a lot faster had Snider asked. Again the colt did just what he had to do. No undue flash or flair and no pretense or swagger.

Only vanity Cy allowed was his lordly head-bowed jog back to the charmed circle where his friends awaited. His greatness needed no showy advertising; but had just done what no other young three-year-old had ever done before or since.

When Jimmy greeted Citation and Snider in the Winner's Circle, he couldn't help but exclaim for all to hear: "My God, what kind of a horse do we have here?"

"I suppose I've been trying to tell you all along, boss," Snider braved to whisper as he removed Citation's saddle. Al couldn't control his enthusiasm any longer, come what may.

"So you have," Jimmy mused, "so you have."

Citation's feat made him the talk of the town, not only of Hialeah, Florida, but of the whole turf world. His presence was immense, his impact electrifying.

It was left to Sunny Jim Fitzsimmons to unmask Cy for the whole world to see. The revered trainer said it simply: "Up to this point Citation's done more than any horse I ever saw—and I saw Man o'War!"

Chapter Five

The Agony and the Ecstasy

"*W*ell, the cat's out of the bag now for sure," sports columnist Warren Brown told Chicago track general manager Bob Henderson when apprised of Sunny Jim's unsolicited praise following Citation's second straight big-league Hialeah victory over older horses.

Brown's commonplace but laconic remark captured perfectly the profundities unveiled by Fitzsimmons's sudden pronouncement that young Cy was equal to, if not better than, the redoubtable—and 'till now sacrosanct—Man o'War himself. Most past comparisons to Man o'War vanished as quickly as uttered. But the esteemed Sunny Jim had gone one giant step further—he dared to suggest that Citation was actually superior to racing's Big Red.

Surprisingly, few decried Fitzsimmons's remark as either outrageous or unfounded. Many thoroughbred greats—including Blue Larkspur, Discovery, Twenty Grand, Phar Lap, Seabiscuit, Equipoise, Gallant Fox, War Admiral, Whirlaway, Count Fleet, Armed, and Assault—had come and gone since Man o'War captured America's sporting fancy; but none was ever considered his equal, certainly not his master.

Sports writers swarmed all over Hialeah following Cy's glossy Seminole triumph. The Joneses were still shell-shocked; owner Wright regarded Cy's brilliance as license to covet yet another Kentucky Derby; Snider was so proud he all but burst his buttons; and Bull Lea and Hydroplane, had they understood their favorite son's heroics, would be strutting like peacocks all over Calumet ground in Lexington.

Unfortunately, Doug Dodson's strange mix of forced-grin and dark moping qualified him as the only ambivalent soul around.

If only Dodson could have curbed his doubts and insecurities—were such conduct governors possible—if only he had realized that once a hot-headed bullet is fired, it can't be recalled.

Doug fired that bullet at the worst, most inopportune time. Anyone with even the slightest interest in racing—especially all news media throughout the country—was captivated by, surely knew of, the game's newest wonder horse and his quiet, modest jockey, Albert Snider.

Jones's awakened amazement in Cy's incredible back-to-back victories over superb fields which included the likes of Armed, Delegate, and Faultless, coupled with Sunny Jim's generous kudos, also help thrust Citation dead-center amid a swelling hullabaloo sweeping the nation.

Unbelievably, Dodson picked that very moment to declare he now wanted Citation back for his own—again! This time Snider vigorously said *no!* "Enough is enough," Al boldly pleaded his case right to the top—personally to both Ben and Jimmy Jones.

And justice prevailed. The Jones boys had had their fill of Dodson's prima donna temperament; Doug had protested once too often. The edict was final: Al Snider would keep Citation. Everyone involved approved of the way Al was handling Citation. The colt was his to keep through the Triple Crown, and as long as Cy stayed healthy. Period!

Moreover, the Joneses, as if to confirm that Al had truly earned his spurs, revealed they were also seriously considering naming Snider as Armed's new jockey for the upcoming Widener Handicap.

Dodson went bonkers!

Worse—Dodson quit; he walked out on Calumet Farm!

It would be unsympathetic to suggest a mighty shout greeted Dodson's idiotic, short-sighted decision to quit the world's most famous stable. To most folks who were familiar with Doug's untimely fits of passion and temper outbursts, a twinge of sadness and a hearty "good riddance" was the general reaction.

Doug threw it all away, angrily watched his fondest jockey dreams disappear as swill down a drain. What a difference a year can make in a crazed man's career when dark emotion is allowed to becloud normal human perspicacity. Doug rode atop the world in 1947 and was now on a "summit plummet" less than two months later.

Doug Dodson's riding career would never be the same. Not that he was ruined as a jockey. Nothing that serious. But there'd be no more money-riding titles; no more Armed, or Pot o' Luck, or Faultless; certainly no more Bewitch or Citation. Those days were gone forever.

Oh, he'd win his fair share of overnight races and features, even a stakes or two. In fact, he teamed up with a Cinderella grass star named Manassas in 1957—John Zitnik's former claimer and dirt-course bust won six straight on the grass that year—to win the rich Arlington Handicap. Two years later, Dodson was aboard Manasses when the six-year-old all but ran down the great Round Table, finishing a dwindling neck shy of the latter in the 1959 Arlington 'Cap renewal.

But Doug's glory days were finished. He remained melancholy, reportedly was almost suicidal when his earthly sojourn ended somewhat mysteriously a few years later. He always condemned his stupidity in quitting Calumet Farm as "a horrible mistake, almost too painful to discuss. They never gave me a second chance; can't say that I blame 'em."

Ironically, Relic—the fleet colt whose owner's daring challenge caused Calumet to "crank up" Citation for a personal duel simply to please two crotchety old egotists—broke down just a few days after Cy's historic Seminole score, never to race again.

Jones's grin said it all: "After all that, we never had to race against Relic—but, by God, we were ready to take on the world."

Dodson's gloomy distress stood in stark contrast to Snider's joyful delight. Their parting wasn't amicable; Dodson's rage was still foaming. Al soon realized nothing short of quitting Calumet himself would assuage his old riding nemesis; Snider decided he'd best keep busy, at the same time count his blessings.

Al several times confided in Arcaro: "I'd give up my life to have Citation for my very own. Cy and I have never lost a race. It's worth a lifetime having him all to myself now. I can't tell you how happy this big guy makes me feel."

Thankfully, no one can really foretell the future, or Snider would never have talked about giving up his life just to have Citation for all his own, no matter what pleasure their relationship gave.

"Al was just so excited about Citation, that's all," Arcaro would always recall. "Like most of us, Al thought life was endless, that he was indestructible. He was young, strong, had just gotten the career break of a lifetime. And he was one helluva rider, too. Made his own breaks; there were no undeserved gifts. He and Cy deserved to be together."

Golf between Eddie and Al became less frequent. "Al never wanted to be too far away from Citation," Arcaro explained. "It wasn't that he was trying to impress Mr. Wright or Jimmy Jones with an 'all work no play' attitude—Al just wanted to be around Citation. Only other real recreation he had was to go fishing once in a while."

It wasn't too long after Citation had pulverized his Seminole foes that stablemate Coaltown, back on the farm, was starting to show off both speed and class for trainer Ben Jones.

Arcaro had done quite well without Calumet in recent years. He rode Shut Out to victory in the 1942 Belmont, also enjoyed phenomenal success with Shut Out's rapid-fire stablemate, Devil Diver, both owned by the Greentree Stable.

Eddie won the 1945 Kentucky Derby at the direct expense of Calumet's Pot o' Luck with the luckless Hoop Jr., the latter breaking down in the Preakness, but not with Arcaro up; Eddie had a prior riding commitment elsewhere for Greentree. Always on the lookout for quality horseflesh, Eddie "picked up" Pavot to annex the 1945 Belmont Stakes for his third "test of champions" victory to that time.

Fast forward to February 18, 1948, and the upcoming Everglades Handicap for three-year-olds at Hialeah. What with Snider on Cy, and Dodson estranged from Calumet, Eddie started expressing interest in the unraced but highly touted Coaltown, a towering son of, yes, Bull Lea, out of the Blenheim II mare, Easy Lass.

Should Calumet's plans proceed as scheduled, Coaltown would be trained by Ben in Kentucky, then shipped in February to Florida to join Citation and company; hopefully Citation and Coaltown would eventually team up to ensure victory in the Kentucky Derby. Wright confessed he'd be happy to win his third Derby "with either colt." Which one didn't really matter to him. All he craved was victory.

Coaltown had finally shaken off the ill effects of the lingering throat ailment which sidelined him throughout 1947. He had grown considerably, was exuberantly frisky, and "the fastest thing on four legs" Ben Jones had ever seen.

Citation was the least interested in Coaltown's growing stature. Cy remained all business, intensely focused on the specific new challenges the approaching Everglades 'Cap proposed.

First, three-year-olds would be traveling the exacting distance of 1⅛ miles—only a furlong shorter than the 1¼ miles Derby—for the first time. That figured no real problem since Cy already had won at 1¹⁄₁₆ miles—just a sixteenth or 110 yards shorter than the Everglades—when he captured the Pimlico Futurity just three months ago at age two.

Second, the Everglades was a handicap, weights being assigned by Hialeah's racing secretary for the expressed purpose of "evening out the field," theoretically "bringing 'em all together as if to achieve a dead heat finish at the wire."

So Cy was assigned top impost of 126 pounds, conceding gobs of weight to the only two "brave souls" who bothered to show up—fourteen pounds to Silvering and seventeen to Hypnos. Cy was tight as a spring thanks to his two bouts with older horses; so, despite the huge weight concessions, his return to action against his own age-class amounted to no more than kid's play.

Snider told Arcaro he didn't ask Citation to "do nothing but win, and win the way he wanted." Cy cruised the 1⅛ miles in 1:49, hardly breaking a gallop, scoring mercifully by one length.

About this time, Coaltown was set for unveiling. Arcaro was interested in the sturdy speed ball, but jockey N. L. Pierson had taken a shine to Bull Lea's newest sensation. So Eddie adopted a "wait and see" stance, knowing he could have Coaltown for the asking, as coarse and unsportsmanlike as such a maneuver would be.

Coaltown was everything Ben Jones said he was. The strapping bay colt raised eyebrows and opened mouths in his racing debut at Hialeah, running off with a record-setting six furlongs in 1:09⅗. Many of the same horsemen who extolled Citation started thinking twice. Citation's paternal tribesman was "for real," would bear watching.

Snider, however, never gave Coaltown a second glance. "He's good and fast all right, but he's no Citation. He can run, but he can't hide, not from Cy he can't. No way."

In fact, Cy was kicking down his stall door; he wanted more action. He had blossomed into an intelligent, intuitive equine machine, with brains and heart to match, eager to compete. So Jimmy okayed yet another February outing—Cy's fourth that month—knowing full well that Cy was still six weeks shy of his actual third birthday.

"Jimmy tells me we're gonna keep our date in the Flamingo," Al informed Arcaro.

"Why don't you let him run a bit?" Arcaro teased. "I've heard a few horsemen complain he never wins by more than a length these days. No use to letting him draw 'em so close, Al."

Snider paused meaningfully, smiled, then nodded to acknowledge Eddie's friendly taunt. "Listen, if I gave him his head, Eddie, they wouldn't know which way he went!"

"Yeah, I've heard that before," Eddie continued the rub.

"You'll see," Snider promised.

Whether Al needed or got Jimmy's permission to "let Cy run a bit" will never be known for sure. For sure, though, was that Citation went out and made a shambles of his Flamingo opposition; as if to prove he could do it anytime he chose.

Just as he did in the Everglades, Cy shouldered top package of 126 pounds, again giving away weight to those courageous enough to step into the same ring with racedom's undisputed champion. This time Cy took no prisoners. He just didn't knock out his field. He annihilated them.

Al rated Citation in fourth early against some sprightly three-year-olds, including Saggy and Big Dial. No need to postpone the inevitable, Snider concluded; he gave Cy a barely noticed hand urge, and the obedient colt dutifully grabbed command at the far turn, exploding to a widening three-length bulge in midstretch.

Then, and only then, did Snider chirp encouragingly, just a tiny bird-like whistle audible only to Citation. Cy shifted into another gear, one he'd never used before—fresh and awesome—and immediately doubled his winning margin—six commanding lengths at the wire in time a fifth of a second faster than his recent Everglades triumph!

"Good thing Cy isn't an older handicap horse," Jimmy chided Al in the Winner's Circle, "else who knows what weight they'd pack on him the next time."

Citation needn't worry on that score; he was a brand-new three-year-old; he'd be carrying scale weight of 126 for the most part all season long. Only a race or stakes allowance conditions, with weight allotted according to races or money won, as well as future encounters with older horses, would affect his weight assignments.

With the February 28 Flamingo in the bag, Citation had earned a well-deserved respite, not that he needed one; nor had he vaguely suggested a rest. A well-oiled machine isn't supposed to tire or wear out even if made of flesh, blood, and bone, and Citation combined wondrous elements of both—machine and animal. If Calumet was to take dead aim on another Derby win at Churchill Downs, their own Louisville slugger deserved the right "to hit for the fences" in as resplendent condition as human hands could make him.

Cy was given the month of March off.

Arcaro would certainly have been forgiven had prior bizarre events combined to make him a devout fatalist, or follower of some other ancillary philosophy that teaches man is nothing more than a helpless pawn of divine but heartless predestination.

Eddie in later years renounced such dogma. Not so much that he got religion, or was convinced many such beliefs originated with ancient pagans, or that the "fate" doctrine foolishly insisted that a person's life, particularly his death, was already "written in the stars." That all helped, but he preferred to trust in what the Good Book taught: that "time and chance," or "time and unforeseen occurrence" as some translations rendered it—most horse people simply call it "luck"—happens to all men. Same can be said for animals, racehorses, too—and apparently without divine intervention by some higher power or powers over which man has no control.

Eddie even quoted chapter and verse to support his belief in man's existence as "a free moral agent"—Ecclesiastes 9:11. He particularly clung to that verse because of its peculiar allusion to horse racing, when the wise man, in this case Solomon, profoundly declared: "and the race does not always belong to the swift."

And Arcaro needed all the help and solace possible if he were to deal with the uncanny chain of events registering before his very eyes, eventually culminating in the shocking death of jockey Al Snider less than a week after winning the Flamingo Stakes on Citation.

For example: had Relic's owner *not* challenged Warren Wright to "crank up" Citation for some silly one-on-one showdown; had Doug Dodson *not* chosen Armed over Citation in the latter's first two hurried starts against older horses; had Doug *not* quit Calumet in a resentful huff, literally making Snider the stable's top reinsman—Citation would *not* have needed the month of March off to be freshened up for his assault on the 1948 Triple Crown. And, quite likely, Al, who couldn't stand being separated from his wonder colt, would *not* have refused Arcaro's offer to play golf on March 5. Al instead choosing to go fishing.

Fame, like life, is sweet and awfully short. Young Al Snider never expected what hit him that fateful day, March 5, 1948. At that time—when he joined two horsemen, trainer C. H. "Tobe" Trotter and Canadian businessman Don Fraser, aboard a frail sixteen-foot skiff—he certainly wasn't anticipating the deadly flash electrical storm which erupted out of the blue off the Florida Keys, brandishing gusty winds, heavy rains, and murderous seas. And at that time, Al Snider enjoyed worthy repute as a rider of the first order, doubtless one of racing's most gifted athletes, surely the game's most envied jockey of his day thanks to a magnificent young colt already lauded by those in the know as the "horse of the century!"

There are stories, theories, reports, and rumors aplenty as to what happened that lethal day. Cries of "foul play" were never substantiated; and even though their boat was retrieved virtually intact less than a week later, the bodies of Snider and his two companions were never recovered, swallowed up in one of racing's greatest mysteries, still unsolved; and as baffling as ever. America's most perceptive minds—as well sundry sleuths, investigators, and writers—remain puzzled as to how and why Snider and his pals could have disappeared without a trace.

No Hollywood script could provide more gripping melodrama as the scenario that surrounded Snider's death. The young rider at that exact moment in time rode tall in the saddle as king of American jockeys, only to have all his hopes, dreams, and joy dashed abruptly in a horrific whirlpool of surreal mystery.

Jimmy and his father, Ben, were stricken by the unreality of it all. And the world of racing mourned its loss. But life must go on, and Citation—the colt upon whose back Snider had not tasted defeat in nine starts—was now in want of something he neither desired nor needed—a new rider.

Chapter Six

Enter the Master

$\mathcal{I}$t didn't take an act of congress to vote Eddie Arcaro in. There was not one scintilla of debate or discussion. Even Warren Wright heartily agreed—Eddie Arcaro would be Citation's new jockey.

Arcaro had already achieved legendary status as America's premier rider by the time life's vagaries dealt Al Snider a mortal blow. The fiery Italian with the nose to make Jimmy Durante jealous had been making turf headlines since the mid-1930s when he started out with a doughty three-year-old Calumet Farm filly named Nellie Flag.

Those were the pre-Joneses days at Calumet, and Warren Wright took an early liking to young, thermal Arcaro, then a rakish nineteen-year-old who candidly thought he "could ride with the best of 'em."

Surprisingly, Nellie Flag and "Banana Nose" were sent off as the favorite in the 1935 Kentucky Derby, the Calumet miss trying to emulate Regret, first and only filly 'til then to win the Derby (1915).

Nellie Flag drew the public's attention on Derby day mostly because of her off-track proclivity; it had rained earlier; the track was exceedingly damp; and Nellie Flag relished mud of any sort.

She might have won it, too, to hear Arcaro tell it, except that she was "horsing," racing parlance for a filly or mare's regular menstrual cycle. Omaha, bred and owned by Belair Stud and a son out of the first crop of 1930 Triple Crown winner Gallant Fox, took advantage of Nellie Flag's indisposition, scored decisively, then went on to become the first and only Triple Crown winner to have been sired by a prior Triple Crown champion.

All this happened, of course, before horses like Sir Barton (1919) and Gallant Fox (1930) had been formally labeled Triple Crown winners, that distinctive title being coined by *Daily Racing Form*'s Charlie Hatton just in time to crown Omaha's 1935 feat.

Born February 19, 1916, in Cincinnati, Ohio, young George Edward Arcaro was an uneducated son of a poor cab driver and couldn't tell one end of a horse from the other. And he couldn't care less; golf was his first and true love. Fact is, he was a feisty thirteen-year-old caddy when a trainer, playing in a foursome to which "that skinny kid" attached himself, suggested, "you're too small to be hauling big golf bags around. You should think about becoming a jockey, you're just the right size!"

Why the suggestion hit home Eddie never could explain. But he didn't sleep that night. The proposition haunted him; he approached his dad the very first thing next morning.

"You're crazy, Eddie," his hard-working immigrant father frowned. "You know all horse players are nuts. But . . ."

That "but" was all scrawny Eddie needed. He hitched a ride to nearby Latonia Race Track and struck up some close attachments with local trainers, agents, grooms, and jockeys. And Eddie Arcaro was off to the races, though it would take some time before he'd start turning heads. Even when he did flash that something special, he'd more often than not screw things up because of his pepper sprout temper.

Eddie finally talked his way into his first actual mount, a horse named Bainbridge, on May 18, 1931—with whom he promptly lost. Losing became young Arcaro's primary occupation; an interminable eight months would elapse before he'd land his first winner—January 14, 1932, at Caliente. The horse was trained by A. W. Booker and was aptly name Eagle Bird, on whose "wings" the Arcaro legend was borne.

Therefore, before he'd team up with Citation in the spring of 1948, Eddie's career had long been in high gear, making him privy to some of the greatest thoroughbreds of all time to that day. Seeing 'em, riding 'em, or riding against 'em.

Horses like Colin, Sysonby, Exterminator, and Man o'War were before his time. But he saw the next best thing—horses like Twenty Grand, Challedon, Granville, Omaha, Cavalcade, Bold Venture, Seabiscuit, Equipoise, War Admiral, and, best of all, Phar Lap!

"In my opinion," Arcaro often said, "Phar Lap had it all over the fine horses who raced in the 1930s. Now I only saw him once, in 1932, the year he won at Caliente, his only start in America. He was, and remained until Whirlaway in 1941, the greatest thoroughbred I had ever seen. I was just sixteen at the time, but he left a lasting impression. I don't think I'll ever forget him."

Eddie had fine words for Triple Crown champs Omaha and War Admiral, also thought Twenty Grand an exceptional colt. He also praised Seabiscuit for his heart, courage, and "especially his persistence."

Explained Eddie: "Seabiscuit was just another horse at two and three, but a real workhorse. I think he started some thirty-five times as a two-year-old, which was unheard of. And he could've been claimed for peanuts at one time. He turned out to be a 'peoples' kind of horse; as he got older and grew to maturity.

"The Biscuit reached his peak as a four-year-old in 1937, winning races all over the country, and something like seven handicap races in a row. What really made him a household name, however, was his famous match race victory over War Admiral at Pimlico in 1938. 'Tis a shame he wasn't good enough to make headlines as a three-year-old—that's a horse's 'glamour division,' you know."

Arcaro's roller-coaster relationship with Calumet Farm, for whom he unsuccessfully rode Nellie Flag in the 1935 Derby, saddled then by trainer B. B. "Bert" Williams, took another sharp turn in the 1938 Kentucky Derby. One of the favorites was Calumet's "legend in the making," Bull Lea himself. But not with Eddie in the saddle.

Arcaro had forged what would be an enduring friendship with trainer Ben Jones, the latter saddling Lawrin, owned by Herbert M. Woolf's Woolford Farm, for that same 1938 Derby, aboard whom Ben hoisted his friend, twenty-two-year-old Eddie Arcaro.

As chronicled earlier, Bull Lea "ran out of gas," as was the speedster's wont, and Lawrin came home a punctilious winner for Jones and Arcaro. Warren Wright was crestfallen.

Intolerant of failure and rapacious for success, Wright set out to hire Ben Jones as Calumet's next trainer. Now "Plain Ben" Jones was no overnight success; he had been an industry mainstay since saddling his first winner in 1909 at Oklahoma City.

By 1913 Jones had expanded his thoroughbred interests to include excellent bloodstock, and from 1922 to 1931 was ranked among the nation's top breeders and trainers. Such was the environment son Horace A. "Jimmy" Jones was born into; and when Wright finally procured Ben as head trainer in 1939, son Jimmy was naturally part of the acquisition.

Things started happening fast. Bull Lea was retired to stud in 1940 after three so-so years at the track. The wonderfully named Whirlaway emerged as the Jones boys' initial big league attraction, first as an enigmatic 1940 two-year-old, then as a charismatic but still eccentric three-year-old in 1941.

Wendell Eads rode most of Calumet's stock that spring, but was no match for Whirlaway's race-day antics, which often included bolting to the outside fence, losing almost as many races as he'd win. Ben Jones gave Eads every chance, right up until the Tuesday of Derby week when Whirlaway again blew the turn in the Derby Trial, finishing second when he should have won by the proverbial country mile.

That's when Arcaro's mutual friendship and respect with Jones took over, and Eddie was hired overnight to ride Whirlaway in the Derby four days hence. Only obstacle requiring hurdling was Arcaro's contractual agreement as first-string rider for Greentree Stable. The latter had no three-year-old of worth at that time; Greentree trainer John Gaver graciously "loaned" Eddie to Calumet and history took off.

Winning his second Derby and his first Triple Crown astride Whirlaway did wonders for Arcaro's orbiting career. It was the final pre–World War II Derby, and Arcaro's magic aboard Mr. Longtail, especially when he converted the late-running colt into an amazing front-runner to win the Belmont—there was no speed in the race—was a work of art.

Unfortunately, even the most gifted "artiste" has been known to stumble, maybe shoot himself in the foot, perhaps even go so far as to crash in flames. In September 1942, the very year following his glowing success with Whirlaway, Eddie was involved in two unfortunate incidents. The first was a violent shouting and shoving match with rider Venancio Nordase during the running of New York's Cowdin Stakes for two-year-olds; the second was an intemperate verbal altercation with track stewards following the explosive track incident. When asked whether he personally intended Nordase any real harm, Eddie thick-headedly swore: "If I could have, I would have killed the sonofabitch!"

America's number one rider, certainly its premier blue ribbon jockey and media favorite, was suspended "indefinitely." The exile lasted exactly one year, during which Eddie was dearly missed by horsemen and racing fans alike. The game wasn't the same, and his was a major faux pas that threatened to end a brilliant career.

Arcaro was genuinely penitent. He resumed his riding career, in many ways still a rounder; but there'd be no more temper tantrums. He still owned a big, wonderful ego, "wonderful" in that he'd no longer anger, intimidate, or alienate friends or fellow industry mates. Rather, he dedicated his very juices of life to assuaging competitive envy or jealousy, at the same time devoting his skills to electrify and galvanize riding and media contemporaries with conduct befitting the sport's most visible and articulate spokesman.

There were star thoroughbreds galore following Whirlaway, including Hoop Jr., Phalanx, Lord Boswell, Shut Out, Devil Diver, Pavot, and Assault, and the promises of greater ones to come. Therefore, the Joneses' call for Eddie to replace the fallen Al Snider was, in effect, no really "big deal." Surely, no cause to celebrate.

Not that Eddie was an ingrate, or so blasé that he'd respond so indifferently to an invitation to greatness, but Snider's death had so painfully scorched his conscience that any kind of expression of exultation might be viewed as inappropriate.

Additionally, to Eddie, Citation was just another champion, albeit exceptional and extraordinary to hear Snider tell it. Yes, Cy could be another Whirlaway, and the colt did boast an amazing record: eight for nine as a two-year-old, four for four as a still-young three-year-old, including two sparkling scores over outstanding older horses—twelve wins in thirteen starts overall, the last seven in a row.

"Cy's record should read thirteen for thirteen," were among Al Snider's last words days before his demise.

But what about Coaltown? Arcaro had heard much about Cy's untested companion. Wasn't he considered the faster of the two when they were both yearlings? Ben had even mentioned Coaltown as a possible Derby mount for Eddie prior to Snider's death. And, suspiciously, Calumet was determined not to team up the two colts, not in the same race, not now for sure. Besides, Eddie always preferred "the fresh horse" over the one hard-campaigned; and he tentatively had agreed to ride My Request.

Not that Eddie had real doubts or reservations the day he and Cy were formally introduced at the barn. Actually, Eddie was immediately impressed by the seemingly sensuous aura—"you could almost touch it"—surrounding the colt as Jimmy held Cy's bridle in one hand, stroking his bay mane with the other.

"He's certainly a good-looker," Eddie smiled. "And those eyes—look at 'em. It's almost as if he's looking right through you, right into your soul." Then, Eddie couldn't help but ask: "Is he as good as Al said he is?"

No doubting Thomas was Jimmy, not since Citation's swashbuckling Seminole rout. "If you won't believe Al," Jimmy replied, "then why not believe what Sunny Jim said. He's an expert for sure. For my money, Eddie, Citation's gonna be, if not already, a real super horse." And Jimmy accented the word "super!"

"Well then," Eddie glanced over the top of his sunglasses, "I'd better be taking him out for a spin, just to see for myself. What's his schedule from now on in?"

"We're just gonna take it easy on him this month," Jimmy affectionately tweaked Cy's ear. "Just easy gallops—you can get on him tomorrow if you like—then start breezin' him in early April."

"How many times do ya plan to start him before the Derby?" Eddie inquired.

"Two, maybe three times," Jimmy replied, much to Arcaro's surprise.

"Wow, you certainly believe in keeping him working, don't you? Doesn't he ever get tired?"

"Nope, not that I can see." Jimmy led Arcaro back to the trainer's car at the head of the barn. "He just loves running. Heck, once he starts racing he don't need much work at all—the racing suits him just fine. Keeps him fit, too."

"Fit as a fiddle, huh?" Eddie laughed.

"Eddie, this colt is like iron," Jimmy confirmed, then added a touch of whimsy: "He's nimble as a cat. Hell, I think he can outrun a cheetah if he had to. And he's as strong as a bull. I can't remember the last time he ever took sick. Never been hurt either."

"He sounds too good to be true," Eddie winked.

"I'm betting he makes a believer of you," Jimmy gently slapped Eddie's shoulder.

"We'll see. We'll see," Eddie said, filled with thought.

Arcaro only three years earlier equaled Earl Sande and Isaac Murphy with his third Kentucky Derby tally astride Fred W. Hooper's lightning-quick Hoop Jr.

Eddie settled for fourth on Lord Boswell in 1946 behind King Ranch's Triple Crown hero Assault, which colt Eddie rode later that year en route to Horse of the Year honor. In 1947, he dropped a Derby squeaker to Maine Chance Farm's Jet Pilot; Faultless was a close-up third. Eddie rode Phalanx that day; subsequently ran third to Faultless and Jet Pilot in the Preakness, after which Arcaro voluntarily "gave up" on achieving any accord with the headstrong Phalanx.

It was an error he regretted.

Phalanx was turned over to a South American rider named Ruperto Donoso. They made beautiful music together, promptly speeding to a booming five-length victory in the Belmont Stakes, which served as springboard to the 1947 three-year-old championship. That very same Phalanx—whose late kick was awesome—was back, bigger if not better, as a 1948 can-run-all-day four-year-old, poised for late-season action should Citation make it that far in one piece.

The Phalanx blunder, added to Arcaro's acceptance of Cy over Coaltown or My Request in his ambition to become the first jockey ever to win *four* Kentucky Derbies, gave way to some understandable edginess as he was lifted aboard Cy for the latter's morning gallop.

Banana Nose Arcaro already had morphed into Heady Eddie; now he was revered nationwide as The Master and ultimately would be hailed as "the greatest jockey of the twentieth century," if not of all time.

Eddie's celebrity, however, had not been easily attained. He learned the hard way, had dutifully paid his dues, then systematically proceeded to win friends and admirers with his raw talent and sheer power, also guts, and—the showiest quality of 'em all—style!

If Eddie Arcaro truly deserved recognition as "The Master," then, to fulfill his most private yearning, he simply had to "look good" at all times—losing as well as winning. Thus was the Arcaro classical "seat" born—a low aerodynamic profile, an athletic body incredibly sculptured into a painfully flattened, almost anatomically impossible shape, built around the ace-deuce style of race-riding (the right stirrup six inches shorter than the left), all combining to create a personal, patented panache on horseback!

Eddie's biggest concern, as he adjusted his tack on Citation, was whether he as rider could help, not hinder, could complement, not detract, from the greatness already ascribed to Citation, a greatness he secretly felt at the time existed more as a dreamy hope than a factual reality. But Eddie was ready to "see the light," were such a "light" actually there to be shown.

Far as Eddie knew, Cy showed him neither bells, whistles, nor fireworks the first time around, a long, easy gallop at Hialeah.

"I'm not sure if I knew what I was looking for," Eddie recalled fondly. "God, he was built beautifully, strong and muscular, but very agile, and fluid in movement. But he was no showman, and no glitter. He just cocked his head, like he was bowing before a king or queen, then went about his business of being a racehorse."

What some might have faulted as a lack of charisma or flair was "just good manners," Eddie explained. "He didn't buck, or rear back without good reason. He never fought the bit, nor did he veto any requests or commands. He was the perfect gentleman, and very formal, always businesslike."

Yet Citation could be playful, sometimes kittenish when being brushed, waggish when bathed, and frisky when hot-walked by his groom to "cool down" after a strenuous work. And he'd snuggle up to those humans he trusted and admired, including groom–exercise rider Freeman McMillan, jockey-rider N. L. Pierson, the Jones boys, Mrs. Wright on occasion, and certainly his old buddy, Al Snider.

At the moment, he wasn't quite sure how he'd feel about Master Edward. Or vice versa.

Arcaro recalled his first impression of Citation: "He was really smart, well-mannered, sorta on the cool side, but not snooty; a bit quiet and reserved; yet full of himself, you could tell, but never a bully. He was so well put together physically, and so well composed mentally, you'd never take him for what Snider really—and I mean religiously—thought he was: 'the second coming of Pegasus,' or something like that."

It was as Eddie and Citation were getting better acquainted that Coaltown, still a question mark in Arcaro's mind, was making waves, and drawing raves, from the thoroughbred community. Jimmy told Eddie that Cy would return to the races in mid-April at Havre de Grace, but the jockey couldn't keep his mind off Coaltown's growing presence.

To say Arcaro was distracted by Coaltown's prowess is putting it mildly.

Coaltown had won his racing debut at Hialeah in Florida unlike any maiden that winter, busting from the gate as if the others were sound asleep, opening up an eight-length bulge before they knew what hit 'em, winning eased up with lengths to spare.

Bursting with confidence, Coaltown demolished his foes in his second outing, scoring "eased up" by twelve amazing lengths!

Just about the time Citation was warming up for his racing return following nearly a six-week break, Coaltown and Ben Jones invaded hometown Lexington; there the flashy speedster, tearing a page from Citation's best-seller, quickly and efficiently disposed of a field of good older horses in the Phoenix Hotel Handicap. He was the talk of the town, and that "town" was the capital of thoroughbred racing.

His speed certified, Ben Jones put Coaltown's ability to handle a distance into a crucible called the Blue Grass Stakes at 1⅛ miles. Calumet's newest sensation proved he was "for real" with a cruising track record-breaking victory in 1:49⅗. Coaltown was a legitimate "triple threat"—speed, class, and distance!

Meantime, Citation and Eddie Arcaro were prepared for their first dance together, the April 12 Chesapeake Trial, a six furlongs sprint pointing up the longer, more important 1⅟₁₆ miles Chesapeake Stakes five days later at Havre de Grace in Maryland.

Arcaro's mind had to be wandering all over the place. Not only was Coaltown an unqualified sensation, but Cy was coming off a long layoff. Moreover, the track at Havre de Grace was oozing mud, which should have been his rider's least concern since Citation had repeatedly demonstrated he "needn't carry his track with him" wherever he went.

Citation carried top weight of 126, conceding four pounds to three-year-old Saggy, whom he had crushed by ten lengths in the Flamingo. Cy also gave big weight gobs to Big Dial and a beast called Hefty, who really didn't belong in the race at all.

Jimmy's instructions to Eddie were simple: "He's all yours, he'll do anything you want him to do. He's been away for a few weeks, but he's ready. He was born ready. Just don't get yourselves hurt."

Eddie had galloped Cy several times in recent weeks, but had relinquished the colt's works and time trials to his various exercise riders in both Florida and Maryland. This would be the first time he'd be fully tasting Cy's might under race conditions.

What should have been a walk in the park turned disastrous. And Master Edward Arcaro had no one to blame but himself!

Eddie had always flatly stated that he's never seen a "good" jockey make a "bad" horse win, but too many times he's seen a "bad" jockey make a "good" horse lose. What it boiled down to: a jockey needs not only a "live" mount, but also the personal skills and savvy *not* to compromise or allow his horse to experience more than his normal share of trouble, or bad racing "luck."

You can count on the fingers of your two hands the times The Master rode so poorly that he'd go sleepless that night because of a troubled conscience. Eddie wrote, then rewrote the book on race-riding. He not only delighted the eye as a competitor but stood alone as a master strategist, figuratively riding four or five other horses at the same time in the same race.

He made his own rules, then broke them, but only when appropriate; he'd usually stick to his guns on personal principles despite a race's many vicissitudes and untoward circumstances.

One of his simplest, most powerful philosophical tenets was: "outside of one, and inside of two." What it meant both in theory and practice was that whether there was one, two, three, or more horses in front of you, *never* duck inside—always outside—the leader for fear of getting shut off. And, if possible, *always* steer inside of two or more, even if it means splitting the *inside* two horses, thus *avoiding* trouble *outside*, particularly if the outside horse bolts, or forces you wide, thereby eliminating all chance.

That having been said, Eddie put it all together, at least he thought he did, only to have it backfire!

Cy was a bit sluggish leaving the starting gate; it took him an extra second or two to find his best stride. He was fourth, only two lengths off Saggy's spirited early pace. Hefty gave chase, then moved right alongside the leader as the field curved around the final turn.

Arcaro had Citation spotted perfectly in fourth, now just three lengths off the embattled leaders. Everything behind Cy was spent, so he took over third. As Saggy and Hefty matched strides contesting the lead, Eddie knowingly violated his cardinal rule, obviously feeling he had "the best horse," and that there was no need to save ground by darting inside the two leaders and risk having to check and possibly finding himself hopelessly penned in.

So The Master chose to swing three wide as the Chesapeake Trial field rounded into the home lane. Cy, as always, was running easily, having the two front-steppers in his cross hairs, ready to pounce and wrest command at Eddie's asking.

Hefty, racing outside of Saggy, apparently changed running leads prematurely, going into a lead with his right foreleg, prompting him to all but bolt to the outside—carrying Citation and Arcaro with him. Eddie didn't realize it then, but all he had to do was take Cy back, allow Hefty his outward course, then dive inside and redirect his colt's energies to collaring the leader.

Eddie, however, restrained Citation until well within the homestretch run; he tardily eased Citation out, passing Hefty inside the eighth pole, at which juncture Saggy, emboldened by the gift of an easy lead with no challengers, shot to a two-length winning margin.

Eddie didn't persevere with Cy, actually wrapped up on his colt, unaware all he had to do was rouse Cy to shift into passing gear and salvage the triumph. Cy missed catching Saggy by a length. Fifty years later, The Master would humbly confess: "What I did that race was dumber than dumber!"

Chapter Seven

Vindication . . . and More!

"*I*t was a race made in hell!" Eddie later recounted.

The media had a field day. Here was Citation, lauded as worthy successor to legendary Man o'War by no less a respected expert than Sunny Jim Fitzsimmons, getting his butt kicked by a horse named Saggy, the same Saggy who only two months ago Cy had destroyed in the Flamingo Stakes.

Eddie graciously took all the blame.

"And he should have," Jimmy Jones would later add in an angry footnote to a notorious defeat whose impact would swell enormously all season long. Citation would be asked to prove his preeminence all over again, this time with no ifs or buts.

Cy had no problem with that challenge, but Arcaro remained troubled. Yes, The Master had flubbed, and he unpretentiously admitted his error. But his "wonderful ego," which he guarded jealously, demanded he both explain the blunder and vow it would never happen again.

"I admit I didn't know Citation that well, and for some strange reason I felt a kind of weird, crazy heat I never felt before. If anything, I might have ridden him too tentatively. And if it weren't for all those 'hundred granders' ahead of us—the winner's pot in the Trial was a nothing $8,300—I could've caught Saggy for sure. But I wasn't about to burn up my colt, not with the Derby coming up.

"Don't hold the loss against Citation," Eddie told reporters, "it was all my fault, pure and simple. And believe me when I say it—it won't *never* happen again!"

Eddie's pledge was not born out of overconfidence. He certainly didn't want to lose Citation to another jock; the colt was last year's two-year-old champion by a landslide, and trainers like Sunny Jim saw him as truly special. But their first race together left more questions than answers, so getting beat was all the more humiliating.

Eddie's affability in defeat soothed what easily could have triggered a media savagery, but the sports folks' honeymoon with Calumet was still in full bloom. Snider's death by misadventure also helped keep race commentary on an even keel. Heck, Citation lost a race everybody knew he should have won. Seemed only right he deserved another chance.

Arcaro devoted himself to "friendly" revenge, but revenge nonetheless, with the Chesapeake Stakes less than a week away. Saggy's connections gloated publicly. And there were a few who felt Citation's loss was genuine. Of course, Saggy would have another chance to prove his worth, this time at 1 1/16 miles. Speed, however, was Saggy's game, and his people all but dared Cy to try and stay with him in the early going.

That "dare" rankled Arcaro and Jones, Eddie particularly since he was the reason Citation lost; Jones also felt the defeat inexcusable; besides, Saggy's peoples' mouthy claims ulcerated his stomach.

It rained the night before the Chesapeake. Again there were those few who foolishly thought Citation was intimidated by "off-track" going, that perhaps "the great one" needed a fast track to do his best?

A muddy track greeted Maryland fans on race day morning. The sun, however, peeked out a hour or two later, drying the track considerably, though the surface had improved only to "good" by post time.

Curiously, although Citation had lost five days earlier as the heavy one-to-three favorite, he made so many fans in defeat that they backed him down to prohibitive one-to-five favoritism for his return bout with quick-starting Saggy. His star had not dimmed one tiny watt.

Eddie had made it his business to "get to know" Citation better in the five days since the Trial. He hung around Cy's stall for hours, even jumped aboard for a brisk three furlongs dash the morning before. What the rider discovered that he hadn't appreciated five days earlier was that Citation could sprint like Equipoise, close like Whirlaway, dominate like Man o'War, shift gears like Count Fleet, "wait" like Seabiscuit, and explode like Phar Lap—and then do it all over again! And again. And again.

Eddie willingly stopped short of calling Citation "a machine." He didn't mind occasionally alluding to Cy as "a well-oiled machine" as tribute to the colt's businesslike focus whenever he took the track. "But Citation was a flesh and blood animal, a horse," Eddie praised, "a thoroughbred horse who, when I knew and rode him as a three-year-old, could beat any horse I've ever seen or ridden—and beat 'em silly—but never with maximum or all-out effort. None of us knew how truly great he was. In fact—damn it, I was one slow learner—it would still take me another race or two to really appreciate what a standout he was."

Eddie asked only one thing of Cy in the Chesapeake: "Help me look good, buddy. You just tell me what you want—I won't screw it up this time. I promise!"

For that matter, Jimmy Jones merely shook his head, though he did crack a smile in the paddock. Trainer and jockey exchanged glances. No words were spoken. Jimmy totally relied on Arcaro's reputation "to never make the same mistake twice."

Cy outbroke the field, which had to leave Saggy in a dither; then, responding to a virtual inaudible "whoa" from Eddie, dropped back to third, but only a length or so behind the leaders. Saggy regathered his bearings, but before he could accelerate, Citation reclaimed command as the field settled up the backstretch.

Not only Saggy, but a couple of other fine three-year-olds, Bovard and Dr. Almac, also gave chase. After six furlongs, Saggy moved to accost easy-running Citation, and, for the briefest moment, actually put his head in front. This time Arcaro harbored no fears, no perceived "heat" or nervousness. In fact, he had yet to ask Citation to run; he just didn't want to give Saggy any excuses. Saggy breasted Citation, and two power-charged dragsters lined up eye-to-eye as if poised at the starting blocks.

Many anticipated a duel in the making. Saggy's jockey sharply roused his charge—and "the race was on!"

Mercifully, Citation neither prolonged the agony nor postponed the inevitable. He delivered the coup de grâce the very instant Saggy issued his courageous challenge. Saggy, to his credit, tried so valiantly, expended so much verve and effort, that he shot his bolt, retreating to finish dead last.

Citation and his increasingly more confident rider proceeded to spread-eagle their field, sauntering home by nearly five lengths. Exoneration, indeed!

Saggy pulled up a little gimpy, was given a much-needed rest, tried making a comeback two months later. His spirit and physical prowess seriously damaged, he retired prematurely, managing to salvage some comforting prestige when ten years later, in 1958, he sired the late-running Carry Back, hero of both his sophomore year's Kentucky Derby and Preakness Stakes (1961).

Curiously, Saggy, who personified speed even in losing to Citation, produced someone like Carry Back, who epitomized endurance at its finest. Such are the mysteries of breeding and pedigree. Yet for all his distance prowess, Carry Back was unplaced in the 1½ miles Belmont Stakes.

Cy's Chesapeake Stakes winning time was serviceable—1:45⅗—considering track conditions. But again time was no indication of his overpowering class. He did win with lengths to spare, mostly because Arcaro didn't want to risk repeating his debacle of five days earlier; but he was merely cantering the final hundred yards, so thoroughly had he outclassed his pursuers from start to finish.

Cy's Chesapeake victory marked his sixth start in exactly two and a half months of his three-year-old season. And had he not lost the Chesapeake Trial earlier that week, he would have been riding a nine-race winning streak, which victory skein should have read fifteen straight were it not for his second to Bewitch the summer before when he agreeably was part of the family "fix" at Chicago's Washington Park.

"Hey, we've got ourselves a win streak," Arcaro teased the Joneses, his head hung somewhat guilt-stricken. "We're now one for one. Not bad, hey? What a way to go into the Derby."

The Jones boys suddenly subdued their laughter.

"Did I say something wrong?" Eddie wondered.

"No, Eddie, we've just been thinking, that's all," Ben spoke for the father-son training team.

"Seriously, I didn't do anything wrong, did I?" Arcaro repeated.

"No, no, of course not," Jimmy chimed in. "The two of you did just fine. It's just that we might have a change in plans, that's all."

"A change—what kinda change?"

The Joneses reminded Eddie that the Derby was scheduled for Saturday, May 1, a good two weeks away, and that Citation seemed to thrive on racing; that, perhaps, it wouldn't be wise to "do nothing" with him—except works—for those couple weeks.

Besides, though they didn't emphasize this fact, Coaltown was on a hot streak, piling up win after win, each more impressive than the last. Plus, Coaltown was a fresh horse, having missed his two-year-old campaign.

Citation and Coaltown would easily make the greatest two-horse stable entry ever in the Derby.

"We just want Cy at his best, is what we're trying to say," Jimmy encapsulated Calumet's concerns.

"Moreover," Ben grinned, "no Belmont Futurity winner has ever won the Derby—so that would be a 'first' for Cy. And guess what? No winner of the Derby Trial, which is scheduled for Tuesday afternoon of Kentucky Derby week—just four racing days away—has ever gone on to win the Derby itself."

"I get ya," Arcaro replied, "you guys want to smash two jinxes all at once. And you think Citation's the one to do it?"

"Yeah," said Jimmy, "and it answers our need to get another race under him. We wouldn't be doing it if we didn't honestly think he was up to it."

Twenty-first century horsemen today would laugh, if not run, the Jones boys out of town were they to actually start the nation's number one three-year-old in so insignificant a race as the Derby Trial, especially since the colt had already seen action less than two weeks before in what was Cy's sixth outing—three major stakes included—of the young season. If Citation wasn't already shipshape then no such animal existed.

Furthermore, the Trial was on the Tuesday before a grueling 1¼ miles Kentucky Derby; no colt in history was good enough to capture both events. And the Trial was no breezy six furlongs sprint. It was an exacting mile, too enervating a task for your average great racehorse.

But nobody familiar with the game ever said Citation "was your average great racehorse." There was nothing "average" about Cy at all, unless it was his general overall physical appearance. There certainly was nothing "average" about his heart, spirit, or class.

Arcaro himself was somewhat bewildered, but he knew better than to question Ben and Jimmy Jones on anything pertaining to thoroughbreds and racing-training regimen. Moreover, Coaltown loomed an even bigger threat off his Blue Grass Stakes romp only the week before, the awesome colt racking up his fourth straight triumph in a surging career that was taking the racing world by storm. Thus, Eddie couldn't help but feel, and agree, that Cy might really need the Trial as a final tightener.

Cy already had humbled such quality two-, now three-year-old contenders as Better Self, Bewitch, Free America, Salmagundi, Billings, My Request, Piet, and Saggy; also a classy array of older stars the likes of Armed, Delegate, Kitchen Police, Sky Blue, Faultless, and Buzfuz.

Coaltown, My Request, and Better Self wisely were being saved for the Derby itself, but among Citation's Trial opponents was a late-developing sophomore named Escadru, also a speedster named Eagle Look. Tuesday's one-mile Trial, therefore, was no cake walk. Cy would have to expend some effort to dispose of his newest challengers.

The dynamic duo of Coaltown and jockey N. L. Pierson were more than just curious onlookers April 27 at Churchill Downs. The pair had forged a marvelous rapport, and Pierson spared no adjectives extolling Coaltown's many virtues, suggesting he may even be Cy's better.

Coaltown actually sported one advantage Citation had forfeited—he was undefeated going into the Kentucky Derby. Thus, by the time Cy and Arcaro took the track for the Derby Trial, Coaltown was the talk of Kentucky. His two Keeneland scores at neighboring Lexington had captivated Kentucky hardboots, who prided themselves as expert judges of prime horseflesh. But like most observers they reserved their final judgment until Citation would dispose of his Trial rivals.

Dispose of them Citation did. Not with arrogance or boastful vainglory. No showboating, no ribbons, no banners, no trumpets or bell-ringing; just skilled craftsmanship and systematic, almost methodical, execution. An effort truly professional and typically understated.

Away alertly—Arcaro sat motionless—Citation skipped into second after the opening quarter, then, without a hint of encouragement from his rider, assumed command, dashing clear by two lengths as the field circled the final elbow. Escadru drew aim at midstretch, only a length or two away, and was still a length or so behind Cy at wire's end.

If Citation were in need of a final workout before Derby day, that's what he got. Only one thing pounded Arcaro's brain as Cy briskly pranced—head bowed proudly—to the Winner's Circle: what might he do if I ever really asked him to run?

Churchill Downs was aglow with excitement and anticipation, wildly intoxicated by racing's newest wonder horse, but equally enraptured by his increasingly enigmatic stablemate Coaltown and their ensuing first-ever titanic clash.

Imagine how afire with expectation America would be were television available; nevertheless, the press came alive with headline newspaper and radio coverage befitting so intriguing an event.

Arcaro's respect for Citation by Derby day eve was firmly established. That night he, along with Ben and Jimmy Jones, also Coaltown's exultant pilot, N. L. Pierson, gathered for a heart-to-heart.

Pierson had never ridden Citation in an actual race, but had worked him several times, was fully conversant with his speed and workmanlike demeanor; he also sensed Cy's competitive spirit, though denied the chance to see it played out in actual hoof-to-hoof combat.

But Pierson was intimately familiar with Coaltown and the colt's speed, stamina, and class. "He's a genuine fireball, and I think he can run all day. No one's ever even come close to challenging or catching him. He's the best I've ever ridden."

In all fairness, Pierson hardly approached Arcaro in terms of having ridden exceptional horseflesh, though he had worked Citation. But the exuberant jockey wasn't alone in his high regard for Coaltown.

Chicago sports writers John P. Carmichael and Warren Brown had a friendly running feud—Carmichael agreed with Ben Jones that Coaltown was "the fastest thing on four legs he'd ever seen," while Brown stuck with his original opinion that Citation was the "greatest colt since Man o'War, if not the best of all time."

If horsemen were polled, they'd overwhelmingly favor Coaltown. For starters, he was undefeated in four starts, including a victory over older horses, plus the recent 1⅛ miles Blue Grass Stakes in which he murdered his field with lengths to spare.

Citation, on the other hand, had already tasted defeat; most recently to an ordinary horse like Saggy. Forget the extenuating circumstances, which included a rare boneheaded ride by jockey great Arcaro. And forget—conveniently—what he accomplished before and since. The record was clear: Citation was the reigning champ, and stablemate Coaltown was the undefeated contender.

If the 1948 Kentucky Derby were an election, exit polls most assuredly would indicate a growing voting trend favoring Coaltown.

Though Arcaro had fast become a devout Citation convert, there remained a vestige of concern. He was sure of two things: one, that Cy had the stuff of which legends were made, and if Sunny Jim Fitzsimmons said he had done more than the great Man o'War, well, that was good enough for him.

Two, from what Al Snider had told him, and from what he saw and felt in just three "rides" aboard Citation, Eddie was absolutely convinced no horse past or present could ever "catch" Cy from behind once he had taken a meaningful lead, or assumed purposeful command.

Eddie's tiny final doubt was this: The rains had hit Churchill Downs, and for sure the track would be sloppy tomorrow, May 1, Derby day.

Citation could handle any kind of "off" track—he'd proved that repeatedly. But so could Coaltown, and Coaltown owned electrifying speed—speed that was genuine, not cheap—and slop usually heightened and reinforced natural speed, making the fleet merchant virtually impossible to catch.

Eddie already knew Jimmy's love for Cy. Ben, however, was closer to Coaltown since he was the colt's primary trainer in Florida and Kentucky. Ben, therefore, was considered more objective.

Eddie privately sought out the great Ben Jones. "I have just one question, Ben," Eddie whispered. "I have nothing but respect for Coaltown's speed, so I must ask: Am I up on the right horse tomorrow?"

Ben smiled. And placing his hand on Arcaro's shoulder, he uttered words of prophetic insight: "Eddie, you can sleep well tonight, because, and you can take this as gospel: any horse Citation can see—he can catch! And he's got perfect eyesight!"

Eddie Arcaro slept like a baby that night.

Chapter Eight

Days of Wine and Roses

$\mathcal{E}$ddie would never again doubt Citation.

Ditto for Citation, though the colt never had any problems with his riding companions. He liked 'em all, particularly Al Snider, whom he knew best. And he was becoming increasingly fond of Arcaro, kindly forgiving The Master for his boo-boo in the Chesapeake Trial. Eddie's professional touch—firm but soft—suited Cy just fine.

It was hard to say whether it was strictly coincidental, occurring as it did just after gaining Arcaro as a pilot, but Citation was undergoing a wonderful metamorphosis as Derby day approached. Almost overnight—similar to a young man receiving a hard-earned college diploma—Cy flowered into a full-bloomed adult, endowed with the wisdom maturity bestows, and wrapped in the virility and sinew that legitimate manhood confers.

With the Derby on deck, Citation also graduated to loftier character and ambition. He was still the same focused, all-business equine of recent past; but maturity had replaced adolescence. His innate intensity remained; tempered, however, by a relaxed casualness that suggested he had come to enjoy work as much as play.

It was as if Cy discerned the Kentucky Derby as avatar to a "higher calling." But there'd be no P. T. Barnum aura of flash or splash; his cultured manliness forbade ostentation, and his physical bearing rarely elicited the "oh's and ah's" accorded such colorful predecessors as Equipoise, Phar Lap, Man o'War, or Whirlaway.

But he'd still jog, canter, even gallop, in full regalia to and from the starting gate, head supremely arched in that familiar bow, proudly delighting his legion of loyal celebrants and worshippers—yes, Cy's unmistakable hallmark: "The Great One is passing in review."

And "The Great One" was on a mission. Coveting and winning the Kentucky Derby was no option. It was a *must*. Racing's implicit dogma commands: The *good* three-year-old, if in racing trim, *must* win his Derby; however, only the *great* ones win the Triple Crown.

For example, over the decades before and since Citation, only a few verifiable greats bypassed the Derby, either by choice (Man o'War), because of injury or unavailability (Kelso, Buckpasser, Tom Fool, Dr. Fager, and John Henry); or because of ineptness at that point in their careers (Sun Beau, Equipoise, Seabiscuit, and Cigar).

However, other notables—Native Dancer, Nashua, Bold Ruler, Round Table, Damascus, Forego, Alydar, and Point Given—managed to rebound magnificently after losing "The Run for the Roses."

And the "Roses Run" indisputably remains the world's greatest horse race, surely the most celebrated, certainly the most ballyhooed. And for good reason: the Derby is a happening, a fever, a mood, a swirl of fantasy, real and unreal at the same time; racing's most clamorous and glorious day, almost fictional, like a figment of imagination; the sport's fantastical Emerald City where the dreams of owners, breeders, trainers, horses, and jockeys can all come true—but just once that year, on that memorable first Saturday in May.

Media battle lines in 1948 were inextricably drawn, not only whether Coaltown could derail Citation and remain unbeaten, more importantly, prove unbeatable; but might not the spunky Eastern colt, Ben Whitaker's multiple stakes hero My Request—who had of all riders Doug Dodson in the saddle—have been cast in the role of spoiler, fully capable of disrupting Calumet's ironfisted hold on this fabled race?

Every sports writer in America—including Red Smith, Joe Palmer, Arch Ward, Warren Brown, Bill Boniface, Joe Kelly, and John P. Carmichael—was caught up in spirited debate. Radio race-callers and commentators Clem McCarthy and Bill Stern also voiced strong opinions. So did the nearly one hundred thousand fans who actually showed up on Derby day, when crowd figures were counted, not estimated.

As far as horsemen were concerned, reason ruled over hope. Only four other three-year-olds, among them My Request, Escadru, and Billings, were sufficiently brave to challenge Calumet's powerhouse entry of Citation and Coaltown, who curiously drew post positions numbers one and two. Number one—which some felt prophetically meaningful—went to Citation, entrymate Coaltown right alongside in number two.

Derby day dawned dank and gloomy. Dark clouds and heavy rains drenched historic Churchill Downs, and the track was fetlock deep in a soupy mix of slop and mud. Umbrellas were everywhere; the sun weakly tried to make an appearance, to no avail. But as Derby post time neared, the rains stopped. And history was about to be made.

Jimmy Jones was characteristically joyful in the paddock, exchanging small talk and Derby trivia with a well-rested and confident Eddie Arcaro. Equally alert, but even more confident, was jockey N. L. Pierson, who nodded as Ben Jones reminded him that Coaltown loved and belonged "on the engine," in front where he's been all his life. Pierson, however, wasn't privy to Jones's remark the night before to a concerned Arcaro regarding "Citation's perfect eyesight."

And there was none of that "let Bewitch win" nonsense of last year. Order of the day: may the better colt win—pure and simple.

Only prerace surprise was that when the tote board, which reported the current odds, opened prior to the race, lo and behold, advance Derby wagering actually listed My Request as favorite over the Calumet duo. Which was not that totally unexpected, however, since My Request rode into the Derby off four straight wins, including the always important Wood Memorial in New York. No slouch he.

By the time the nostalgic strands of "My Old Kentucky Home" filled the arena, and the six three-year-olds who were suited up for battle paraded past the stands, heading for the starting gate at the top of the Downs' quarter mile homestretch, Citation and Coaltown had been reestablished as two-to-five choice, lowest in Derby history, with My Request still respectfully regarded as four-to-one second choice.

So overwhelming was the Citation-Coaltown twosome, Churchill Downs impresario Matt Winn felt obliged to impose "win betting only" on the 1948 renewal. But those were days when thoroughbred racing still had a magical grip on the nation's sporting interest. Gambling was secondary to the impelling test between two super colts in the world's most glamorous race.

Only thing Eddie knew, or cared about, was that he and Cy had the rail and that Coaltown and his cocksure rider, N. L. Pierson, were poised right alongside. "The rest [of the field] meant very little," Eddie ceded, but not ungraciously.

"Ben in effect had surgically removed any remnant of doubt from my soul," Arcaro smiled, gently massaging his coy smugness. "I went into the Derby totally convinced I was riding a super horse, no matter how fast, or great, Coaltown might be. And he was a great one, too.

"Mostly, though, I was confident in Cy's ability. I was convinced I could use him any which way I wanted. So I figured the best way to neutralize Coaltown's speed was to make him use it right from the get-go. Now normally that would mean hurting my horse, using him prematurely, compromising if not ruining his chances later on when the real racing began. But Citation was Superman in a dark bay cape, as far as I knew and believed. So I roused him right at the start."

Citation actually outbroke his avowedly faster playmate, forcing Pierson to urge Coaltown to the fore in the long run down the home land the first time. "Yeah, I made Pierson and Coaltown prove they had their running shoes on, which they did by the time we shot under the wire the first time, then banked into the club turn with a mile to run in the race."

Eddie eased back on Cy, "otherwise he would have gone on with Coaltown on his own, which I didn't want him to do. Besides, I wanted to see what My Request, also Billings, were up to. Both were being fairly energetically handled to stay within shouting distance of Coaltown, so I figured they'd be of no account today." Eddie figured right.

Thus, by the time Coaltown blazed by the opening half in :46⅗, the long-striding leader had sped to a four- or five-length advantage, Pierson sitting confidently on his unbeaten steed. The field sped another quarter, leaning into the far turn with only a half mile to run, and Coaltown's lead had burgeoned to six over Citation, the latter at that juncture just a length ahead of My Request.

Crunch time had arrived. A half mile remaining. And the match race which everyone fervently awaited—was on!

"Cy was a Cadillac, fully equipped and powered," Eddie would reflect, "while Coaltown was a high-toned Buick, as capable as could be, but my machine was more superbly built, with extra gears and greater built-in muscle.

"Cy was begging to run. Oh, he was rippin' off the furlongs at a fancy clip himself, as fast as could be expected in all that slop and mud. But

Coaltown seemed miles ahead of us as we left the half-mile pole. So I touched Cy's shoulder with the whip, just a touch mind you, then whispered in his ear: 'Cy, you can see him up there, can't you? Okay, now do your thing—go catch him!'

"And right off the bat, Cy was gone! So fast—like a bullet—he scared me. He left My Request, Billings, and the others like they were walking. I looked ahead through mud-spattered goggles—Pierson knew we were flying, and he really got into Coaltown. Now Coaltown had never before been asked to give his all. And he was no slouch. He was a champ, would be in years to come, and he had no slows, no letdown, certainly he hadn't run out of energy.

"Simply, and there's no other way to put it, Cy simply was running twice as fast as Coaltown!"

America's favorite race-caller was Clem McCarthy, the gravelly voiced announcer whose natural exuberance and throaty heel and spur radio "calls" did much to popularize the sport on broadcasts made possible by the Gillette Safety Razor Company.

McCarthy could be forgiven if he faced the 1948 Derby call with a modicum of trepidation, even if only saddled with the chore of calling a six-horse field. Only the year before, the 1947 Preakness, Clem had mistakenly called Jet Pilot the winner when it was Calumet's Faultless who actually finished first in the middle jewel of the Triple Crown.

The reason for his gaffe: the similarity in colors. Faultless was adorned in Calumet's devil's red and blue, while Jet Pilot was bedecked in the cerise of Maine Chance Farm. Actually, the two sets of silks weren't that strikingly similar, but if that was Clem's excuse, imagine his concern calling both Coaltown and Citation, each wearing silks that were, with the exception of their caps, identical.

But Clem stumbled not, nary a single misstep, and his CBS 1948 Derby call as Coaltown led Citation into the stretch colorfully captured the occasion: "And they're turning for home . . . Coaltown and Citation are head and head . . . and it looks like Eddie Arcaro has got his Derby . . . they're coming down home together . . . riding each other close . . . and it's Citation coming to the front . . . he's everything they said he was . . . he's going to win with his ears pricking . . . it's Citation by two . . . and he's pulling away . . . and the other horse Coaltown is hanging on gamely . . . and that's all he can do is to hang on gamely for second . . . 'cause it's all Citation in the Derby."

Certifying his greatness, Citation imperiously and with precision and aplomb ran down Coaltown in the upper stretch, mercilessly decked him for the count, requiring just two slight whacks from Arcaro's whip approaching midstretch to validate his colt's superiority.

Eddie took a relaxed hold on indefatigable Cy inside the final sixteenth, but effortlessly still added to his winning margin, splashing under the wire by 3½ lengths in 2:05⅗, an eased-up final clocking after Coaltown had reeled off six furlongs in 1:11⅖ before being collared by Cy at the mile in 1:38 flat, amazing fractions considering the tiring surface.

Greeting Citation, who generously shared the Winner's Circle with his conquered stablemate Coaltown, were Warren and Lucille Wright, their myriad friends and family, and, of course, Ben and Jimmy Jones.

Jimmy took credit as Cy's trainer of record, a magnanimous gift from his beneficent father, the latter "just that"—a gracious, loving patriarch who never missed an opportunity to lavish praise and honor Jimmy's way.

Margaret Glass, a still-spry retired octogenarian and a rare remaining Calumet Farm historian, vividly recalls her days as farm secretary, and, as far as Warren and Lucille Wright were privately concerned, the stable's de facto general manager without portfolio.

Margaret kicked off her long tenure at Calumet in 1940, the year Bull Lea served his first mares. She made sure that farm activity, from her secretary-accountant's point of view—including contacts and contracts involved in the farm's breeding and rearing of thoroughbreds—whirled right along. Among her duties, in addition to keeping the Wrights happy, were bookkeeping, accounts payable, travel arrangements, and the sundry toils and trials involved in keeping the world's greatest breeding kingdom running.

"Ben was a tough but shrewd taskmaster when it came to training horses," Margaret recalled, "but he was the perfect 'father figure' in more ways than one, especially with his son Jimmy. When Jimmy was serving with the Coast Guard in the early 1940s, Ben kept him on 'his own' payroll. Every payday without exception, Ben told me to send half of his 10 percent trainer's fee to Jimmy wherever he was stationed. And I know Jimmy appreciated it, as he did everything else his father did for him.

"So Ben, feeling he had accomplished more than he deserved, first at Woolford with Lawrin in 1938, then with Whirlaway, Armed, Twilight Tear, Pensive, Twosy, Fervent, and Faultless from 1941 onward, didn't

The classic Citation pose—neck arched and head bowed. Whether for exercise rider Freeman McMillan or his many jockey corps members, including Eddie Arcaro, Steve Brooks, and Al Snider—Cy was always regal, equine poetry in motion. (*Courtesy of Keenland-Cook*)

Citation enters track with his first jockey, the ill-fated Al Snider. The occasion was the September 30, 1947, Futurity Trial at Belmont Park in New York. The team of Citation and Snider were undefeated in nine starts covering 1947 and early 1948. (*Courtesy of Keenland-Cook*)

Minutes later, Cy and Snider combined to register an authoritative victory over Gasparilla and Up Beat in Belmont's Futurity Trial. The race was run down Widener course with Belmont stands in the background. (*Courtesy of Keenland-Cook*)

Less than a week following the Trial, and wearing the same number 2B, Citation stands victorious in the winner's circle with owner Warren Wright (far left) and trainer H. A. "Jimmy" Jones. The Belmont Futurity was Cy's seventh win in eight starts as a 1947 two-year-old. He'd win another, the November 8 Pimlico Futurity, to close out an eight-for-nine season as America's two-year-old champion. (*Courtesy of Keenland-Cook*)

Now closely associated with master jockey Eddie Arcaro, mighty Citation rolled imperiously through the slop on May 1, 1948, to register a brilliant 3½ lengths victory in the Run for the Roses, the heralded Kentucky Derby. Stablemate Coaltown and eastern threat My Request were far back in second and third. (*Courtesy of Keenland-Cook*)

There were smiles aplenty as the father-son training team of Ben (right, in white hat) and son Jimmy escort handsome Citation and his beaming rider, Eddie Arcaro, to the charmed circle following victory in the 1948 Kentucky Derby at Churchill Downs in Louisville, Kentucky. (*Courtesy of Keenland-Cook*)

A familiar scene—one for the ages—trainer Jimmy Jones leading Big Cy and his immortal jockey Eddie Arcaro to their "home away from home,"—the Winner's Circle, this time in the April 27, 1948, Derby Trial at Churchill Downs. (*Courtesy of Keenland-Cook*)

Citation leads only three challengers as the field pounds under the finish line the first time en route to victory in the 1948 Preakness Stakes at Pimlico, the second leg of racing's fabled Triple Crown. In his wake at this stage are Vulcan's Forge (covered up by Citation), followed by Bovard and Better Self. (*Courtesy of Keenland-Cook*)

This is more like it—mighty Cy all by himself in the Preakness, scoring by nearly six commanding lengths. The track was listed as "heavy," but no deterrent to Citation. The others—Vulcan's Forge, Bovard, and Better Self—were hopelessly outclassed. (*Courtesy of Keenland-Cook*)

With this galloping eight-length victory in the June 12 1½ miles Belmont Stakes, peerless Citation became the eighth Triple Crown champion in the annals of thoroughbred racing. It was the second Triple Crown triumph for his redoubtable jockey Eddie Arcaro. Unbelievably, there'd not be another Triple Crown champion until a quarter-century later and 1973's victory by Secretariat. (*Courtesy of Keenland-Cook*)

"Hail the conquering hero!" Leigh Bettson (second right), president of Santa Anita Race Track, and New York racing icon George D. Widener (far right) jointly salute (left to right) trainer H. A. "Jimmy" Jones, Calumet Farm owner Warren Wright, and jockey Eddie Arcaro following Citation's June 12 Belmont Stake victory. Citation thus became the sport's eighth Triple Crown kingpin. (*Courtesy of Keenland-Cook*)

A familiar picture—this one two weeks prior to Citation's romp in the Belmont Stakes. Cy and Eddie Arcaro, joined as usual by trainer Jimmy Jones, were perfection personified, winning the Jersey Stakes by 11 lengths in track record time for 1¼ miles at Garden State Park in New Jersey. (*Courtesy of Keenland-Cook*)

Launching an unprecedented four-day victory run at Belmont Park, Citation with his curious rider Eddie Arcaro glancing back to assess damage to First Flight and running mate Coaltown, trimmed the fastest sprinters of his day with an easy victory in the September 29, 1948 Sysonby Mile. It was one of his many undefeated forays against older horses and a veritable "tune-up" for the grueling two-mile Jockey Club Gold Cup just three days later. (*Courtesy of Keenland-Cook*)

Citation's seven-length victory in the October 2, 1948, two-mile Jockey Club Gold Cup was a mere formality for America's Super Horse. Again joined by jockey Eddie Arcaro and (left to right) Jimmy Jones, Warren Wright, and Ben Jones, Mighty Cy accomplished in four days at Belmont Park what no other thoroughbred past or present had ever done. On Wednesday, September 29, he defeated the nation's fastest older sprinters at one mile, and on this day, Saturday, October 2, he humbled the world's grandest older stayers at a two-mile marathon. (*Courtesy of Keenland-Cook*)

Getting a bit boring? No way! Not for (left to right) Eddie Arcaro (in the saddle), Jimmy Jones, Warren Wright, and Ben Jones. Two weeks following his Jockey Club Gold Cup rout, Big Cy was back to work—winning the 1⅝ miles Empire Gold Cup in a gallop. It was Cy's twelfth straight win as a 1948 three-year-old. He'd win three more that season to go into temporary retirement with 19 wins in 20 three-year-old starts, and 27 wins and two second-place showings in 29 lifetime outings. He was, and would remain, in a class by himself! (*Courtesy of Keenland-Cook*)

Citation returns from a whole year layoff following serious injury to cap his "first" comeback as a 1950 five-year-old, capturing the Golden Gate Mile Handicap under 128 pounds with a new world clocking of 1:33 3/5. With Steve Brooks aboard, Citation defeated Bolero by three-parts of a length and at the same time displaced Stymie as the world's all-time money-winning champion. Retirement seemed the decent thing for Calumet's heroic "cripple," but owner Warren Wright was obsessed with Cy becoming racing's first equine millionaire. (*Courtesy of Keenland-Cook*)

want Jimmy to feel left out. Ben sorta felt he'd promote himself to 'general manager,' thereby making Jimmy the stable's number one trainer."

Ben's self-styled "promotion" didn't sit well with the farm's nominal back-home general manager Paul Ebelhardt. Paul at first was ranked "farm manager," but, with Warren Wright's blessings, became known as "general manager," bestowing the title of "farm manager" to Bill Raetzman, the latter really in control of Calumet's breeding-nursery operation.

Wright did some fancy juggling. He didn't want Ebelhardt's nose out of joint; and he certainly didn't want to countermand the wishes of racing's most renowned trainer. Ebelhardt kept his general manager title as regards farm activities; Ben would rule as general manager and chief trainer once the horses became race-worthy.

"Things weren't always that perfect, not even in our own paradise," Margaret joked.

One thing was certain, however. Citation was now an accredited superstar. No more reservations about whether he could cope with Coaltown's acclaimed speed. He had taken on, and conquered, a star-studded three-year-old division; but then so had numerous classy three-year-olds before him.

Racing was knee-deep in the lore and legacy of bona fide "glory days." War Admiral, Man o'War's greatest son, had swept the 1937 Triple Crown. Four years later (1941), Whirlaway swamped his foes in annexing his Triple. Two years later (1943), Count Fleet murdered his opposition in the Derby, Preakness, and Belmont Stakes. Three years later (1946) racing's "Club-Footed Comet" Assault stole the nation as turfdom's seventh Triple Crown kingpin. Now, just two years later—no fewer than eleven years since War Admiral starred as the first of four rapid-fire Triple Crown champions—Citation exploded on the scene.

Therefore, whereas Cy's monumental Derby score over so highly regarded a colt as Coaltown was generally rated as exceptional, racing's newest sensation would have to sustain his brilliance if only to retain respectability, Sunny Jim's accolade notwithstanding. That's how numerous great horses were those days.

Many sports devotees, however, started to suspect, if not perceive, a singular sublimity in this average-looking horse who insisted on going about the risky business of winning without undue fanfare. Throw out his two "excusable" defeats and American sports aficionados would be looking at an unbeaten seventeen-for-seventeen Kentucky Derby winner, and a virtual shoo-in as the eighth Triple Crown winner in American history.

When queried by sports experts as to whether Citation possessed the wherewithal to win the Triple Crown, Arcaro tersely replied: "There's nothing Citation can't do, and you can quote me, too."

Quote Eddie they did. Sports pages were ablaze with commentary and opinion about the sport's newest phenomenon. Another Triple Crown winner was one thing—most experts were already conceding that inevitability—but possible ranking as "the greatest horse who ever lived"—that became the *big* sixty-four-dollar question.

Adding fuel to the conjecture was jockey N. L. Pierson's sporty support of Citation's awesome Derby supremacy: "Citation beat us fair and square. We have no excuse. My colt was right on top of his game. We took an easy but commanding lead. He loved the track; that was no excuse. And he was still running strongly when Citation came to us turning for home. He never threw in the towel. I asked him for his best, and he kicked in just like he's always done.

"Citation was just something else, that's all, actually more like something from another world. He went by so easily, I think my colt got the shakes. He never really knew what hit him!" It was a gentlemanly confession.

Elmer Polzin of the *Chicago Herald-American* put it this way: "What really impressed me was Citation's determination and single-mindedness once he set out to collar Coaltown. He was relentless, almost ruthless, and so dedicated that I still get chills thinking about how he turned on the power from the far turn to the wire!"

Arlington-Washington magnate Ben Lindheimer didn't have to feather his nest cajoling Warren Wright to assure Citation's summer presence in Chicago should all go well with Calumet's superstar. But business, not friendship, insisted Lindheimer ascertain that both the Arlington Classic and American Derby remained a priority on Citation's schedule should he successfully covet both the Preakness and Belmont.

Lindheimer sought to keep Chicago's approval rating high—two of racing's last three Triple Crown winners—Whirlaway (1941) and Assault (1946)—shortly thereafter wound up at Arlington, ironically both colts losing in spectacular upsets: Whirlaway finishing second to Attention in the Classic, after which Assault astonishingly ran dead last to an Illinois colt named The Dude in the same race.

Only marvelous Count Fleet, who easily swept his 1943 Triple Crown, failed to "start back" at Chicago's Arlington Park, not that he didn't want to. An injury incurred while running off with the Belmont forced the cleverly named John D. Hertz son of Reigh Count-Quickly, by Haste, into premature retirement.

"Citation will be at Arlington and Washington win or lose," Wright promised Lindheimer, "but we have every intention to keep on winning everything in sight."

The only caveat in Citation's armor, espoused especially by only a few media members who for whatever reason were disinclined to jump aboard the Calumet bandwagon—unaccountably at times including *Daily Racing Form* columnist Charlie Hatton—might be his hectic schedule. Some felt he was "over-raced," that no ordinary animal could stand his punishing grind of racing without some let-up.

Wright even questioned the Jones boys. They responded harmoniously: "Citation's as sound as the day he was foaled. He loves to compete, and he keeps himself in good shape mentally as well as physically. And he never overextends himself. He's yet to come back from a race even vaguely tired. We don't think he even knows how really great he is."

One need not be a Phi Beta Kappa to conclude Citation "looked like a lock" to win the 1948 Triple Crown. He had thoroughly demolished every three-year-old thrown at him; and his class was enhanced by the easy manner in which he toyed with older stars Armed, Delegate, Kitchen Police, and Faultless prior to drawing bead on the Derby itself.

Chicago Tribune sports editor Arch Ward particularly "admired Cy's fervor in manhandling unbeaten Coaltown" in their Derby showdown. By the same token, scribes Joe Palmer, Warren Brown, John P. Carmichael—even "doubting Thomas" Charlie Hatton—had rated Coaltown "a potential great" prior to his stunning Derby defeat.

Ben Jones was happily afflicted with "Derby fever," as were son Jimmy, Warren and Lucille Wright, and the whole Calumet family. Ben had won with Lawrin and Whirlaway in 1938 and 1941, respectively, with Arcaro aboard both times; then with Pensive, little Conn McCreary up, in 1944. Now Citation won, which made Arcaro the Derby's only four-time winner, three of those scores astride horses with whom Ben Jones was personally involved.

The Preakness was scheduled two weeks after the Derby, May 15; its distance was 1³⁄₁₆ miles, or a sixteenth of a mile—110 yards or 330 feet to be exact—shorter than the Derby. Calumet already had decided not to start Coaltown, for two reasons: one, his was a lofty, prideful mien, a vanity which could not survive repeated insults from a compatriot once regarded as a lesser. They didn't want to break his spirit. And two, there were other rich worlds to conquer; since Citation couldn't be in two places at the same time, they'd deputize Coaltown to pick up any extra reward money available.

Of the three Triple Crown events, the Preakness usually wielded the least spectacular draw, unless, as in Citation's case, an exceptional animal was overwhelmingly favored to add racing's second jewel to his crown en route to what the sports world eagerly sought—another Triple Crown champion, not realizing at the time how elusive such a quest would become.

Cy wore his garland of Derby roses proudly during the two-week break leading up to Preakness Day, two weeks in which horsemen searched their souls as to whether to "go" or whether to "stay" the execution which loomed unavoidable in Maryland's big race at Pimlico.

Opponents, including Coaltown, dropped by the wayside, even though the Preakness was counted upon to annually unveil new or fresh obstacles for the Derby winner to hurdle on his way to the Belmont Stakes a little later down the road.

One bold upstart emerged—his name was Vulcan's Forge, rarin' to go as a lusty three-year-old, remembered for his victory in the Champagne the year before. And a desperate Doug Dodson, still smarting over his break with Calumet Farm, would ride him. Vulcan's Forge later would win the Withers, and in later seasons proved his mettle as a crack handicap performer, winning such blue ribbon events as the Suburban in the East and the Santa Anita Handicap in the West. Vulcan's Forge and his affinity for the late run made him a well-credentialed adversary.

Bovard and Better Self wanted another crack at Cy. Therefore only four horses went postward. Interest, however, skyrocketed. Maybe Sunny Jim Fitzsimmons was right after all? The sports world woke up to the reality that Citation was a legend in the making. Could this dark bay colt really be "The Greatest Thoroughbred Who Ever Lived"?

The Preakness weatherman—probably the same guy who worked the Derby—was up to his old high jinks again: ominous skies, torrential rains, and a track, this time, unlike any other. Not slop or mud, but one rated "heavy." Arcaro said it looked like "molten cement."

Track condition, however, had become Cy's least worry. "He's like the mailman," writer Elmer Polzin predicted, "neither rain, snow, sleet, or slop, mud, or even heavy going, will stay his rounds."

Citation showed up Preakness Day in all his glory. The turnout was huge, the press clamoring to chronicle another mammoth performance, no matter how adverse the weather or track condition.

Racing historian Peter Winants referred to Cy's Preakness victory as a "laugher." Winants meant no disrespect for those who toiled fruitlessly in Cy's wake. Winants's expression was one of mirth rather than derision, though Cy hardly stopped at the finish to salute or "high-five" his three leg-weary combatants as they struggled home under the wire.

For Arcaro, Cy's Preakness was "just another eye-opener." Eddie went into the race with his sights covertly affixed on the Belmont Stakes, which, as racing schedules would have it, was a good month away, on June 12. "The Belmont was our 'must' event," Arcaro recalled, "not that we didn't recognize that there'd be no Belmont or Triple Crown without first winning the Preakness. But the way I felt, and by no means was I belittling those who tested us in the Preakness, but the only way we could lose is if Citation fell at the eighth pole.

"But then, Jimmy had already bragged that 'Citation could fall down, and still get up to win if he wanted to.'"

Eddie wanted to prove once and for all to himself that Citation was the "pushbutton" colt Al Snider swore by. "Actually, I was one up on Al, since just prior to the Derby Ben Jones promised me 'any horse Cy could see, he could catch.'

"I already knew that no horse alive could ever catch Citation if he didn't want to be caught. I don't mean him being headed while I'm rating him, or asking him to lay third or fourth early behind some genuine speed; I mean once we took the lead on purpose, on the turn, or in upper stretch—no horse could ever bring him down!

"So—and Jimmy gave me no orders—I decided to let him control the Preakness right from the start. Hell, the distance [1³⁄₁₆ miles] was no problem, but I didn't want him getting bogged down in all that gook if we could help it. So I sent him at the start. No real urging, just a nudge to let him know he should take command as pacesetter. He was docile as a lamb. He grabbed the lead passing the stands—never once looked back—and never throughout the trip did he work up even one drop of sweat."

Better Self and Bovard pressed Citation early. It was utterly astonishing to see their riders alternately pumping and pushing, eventually strapping their mounts to stay within hailing distance, while up front Arcaro sat motionless as Cy deftly churned through what looked more like a plowed field than a race track.

Cy settled up the backstretch 1½ lengths ahead of his three pursuers. He later opened up two lengths, then three, slowed down the pace just a speck, and was still two lengths in front in midstretch when hard-hitting Vulcan's Forge came a-charging!

Vulcan's Forge was never more fearless or determined, but he not only failed to gain an inch on Citation, but unbelievably found himself actually losing ground—and he was "full out" while Cy was just galloping. Cy dashed under the finish wire by nearly six lengths, Arcaro craning over his right shoulder to assess the damage done.

Arcaro's broad smile as Cy proudly bowed before an appreciative crowd certified the colt's full arrival, if not as Horse of the Century, at least Horse for the Twentieth Century's First Fifty Years.

It was generally agreed that Sunny Jim Fitzsimmons knew his horses, that his remarks were prophetically accurate. What people didn't know, though, was that the best was yet to come.

Chapter Nine

"Boss, That Hoss—He Ain't Human!"

*A*rcaro was keeping his word, "Citation won't ever lose again," and remained true to his promise "never to make the same mistake twice."

Not everybody was an immediate proselyte, however. There were a few disgruntled holdouts. A skeptic here and there. A wearisome curmudgeon. A sports ne'er-do-well. A racing naysayer. A cantankerous critic unwilling to give credit where credit was due, withholding praise from the praiseworthy, denying awe to the awesome.

They—a few of them sophistic Easterners openly contemptuous of any horse or stable that dared to extensively race and excel anywhere west or south of the Great Lakes—seemingly demanded more proof, that they'd stand convinced only if Citation could win the Belmont Stakes in New York State.

Snobbery precluded "acclaim or acceptance" unless Citation's reputation for greatness be unequivocally confirmed in the third and final leg of the Triple Crown. Truthfully, the Belmont deserved its lofty rating: its 1½ miles was "the true test of champions."

Never fully explained was self-proclaimed *Daily Racing Form* guru Charlie Hatton's carefully hidden disrespect for Citation's impact on American racing. Hatton refused to put Cy in the same league as Man o'War, later would exalt Native Dancer as "greatest ever," only to amend that claim to deify Secretariat during the writer's final days on earth.

In Hatton's defense, it's that varied difference in opinion that makes horse racing. Thus, one could only imagine what Citation's achievements in the Belmont, in subsequent encounters in Chicago, again back in New York, Maryland, and finally California, did to ruffle Hatton's plumage and painfully wound his psyche.

Citation, however, was an equal-opportunity horse. He treated fan and critic alike, always giving his best.

Surprisingly, New York welcomed Calumet, the Jones boys, and Citation with open arms. Many fondly recalled his superiority the past fall when he swept both the Belmont Trial and Futurity with power to spare.

Sports fans in the 1940s had come to expect a semblance of perfection and constancy from their champions. Winning the Triple Crown was a legitimately achievable accomplishment, not the virtually impossible feat it was about to become in the years to come. "Great colts win the big races!" was the universal battle cry.

There was one fly in the ointment, however. Weird scheduling allowed a full month between the Preakness and the Belmont. Most future horsemen would have done obeisance to such a calendar anomaly, so fearful would trainers become, deploring the fact that "there wasn't enough time between Triple Crown events" to keep their charges fresh.

Therefore, the Joneses may very well have been arrested for animal abuse were they operating fifty years later.

"Heck, we can't keep Citation in his stall a full month," Ben and Jimmy chimed. "That would be criminal the way he looks and feels. The big guy wants to run. Not to run him would be an insult to his manhood."

Their attitude nearly caught Arcaro by surprise. Sylvester Labrot Jr.'s Bovard, who had been vainly chasing Citation all spring, was being pointed for the Jersey Stakes—later to be renamed the Jersey Derby—on May 29 at Garden State in neighboring New Jersey. Bovard's people contacted Eddie, hoping to get The Master to ride their luckless colt in the 1¼ miles stakes for three-year-olds.

Eddie said, "why not," but before shaking hands on the deal he called Jones for clearance.

"We were just about to call you," Ben chortled. "Sign no deals, Eddie, 'cause it looks like we're gonna start Cy in that very same Jersey Stakes."

Arcaro wasn't half as stupefied by Ben's decision as were the media, whose collective hair stood on end—why risk injury or the danger of "over-racing" with the Belmont so close at hand?

Eddie merely shrugged his shoulders. He trusted Ben's and Jimmy's judgment on such matters. The Jones boys certainly understood how cherished another Triple Crown trophy would be adorning Warren Wright's already crowded mantle.

Arch Ward and Warren Brown called Wright personally, unwisely by-passing Ben and Jimmy. They reminded Wright that Citation, despite his reputation as a "workhorse machine," was one race away from unique fame, that the colt had already started no fewer than nine times in less than four months as a three-year-old. Did he really need the extra work?

Wright, of course, had no qualms seeing Citation strut his stuff in New Jersey. He'd never call the Joneses on the carpet by questioning the wisdom of their decision. Ben Lindheimer did the right thing; he called Ben Jones directly. But Lindheimer had an arcane motive: he didn't want anything to happen to Citation before Calumet would ship to Arlington and Washington Parks for its annual Chicago summer campaign. Lindheimer was not blind to Citation's swelling celebrity, particularly if he were to capture the Belmont as racing's eighth Triple Crown hero.

Joe Palmer, Red Smith, and Charlie Hatton—the latter credited with titling the Derby, Preakness, and Belmont as the Triple Crown in 1935—likewise were astonished, at the same time galvanized, at what confidence Ben and Jimmy Jones exuded in their young superstar. Palmer and Smith reportedly critically admired the trainers' nerve; Hatton kept much of his disdain to himself.

Regardless, Citation arrived at Garden State in full battle garb, eager to include Eddie Arcaro in his top weight assignment of 126 pounds, un-intimidated by the fact that he'd have to concede as much as twelve pounds to his rivals.

But—wonder of wonders—Cy would catch a fast track to do his thing—finally!

The fast track presented a momentary temptation to "give Cy his head," to let him run "a little," and show off for his legion of admirers.

Arcaro knew better, though he did proffer the idea smilingly to Ben and Jimmy in the paddock that May 29. No, the Jersey Stakes was "just another workout" for Citation, "just to keep him fit, just to give him the exercise he needed so he wouldn't grow stale" while waiting for the Belmont Stakes. Ben especially made that point clearly.

CBS included the Jersey Stakes in its regular Gillette Cavalcade of Sports radio racing coverage, again with Clem McCarthy on the call. Cy had become an American institution, not only because of his dominance and brilliance, but also because of Al Snider's tragic death, which led to the unforeseen teaming up of Citation and jockey legend Eddie Arcaro.

"I'll take it easy with him," Eddie assured Jimmy Jones when the latter gave him "a leg up" into Cy's saddle. "Some day," Eddie grinned, "some day, you know, we're just gonna have to let him run full out." Then Eddie added assuredly: "But not today, yes, I know. Today's just a work."

But what a "work!"

Cy left the gate with the first flight, then took a short lead as the field pounded into the clubhouse turn. The top package of 126 pounds was merely a feather on his brawny back, and he settled up the backstretch with just over six furlongs yet to travel bouncing along easily with a three-length bulge, Eddie barely moving his hands, almost tugging at the reins.

How Eddie loved to recall: "We passed the half-mile pole, leaning around the far turn, and Cy was now four or five lengths to the good. I never once looked back, never worried either, because he was in full charge, and once he took charge, no horse living could ever catch him from behind."

"Normally I'd judge the fractions pretty accurately, but I needn't that day—he was just loping along.

"Suddenly, we were at the eighth pole in midstretch," Eddie continued, "and suddenly we were all by ourselves, and I mean 'all by ourselves.' We were some eight lengths ahead of a horse called Macbeth, and old Bovard himself, and so I looked back, just once—I never meant for him to be that far in front!"

So Eddie grabbed more rein, hauled back on Cy more seriously. "I totally eased him up—you'd have to see it to believe it—from the eighth pole to the wire, and the big guy still was reaching out for ground without any urging or trying. Citation was eleven lengths in front—it was a runaway—after a mile-and-a-quarter over a fast but deep, tiring track, a track not conducive to speed."

Still—Citation breezed the classic 1¼ miles in 2:03 flat, a new track record, shattering the old mark by one and three-fifths seconds. And he did it as if he were merely taking a leisurely stroll through Central Park!

"Sorry, boss," Eddie remarked to Jimmy after Cy's hallmark head-bowed canter to the Winner's Circle. "I give you my word, the big guy never left a gallop the whole way around."

Jimmy's smile in return assured Eddie that the great rider had done no wrong. "If this hoss gets any better, some day we're gonna wind up running against ourselves," Jimmy effused, not then realizing he was uttering a soon-to-be-fulfilled prophecy.

"If Citation isn't the greatest four-legged athlete of all time," Warren Brown shared with writing cohort Elmer Polzin, "there simply ain't no such animal!"

Polzin concurred wholeheartedly. He was an unabashed Calumet convert; anything the stable unleashed was fine with him—Whirlaway, Twilight Tear, Pensive, Armed, Faultless, Bewitch, and Coaltown. The latter, incidentally, was dodging Cy following his Kentucky Derby drubbing; he immediately returned to his winning ways, eventually annexing the Swift, Drexel, and Jerome Handicaps, an omen of greater things to come as a 1949 four-year-old.

Polzin, though, did have one minor concern, and he wasn't alone. Racing-breeding pundits couched it this way: they were fearful Citation just might use the Belmont Stakes to "step on his pedigree."

His daddy, the fabled Bull Lea, was peerless as a sire. But a couple red flags had been hoisted. Bull Lea as a racehorse was a veritable speedball; distance was not his forte. Now he had sired a bevy of outstanding champions, including Twilight Tear and Armed, 1944 and 1947 Horse of the Year, respectively. Armed's career had covered multiple seasons, the gelding piling up stakes and handicaps like a resourceful squirrel collecting nuts for the winter.

Armed, however, like most sons and daughters of Bull Lea, had never won at more than 1¼ miles, though in fairness the rugged competitor never really had occasion to race beyond that distance. No disgrace there; none intended. But Citation would have to negotiate 1½ miles in the Belmont two weeks hence if he were to authenticate his already proclaimed reign as America's greatest horse of all time.

Questioning Bull Lea's ability to father a horse capable of winning at 1½ miles was nothing more than sports ballyhoo. It sold papers, was fodder for the rumor gristmill, and was good for business. Racing was America's number one spectator sport those days, and debates over whether Cy could go the Belmont distance helped attract an inordinately enormous throng to Belmont Park the afternoon of June 12.

By post time for the Belmont, guys like Elmer Polzin, Arch Ward, and Warren Brown were confident Citation could turn the trick. Most complacent of all were Mr. and Mrs. Warren Wright, Ben and Jimmy Jones, Paul Ebelhardt, Margaret Glass, and sundry other members of the Lexington, Kentucky home team invited to Belmont to see history made.

Only distraction that day was the fact that seven so-called presumptuous challengers were entered against Mighty Cy, a large field by any calculation, compiled as if by secret conspiracy to deny the Calumet colt his rightful claim to thoroughbred immortality.

There, of course, was no such conspiracy, just that owners and trainers started believing, actually hoping, that all that hogwash about Bull Lea's suspected inability to sire a horse capable of going farther than 1¼ miles might be true.

All of Citation's usual three-year-old challengers, including late-running Escadru and hard-knocking Better Self, showed up for one last tussle. There were newcomers, too, like Sam Riddle's high-spirited Faraway, whose blistering speed it was hoped just might soften Citation up for a late-stretch upset.

By Belmont time, Arcaro was so sure of Citation's power he jokingly predicted the only way the colt could lose is if "I fell off at the start." Simultaneously, Jimmy Jones in the paddock kiddingly warned Eddie— "The Triple Crown's ours, so just don't fall off!"

By Belmont time, also, Cy had acquired a curious habit of resting in the gate while the horses were being loaded. "It was like he consciously was 'taking a load off,'" Eddie remarked. "He was so cool, so casual, he'd support his body against the side of the stall, like an athlete crossing his legs, leaning against a wall—resting, awaiting the word 'go!'"

Citation drew the inside post in the Belmont field of eight, so he was the first to move into his stall. Arcaro adjusted his goggles, and just as in the recent Jersey Stakes, the track condition was fast, which was the least of Cy's concerns. And he leaned against the stall.

At that very moment, Citation was in full blossom as a racehorse. Historian William H. P. Robertson in his classic book *The History of Thoroughbred Racing in America* described him thus: "Although he lacked the size, eye-catching color or flourish of [Man o'War], Citation certainly was a handsome animal of adequate proportions: sixteen hands, 1,075 pounds, girthing seventy-four inches, with a stride that averaged twenty-five feet. He was put together so neatly that no single feature stood out, the total impression being one of smooth, muscular power." And that power was about to be unleashed!

But not before he'd nearly fall on his head leaving the gate!

For Arcaro and Jimmy Jones it was no longer a joking matter. Cy stumbled badly at the start, nearly unseating Arcaro. The Master had to use all his agility and athleticism to keep his equine friend upright.

"It could've been a lot worse," Arcaro said. "The misstep was real, and his nose went toward the ground, but he's a superb athlete, and he took the whole incident in stride. In fact, he never really lost but one stride. He recovered amazingly fast—so we both decided, almost simultaneously, that we'd go right to the lead, and mean it."

What Eddie meant by "meaning it" was to invoke Citation's imperishable truth that no horse could ever catch him from behind once he assumed "meaningful" command. That certitude shared equal billing with the irrefragable belief and knowledge that "any horse Cy could see, he could catch!"

Now they'd all have to catch Citation. Faraway lived up to his advance notice and was whipped by Teddy Atkinson to press Citation in the early stages. Once again, Cy would run only as fast as needed, in this case, to retain command, but with a two- or three-length lead he was committed not to relinquish as a result of the ragged start.

The Belmont crowd, aroused by the spectacle of Citation stumbling at the start in full view of the stands, went wild, fearful expectation and wonderment stirring the arena. Horse by horse, after Faraway, especially Better Self and finally Escadru for whom the 1½ miles seemed tailor-made, they challenged Citation, as if by relay.

Joe Palmer described it like no other: "Citation was passing the half-mile pole three lengths ahead. Behind him, Arnold Kirkland swung Escadru to full stride, and around the last turn the margin shortened.

"Three furlongs away, it was a scant two lengths, and the whole, long, searching Belmont stretch lay ahead. No Bull Lea had ever managed to top twelve furlongs, and I thought, with an odd constriction, that quite possibly Citation's banner was coming down.

"I had watched Citation grow in stature for almost a year, with the slowly crystallizing hope that here, at long last, was the horse we'd been looking for since a great golden chestnut (Man o'War) roared to a stop at Kenilworth Park back in 1920.

"He had come to Belmont with undiminished brilliance, because those minor affairs behind Saggy and Bewitch had no more real significance than Upset's Sanford Stakes. Class and speed he had shown in abundance, and the test of stamina was at its straining utmost, there on the turn. And Citation was yielding ground, with more than a quarter mile to go.

"I knew he might stagger in, but if Citation was the horse I thought he was, that would not have been enough. A gasping, barely won victory would have been almost as bad as a defeat, and I would have been sorry for either.

"I could not see Arcaro move, but with some slight dropping of the hands, he released the swelling energy of the great racer beneath him. Citation opened away. He was three-sixteenths out, but he was home.

"The Belmont crowd began to roar before he hit the furlong pole. This observer dropped his glasses, climbed over assorted cameramen, and went downstairs to get into the champagne."

Palmer's story was great. But Citation's Belmont triumph was even greater. He led every step of the way, cruising along by two or three lengths at every call, repulsing bid after bid, demoralizing Escadru in upper stretch, crushing Better Self in midstretch, striding clear past the sixteenth pole, winning "eased up" by eight lengths, equaling Count Fleet's track record of 2:28⅕.

"Eight lengths?" Arcaro responded when told the margin, "why, it could have been eighty if I had asked!"

Citation's Triple Crown victory electrified American sports. Easterners in general, New Yorkers in particular, also lifted their voices and glasses high in a willing toast to Mighty Cy as the world's most celebrated thoroughbred.

Arcaro was especially vocal and articulate. He was alive, aglow with the spirit as racing's first two-time Triple Crown riding champ. When asked by Bill Stern on radio following the Belmont to "compare his two Triple Crown winners, Citation and Whirlaway," Eddie replied with gusto and customary frankness: "Hell, Citation can carry the both of us, and still beat Whirlaway!"

Give Charlie Hatton credit. He too was "impressed" with Citation's Belmont romp, and though he wouldn't favorably compare him with Man o'War, he did acknowledge the ease and authority in which Cy disposed of his seven adversaries.

Trainer "Canny" Max Hirsch, who had saddled two Kentucky Derby winners—Bold Venture and the latter's son, Assault, who only two years earlier (1946) won his own Triple Crown—jumped aboard the bandwagon piloted by Sunny Jim Fitzsimmons, stating incontrovertibly: "There's never been a horse like Citation!"

But it was left to a lowly groom in the employ of internationally famous horseman Alfred G. Vanderbilt, who, after witnessing Citation recover from a near-tragic stumble only to go on and win the Belmont in awesome fashion, to utter perhaps the finest compliment of all. Turning in disbelief to Mr. Vanderbilt, that oldster sighed: "Boss, that hoss—he ain't human!"

Chapter Ten

Human After All

*H*ow would sports fans have reacted were they privy to the incredible fact that racing wouldn't crown its next Triple Crown winner for another twenty-five years? A quarter century later, 1973, before a hungry television audience, Secretariat would fill Citation's big shoes.

Deservedly, too, but not without help from a starved public, yearning to glorify any animal able to infuse life back into a sport which had struggled too long minus the game's noblest attainment, a Triple Crown hero worthy of inclusion in an elite club made up of Sir Barton, Gallant Fox, Omaha, War Admiral, Whirlaway, Count Fleet, Assault, and its latest, greatest member, Citation.

What Citation might have achieved in popularity were television available to the masses in his day, is anybody's guess.

Cy's dominance as a three-year-old easily raised the bar for what Secretariat would accomplish at the same age twenty-five years later. Surely, Secretariat's sensational thirty-one-length victory in the Belmont in world record time was a singular touchstone of equine greatness. For the sake of argument, however, Citation's two early conquests of older horses, the quality of which Secretariat neither met nor defeated, provided fuel to compare the two great colts, though most observers admit such comparisons to this day are at best futile.

Historically, however, what Citation proceeded to accomplish as a three-year-old following his Triple Crown win was unprecedented, doubtless unequaled by any colt before or since, validating his fame and reputation as the greatest horse to ever look through a bridle.

Cy came out of the Belmont kicking and squealing like a frisky new-born colt. He had just racked up his sixth straight—tenth of eleven—win of the year, his eighteenth in twenty lifetime starts, and he was growing stronger and smarter with every outing.

When Calumet and Citation arrived at Arlington Park in mid-June, Elmer Polzin was at the forefront of the brash media throng greeting the stable's world-famous contingent of outstanding horseflesh.

"Ben Lindheimer of Arlington and Washington was on hand, of course," Polzin recalled, "making sure the track's newest meal ticket was safe and sound; more importantly, ready for battle."

When Citation disembarked from his private van, he paused to survey the nosy media, including cameramen whose flash bulbs exploded incessantly, lifted his head high, pulling ever so playfully on the shank firmly gripped in Freeman McMillan's hand.

"Cy then let loose a whinny heard around the stable area," track official Bob Henderson confirmed, "as if to say: 'hey, look, fellas, I'm back, and I'm loaded for bear!'"

Normally a gentleman, what horse people call "a good actor," Cy politely and immediately resumed a placid pose—more lordly than statuesque—quietly, and with manly dignity, following McMillan's lead down the ramp to the barn annually reserved for Calumet's A-team.

Arch Ward reminded Lindheimer that two of racing's last three Triple Crown winners—Whirlaway and Assault—subsequently suffered their first defeats at Arlington in Chicago, both colts losing the Arlington Classic in rousing upsets. Lindheimer, mildly annoyed by the suggestion of a possible "Triple Crown–Chicago jinx," gained a measure of satisfaction when he reminded Ward that both Assault and Whirlaway had won elsewhere following their Triple scores before invading Chicago, that perhaps the colts were tired by the time they checked in at Arlington Park.

"Plus," Henderson came to his boss's defense, "Whirlaway and Assault were 'merely great' horses. We're not just talking 'great' with Citation. We're talking 'greatest'!" Henderson wasn't just idly singing Citation's praises. Every sports fan and media member from Florida to California regarded Cy's claim to greatness as genuine. No one—nowhere—honestly ever expected him to lose again. Except, perhaps, Charlie Hatton.

For the first time, observers had started to take cognitive note of the "physical" Citation. He was full-grown, totally mature, perfectly coupled, molded, and built; muscular and sinewy, yet not prodigious to detract from his fluid way of movement.

"The horse must be made of iron," Warren Brown volunteered.

"Or maybe steel," echoed John P. Carmichael.

Years later Bill Nack of *Sports Illustrated* stated that to do what Citation did as a three-year-old, "He had to be made of titanium!"

No, Cy was flesh, blood, and bone, but a wonderful combination of all three components, so marvelously mixed and blended as to forever defy explanation or duplication.

Ben Lindheimer opined that if Hollywood had invented the sport of horse racing, Calumet Farm in Lexington would be movieland's chosen picturesque homey scene, a setting of verdant beauty and pastoral charm; Ben and Jimmy Jones would be cast in the father-son role of training icons; and Citation would be the filmland's ideal depiction of "the perfect thoroughbred" who could do no wrong.

Shortly upon arrival at Arlington, Ben authorized Jimmy to announce Citation's upcoming racing schedule. Everyone knew both the Arlington Classic and the American Derby for three-year-olds were "must" events if Cy were to continue his relentless domination of his own age group. What they didn't expect, though, was Jimmy's declaration: "Citation's in such fine form—he never had to take a deep breath in the Belmont—that we're thinking of starting him against older horses in the Stars & Stripes in about two weeks. Any questions?"

"Will that mean he won't be going in either the Classic or Derby?" one reporter inquired.

"No," Jimmy actually nodded, "no, he'll still start in the Classic and American Derby. We just feel he's so good right now, that he'll relish taking on older horses again—just to stay razor sharp."

Jones's statement left the media "bewitched, bothered, and bewildered." No outstanding three-year-old colt—past, present, and perhaps future—had ever taken on and whipped quality older competitors as did Citation back in February at Hialeah before training his big guns on the Triple Crown, which he captured so easily.

Now Citation, unlike other champion three-year-olds who'd automatically await the fall in which to challenge older handicap stars, was returning to action against his elders—and in a handicap race no less!

That meant Citation would have to tote high weight, this time conceding precious pounds to older, established handicap campaigners. A few onlookers feared a spirit of "overconfidence" had invaded the Calumet camp.

"Call it 'overconfidence,' if you like," Arcaro said in a pre–Stars & Stripes interview. "But you'd be wrong. Mr. Wright really couldn't care less—as long as Cy was up to it. But Ben and Jimmy Jones truly believed Cy was 'the horse for the ages,' the most remarkable racing machine God ever created.

"As long as he was sound—and he was sound as a bell—they knew no horse in the world, no matter how much older or more experienced he was, could ever touch Citation. And I felt that way, too, with no reservations. And he'd beat 'em up front, or from off the pace. No horse alive could bring him down from behind. And if he could see the leaders, with that 'perfect eyesight' of his, by God he'd catch 'em!"

Arlington's racing secretary and handicapper held Citation in such high esteem that he assigned the colt top weight of 119 for the 1⅛ miles stakes, which impost was equivalent to 129 on an older horse. He went postward with his own older multiple stakes-winning stablemate Fervent, who the summer before ran off with the American Derby at Washington Park, giving Fervent three pounds by the scale—and actual weight to others, including Loujac, the only other intrepid three-year-old in the starry field.

What should have been just another brilliant display of speed, stamina, and class—the July 5 Stars & Stripes Handicap at Arlington Park—turned out to be Cy's longest day, certainly his hardest race, and a potential nightmare.

There was an early-morning incident two days before the race—the impact of which was never fully denied nor confirmed—that might have had some bearing on the pain and misery Citation and his entourage were to suffer in the holiday weekend Stars & Stripes.

It was about 7:30 in the morning: hundreds of excited thoroughbreds jammed the track as they did each morning, bright and early. Groom–exercise rider Freeman McMillan was aboard Citation, accompanied by Jimmy Jones astride a stable pony. The four of 'em were leisurely strolling along; Jones had no specific workout planned for Cy.

Reports remain sketchy to this day, but there was clamorous commotion, shouts and yells from concerned horsemen, jockeys, and exercise riders. Apparently a green two-year-old filly had been spooked by someone or something. She forcefully reared back in fear. She would have posed no real danger to the other thoroughbreds had cooler heads prevailed.

But her nonplussed exercise rider was unseated, tossed in the air like a rag doll, his feet loosed from the stirrups. Had she totally separated herself from him, she probably would have run off, eventually corralled by one of the track outriders officially assigned to guard against such an emergency.

The upended rider tumbled earthward, still clinging to the filly's reins. He landed on his feet, refused to yield the reins, and, as she started to run from him, he steadfastly ran alongside, the two veering wildly to where Cy and his escort were walking.

The filly obviously was uncontrollable, but she meant nobody any harm. Frightened, her fear aggravated by an insistent rider yanking on the reins in a futile effort to haul her in, she plowed broadside into the pony Jones had angled out as buffer between her and Citation.

Cy was smacked solidly just above the right shoulder. The pony, however, took the brunt of the impact, reeling dizzily. Both McMillan and Jones, though rocked by the collision, felt their horses fortunately had escaped unscathed.

Back at the barn, the stable vet gave both animals, particularly Cy, more than a perfunctory examination. They were both fine, uninjured, far as he was concerned. So Cy returned to the business at hand—the upcoming Stars & Stripes.

The holiday attraction, always top-drawer among Chicago stakes headliners—previous winners included Equipoise, Discovery, and Armed—had never been won by a young three-year-old. Thus, the 1948 edition loomed bigger than ever. The usual holiday crowd brimmed with thousands of additional fans anxious to see America's super horse do his thing.

Among Cy's older foes was the 1946 American Derby winner Eternal Reward, now five and bolder than ever, in receipt of three actual pounds from Citation, not to mention the age-weight-scale difference.

But Jimmy Jones and Arcaro were confident nothing could contain racing's bay tornado. "By then," Arcaro assured, "not only us—the Wrights and the Joneses included—but horsemen everywhere, anybody who knew the game, knew Cy's mightiness, that he had truly lived up to his reputation as the greatest horse who ever lived. I honestly expected him to breeze home as always."

Eddie decided he'd allow Cy his own sweet time early in the race. "There was tons of speed, including the fleet merchant Knockdown, and Loujac liked to hear his hooves rattle. Eternal Reward and others, like Pellicle—and we were giving five-year-old Pellicle thirteen pounds—loved to run late. I wanted Cy fresh as possible throughout the race."

Eddie's confidence was mildly shaken by "an uneasy feeling while we were limbering up on the track minutes before the race." He sensed all was not right, but couldn't pinpoint the problem. "Cy just didn't have his old vitality—and yet he did. It was really strange."

Now Eddie wasn't so insensitive to proceed with the race if he felt Cy wasn't right, could be hurting, or, for whatever reason, wasn't up to his best. "Suddenly, the old vim returned." Eddie explained, "He back-kicked like a yearling—seemed like his old zeal was back. I thought maybe he was just having a bad day, like us humans have from time to time. Otherwise, I wouldn't have taken him to the gate, and Jimmy would've scratched him for sure."

Citation fulfilled his obligation in the Stars & Stripes. It was a victory, to be sure; but a Pyrrhic victory, sad to say!

He was jostled slightly at the start, was subjected to close quarters, with some bumping, going around the first turn; but nothing to worry about, just a race roughly contested, at least in the early stages.

Knockdown was nimble of foot, had been since he helped set the pace in Assault's 1946 Kentucky Derby triumph two years earlier, and went about establishing a comfortable early lead with Loujac in prompt pursuit. Cy had completely recovered from earlier traffic congestion, roaring from fifth, some six lengths off the leaders, to third, less than a length away as he negotiated the far turn.

"We were sitting pretty," Arcaro beamed, "and we had Knockdown and Loujac measured perfectly. And Cy appeared to be going easily, no special effort I knew of. Once we straightened away, I nudge him, just a slight push, and he took off as always."

Citation swept by the leaders with his usual exuberance, opening up two lengths on the pack approaching the furlong pole, an eighth of a mile from pay dirt. "He was home free!" Eddie assumed. "I knew it, and he knew it. Then something happened, but I wasn't sure what.

"He started to slow down, letting up, something he'd never done be-fore. It was as if he was waiting for the others. And the others—Eternal Reward and Pellicle—were flying. They meant business!"

As a result, Eddie did what he had never really had to do before. He unhoused his whip for some serious flailing.

"I had no inkling, no idea at all, that he had hurt himself, otherwise I'd never had gotten into him like I did. For some reason," Arcaro deplored, "I thought he was just loafing. Now I've been around horses before who loafed when they got the lead. But not Citation. He didn't know the word 'loaf.' I should've known better."

Urged on by Eddie, Citation also spied Eternal Reward and Pellicle's late presence. They were two lengths behind inside the sixteenth pole and charging. They were still two lengths back at the wire, still charging! Even though Cy was hobbling, they didn't—even hurt he wouldn't allow it—they couldn't gain an inch!

Cy not only refused to be caught despite ostensibly having suffered a serious and painful injury, he manfully retained his two-length margin to the finish, equaling Armed's track record of 1:49⅖ set only the summer before, a truly titanic effort, all circumstances considered.

"Cy slowed down soon as we passed the wire," Eddie continued, "began to limp noticeably. I saw him nodding his head in pain. God, I felt terrible; I felt like crying."

The fans jammed the Winner's Circle where Cy was led by hand by Arcaro. Ben and Jimmy were wide-eyed and slack-jawed. The crowd gave Citation a standing ovation; most of them realized that he had won despite obvious distress. Even Warren Wright's usual exuberance was creased by a frown. Ben Lindheimer cracked a smile, soon replaced by growing concern that Citation's magnificent, record-tying triumph over older horses may have come at too great a price. Still, he seemed okay.

No one could ever actually pinpoint the exact time of injury. Was it precipitated two mornings earlier when Cy was roughed up by that runaway filly? Or when bumped going around the first turn in the race itself? Or when put to an all-out drive when Eternal Reward and Pellicle issued their late bids? Or a combination of all of the above? Whatever the cause, the "iron horse" was indeed injured!

Every expert veterinarian was at Cy's beck and call. They determined that he suffered a wrenched hip muscle and a sprained ankle. Painful, to be sure. Calumet regularly employed a trio of top-flight vets—Charles Hagyard, Art Davidson, and Bill McGee—plus a bevy of track and regional vets experienced in Cy's type of injury.

The good news: Cy's wound, while painful, was neither life-threatening nor career-ending. At least, that was the preliminary diagnosis. The bad news: Cy would be lost to racing for a spell; he had to be treated; he'd need time to convalesce and rehabilitate.

Fast forward to today. Translated, that would mean the horse probably would be lost for the season at least, if not retired to stud, taking into consideration his breeding value. That is, if Cy was your ordinary *great* horse. Which, of course, he was not!

Warren Brown, Elmer Polzin, and Jack Drees visited Cy at his barn where the stringent odor of liniment lingered everywhere. Vets and grooms moved about briskly attending to the sport's most valued patient.

Only Polzin lived long enough to discern the happy analogy with a present-day action-movie hero, Arnold Schwarzenegger, who uttered what Citation had expressly written all over his handsome face: "I'll be back!"

Incredibly, Mighty Cy was back to the races six weeks later!

Maybe he was made of titanium after all?

Chapter Eleven

He's Back!

$\mathcal{T}$he eagerly awaited news that Citation was ready to resume his racing career echoed throughout the world of sports.

"That colt's totally amazing," Arch Ward told Ben Lindheimer, the two sports entrepreneurs heaving a sigh of relief that "the big horse" was back in training.

One sour note: During Cy's absence the Arlington Classic was renewed without him. This was a race Calumet especially coveted ever since 1941 when Attention dealt their Whirlaway a stinging defeat that helped verify Arlington's reputation as "The Graveyard of Champions."

The Jones boys subsequently saddled Twilight Tear and Pot o' Luck to capture back-to-back Classics in 1944–45. The Stable's Free America was back in training but not in time for the 1948 Classic, which was annexed in front-stepping fashion by J. A. Goodwin's brilliant speedster, Papa Redbird, trained by J. M. Goode and ridden by Bobby Baird, the finest "speed" jockey of his day. Baird loved "to go to the front and improve his position." He and Papa Redbird were soul mates.

Baird knew better—least he should have—but he couldn't control his zeal: "Good thing Citation was injured—'cause I don't know if he could have handled Papa Redbird in the Classic. Our horse is fresh, wasn't quite ready for the Triple Crown, but he is now, believe you me." He won the Classic by five in 2:03 for the classic 1¼ miles.

"Them's were fightin' words" to Citation's ears. Nobody loved a challenge better than Cy. But he had some serious "cranking up" to do before facing the starter so soon after being laid up.

Much like Wright responded to owner Eddie Moore's challenge to match swords with Relic back in February, the spunky master of Calumet was eager to make jockey Baird "eat his words," and "as soon as possible." Again Jimmy Jones went to work.

Four weeks into his recovery, Citation appeared as good as ever. As expected, he put on a few extra pounds; a devoted team of vets, grooms, and handlers, in addition, of course, to the Joneses, affectionately doted on his every wish from dawn to evening.

"We really didn't do much with him as far as exercise was concerned," Jimmy commented. "Sore and sprained muscles aren't like breaks or fractures; you gotta be careful not to aggravate the injury, which you could do by returning him to training too soon. We breezed him for the first time in mid-August, about five weeks after he had been hurt. He looked and acted great, as if he was never away.

"So we told Mr. and Mrs. Wright we saw no reason why we couldn't make the American Derby on Saturday, August 28. They were eager to see Cy under colors again. So was Ben Lindheimer. Mostly, though, we did it for the fans and the media, who had taken him to their hearts. It would be his last Chicago appearance, at least this year."

At the last minute, however, eight days before the 1¼ miles American Derby, Jimmy decided he'd better get a final tightener under Cy's belt, "just to make sure he's come all the way back."

"Remember, Papa Redbird had won the Classic, also at 1¼ miles, with lengths to spare. He was sharp as a tack, and his jock, Bobby Baird, bragged he could beat Cy, hoping, I'm sure, that our colt had lost something while being laid up all that time," Jimmy reasoned.

Moreover, Calumet's Free America was back, deserved another shot at Citation since finishing a head shy of the latter when Bewitch, Citation, and Free America turned in their historic 1-2-3 Futurity finish right here at Washington Park exactly a year ago less five days.

And there were other presumptuous three-year-olds, including Walmac farm's long-winded Volcanic, eager to test Citation's mettle. If Cy did have an Achilles heel, it may have been exposed by his long layoff. Or so Volcanic's people hoped. And if—not that anyone wished him any harm—he hadn't totally healed, the American Derby just might be the race to catch Cy *not* at his best.

Jimmy countered those fears by entering Citation in a $4,000 overnight six furlongs allowance sprint on August 21, one week before the August 28 American Derby. The decision was so sudden, it not only caught the local racing fraternity by surprise, but Eddie Arcaro also.

Eddie was back in New York, had agreed to ride in a Saturday stakes at Belmont Park on that Saturday. He probably could have reneged on that commitment, but was dissuaded by Ben Jones, who told Eddie by phone: "It's just a short allowance sprint with an ordinary bunch of three-year-olds. Cy'll have 'em for breakfast. Let's let Pierson ride him. Naturally, you'll be back on him next Saturday for the Derby."

Eddie reluctantly agreed. He was totally committed to Cy, jealously fought against handing him over to anyone, even for an unimportant spin like Saturday's warm-up. Eddie complied, but not before insisting on talking to N. L. Pierson directly by phone.

"I told N. L.," Eddie recounted, "that I promised Cy'd never get beat again, and that I didn't want that promise broken, that all he'd have to do would be to let out a notch on Cy if things heated up, or even got close. Pierson gave me his word, then—and this was mighty nice of him—thanked me, and I mean really *thanked* me, for giving him this great privilege to ride Citation in an actual race."

It's still doubtful anyone remembers the nominal stakes feature that Saturday at Washington Park, because all eyes were on Citation's return to the racing wars.

"I felt like it was the Kentucky Derby all over again," Pierson confessed, "but this time I was riding 'the big horse.'"

Fans lined the rail to get a closer look at Cy; he knew what they wanted. "He cocked that head, arched his neck, then bowed to 'em all as they squealed in delight," Pierson recalled. "He took his trademark pose and proceeded to gallop the length of the stands just like that. It wasn't until we got around the first turn and started heading for the starting gate that he broke the pose and started galloping."

And he "galloped" in the sprint, too. With his rider's cooperation, Cy broke a bit tardily from the gate, then took over second about two lengths off the high-flying leader. By the time they swung around the far turn, Cy had only King Rhymer to catch, with a horse named Speculation another three lengths back puffing vigorously to keep up.

Pierson had experienced Cy's fluid glide in workouts, but never in actual competition. The colt's stride was powerful but smooth, resolute but effortless, awesome yet graceful. "He felt like a brand-new, super-charged Cadillac," Pierson cheered.

Citation poked his head in front in upper stretch; Pierson, privy to Cy's legend of never having been caught from behind, started counting his chickens. Confidently, but apprehensively concerned "not to screw up," Pierson deliberately let out a notch a furlong from home. Cy lengthened stride ever so imperceptibly, dashing clear in the final hundred yards by 2½ lengths before King Rhymer in 1:10⅘. Speculation was another four lengths away in third.

Racing fans thrilled to the unequivocal announcement: "The king is back—long live the king!"

Pierson had never before experienced Cy's brand of greatness. Unlike "name" jockeys Arcaro, Johnny Longden, Earl Sande, George Woolf, Ted Atkinson, Conn McCreary, and, more recently, Al Snider and Doug Dodson, Pierson enjoyed only rare association with outstanding horses.

Yes, N. L. had ridden Coaltown, second only to Citation among the nation's thoroughbred elite; and two years earlier he was a last-minute substitute on Armed when the grand gelding won the Sheridan Handicap here at Washington Park. Later this very summer he'd win the Washington Park Handicap for Calumet aboard Fervent.

Pierson was diffident, modest, certainly not renowned for his erudition, but with rich simplicity he told anybody who'd listen: "Citation's the most magnificent horse I've ever been around. Yes, 'magnificent' is the word— it's the only way I know how to describe him."

Papa Redbird's connections, while duly impressed by Citation's powerful return to action, remained unruffled, surely unintimidated. The supreme confidence that owner Goodwin, trainer Goode, and jockey Baird displayed in their high octane speedster was admirable, indeed.

In addition to the Classic, Papa Redbird had also captured the Dick Welles Stakes, again with speed to spare. What made him doubly formidable, similar to Coaltown's role in the Kentucky Derby, was that the American Derby possessed no other viable speed; he'd virtually have his own way right from the start. And genuine speed, which was Papa Redbird's stock in trade, if unopposed, is always dangerous.

Citation's old buddy, Free America, was a bona fide "one-run" colt; that is, a horse whose stretch-running modus operandi was etched in stone. So he'd not be around to assure a realistic early pace. And the race's other major contender, Volcanic, also packed a fearsome late kick.

Additionally, while Jimmy Jones in his comparatively youthful innocence considered Citation "honed to perfection" for his return to major stakes action, father Ben was more cautious, also a great deal more realistic in his evaluation of Cy's present physical condition.

"Mentally, also emotionally, Citation's at the top of his game," Ben privately shared with Arcaro a few days before the American Derby. "But then he's always right up there"—Ben pointed to his head—"his brain never fails him, nor does his confidence ever waver. He knows he can beat any horse alive. Nothing, no one, no one animal, ever makes him nervous or afraid.

"I'm just a bit worried about him physically," Ben continued. "Horses don't talk, although sometimes I think Citation could if we let him, so I'm really not all that sure he's 100 percent. Now, at 50 percent he can beat any horse in the world, and we know he'll give as much of himself as necessary to get the job done. I just don't want him straining himself like he had to do in the Stars & Stripes after he hurt himself. It's your job, Eddie, to nurse and pamper him Saturday."

When all was said and done, what Ben simply suggested was that Eddie apply The Master's touch, work his magic, and give Citation the "assist" he might need to continue his regal reign without undue exertion or excessive striving.

Not since Eddie guided Lawrin for Ben Jones to win the 1938 Kentucky Derby had either Ben or Jimmy ever given Arcaro orders or detailed instruction on how to ride any of their charges. They'd be the last to forget "the Arcaro miracle" performed by Eddie on Whirlaway to win the Belmont Stakes en route to sweeping the 1941 Triple Crown.

Thanks to Ben Jones cutting away Whirlaway's left blinker in the paddock prior to the Derby, Whirlaway ran straight and true as he and Eddie stormed four-wide approaching the top of the stretch to register a record-breaking eight-length victory in Louisville.

Arcaro then won the Preakness in typical Whirlaway style, lagging twelve lengths behind the field until settled up the backstretch, after which Eddie and Mr. Longtail adroitly threaded their way inside, between, the outside of horses for an authoritative five length tally.

Only three horses challenged Whirlaway and Arcaro in the Belmont, and it was obvious long before they left the gate that the three challengers were determined to set a snail's pace by way of neutralizing the colt's famed late kick. Ben gave no orders to Heady Eddie in the paddock, just encouragement couched thus: "Go out there, Eddie, and win us a Triple Crown!"

Arcaro, who had "a clock in his head"—it was a Rolex, too—instantly sensed the slow pace, and, from dead last after the first quarter, astonishingly swept by his three "clever" rivals, opening up an incredible seven-length lead. Whirlaway on the lead so early in any race was unheard of!

His opponents flabbergasted, Whirlaway, thanks to some brainy strategy by a rider fast gaining repute as The Master, led throughout to record an easy, romping Belmont triumph.

So when it came time for the American Derby, Citation's first race after his recuperation, Eddie knew what must be done.

Such legendary military tacticians as Hannibal and Alexander the Great had nothing on Arcaro when it came to expertly plotting "equine warfare." Eddie was nonpareil as a jockey strategist. He'd studiously examine each race; he'd analyze the *Daily Racing Form* past performances; then attempt to "read" the minds of his riding opponents.

"I'd try to 'ride' all the other horses in the race, too," he cooed. "If I thought I knew what the other jocks would do, or try to do considering the quality and ability of their horses, I'd be in a perfect position to judge, or assess, the race, its pace, and then decide when and where to make my move.

"Now, I had no real concerns with Cy. He towered over every other horse. I honestly believed he could not be beaten. My only job was never to let him run full-out, which I never did, except when confused and disturbed when he hurt himself during the Stars & Stripes. I didn't want that to happen again. So if we were to win the American Derby—and there was no doubt in my mind that we would—we'd have to win it without stress or strain."

The 1948 American Derby aroused and arrested the nation's sports spotlight. The greatest colt of the first half of the twentieth century was on a comeback of sorts, having suffered the first injury of his remarkable career. Fans everywhere—imagine the attention were television available—wondered whether he had "the right stuff" to cap his return with victory over the likes of Papa Redbird, Volcanic, and own powerhouse stablemate Free America.

The Joneses said the American Derby would be his last race against his own age group. "From now on, Cy will take on older horses, and at any distance," they confirmed. To race aficionados there was nothing grandiose about that statement—Cy already had whipped older horses in three prior bouts, including the recent Stars & Stripes.

Warren Wright's bottom line, of course, was winning; the Jones boys, however, were determined to certify Citation's enthronement as "The Greatest Thoroughbred Who Ever Lived!"

The time-honored American Derby was founded in 1884 and won by the champion filly Modesty, ridden by the greatest rider of his age, Isaac Murphy, who also just happened to be America's first great black athlete.

The race's roll call of winners already was a Who's Who of American thoroughbred racing by the time Citation took the track: Emperor of Norfolk, Dodge, Reveille Boy, Cavalcade, Black Helen, Whirlaway, Alsab, Eternal Reward, and Fervent, the latter scoring only the year before (1947). The stakes was steeped in tradition.

The Derby also was an allowance stakes, which meant Citation would shoulder top weight for a three-year-old (126), conceding valuable poundage to the others, including eight precious pounds to his own late-running stablemate, Free America.

Free America, incidentally, was poised for the ultimate effort. He was the one who supposedly was "running all over Bewitch and Citation" nearly exactly a year ago (August 16, 1947) in Calumet's historic 1-2-3 Futurity finish at Washington Park. A few still harbored the hope that he could—a year older and wiser—spring the upset of the ages.

Neither Free America's presence, nor that of the vaunted Volcanic, fazed Arcaro as much as Papa Redbird's blazing speed. Ben took notice of Eddie's concern—in reality more of a nuisance than a fear—and casually reminded him: "Remember, Eddie, any horse Cy can see he can catch."

Arcaro smiled, completing Ben's adage: "And he's got perfect eyesight, right?"

And to himself, Arcaro added: "And once Cy's in front no horse can bring him down."

Jimmy Jones put the frosting on the cake: "Okay, Banana Nose, show 'em all what we're made of."

Eddie leaped aboard Citation, and the crowd emitted a deafening din when Citation entered the track—neck arched and head bowed to receive and acknowledge his loyal subjects.

Citation obediently took his slot in the starting gate. Almost immediately he shifted his weight to lean against the inside portion of his stall. Eddie made sure Cy's feet weren't crossed; he wanted no repeat of the Belmont Stakes near-mishap.

Bobby Baird aboard Papa Redbird gave Eddie a wink. Nothing pugnacious or contentious. A sorta "may the best man win" wink. Eddie nodded, pulling his goggles down from the brim of his cap. "Cy couldn't have been any more relaxed unless he were Perry Como himself," Eddie would later recall. "Don't get me wrong," Eddie explained, "he was all business, no play. But he was also all confidence, a true professional."

"And they're off!"

And Papa Redbird catapulted to the lead with no coaxing from Bobby Baird. Cy, however, was taking his time, as was Free America, the latter losing ground early as was his custom. A colt named Reborn raced second in the early going.

"We had nothing to run with us early," Baird said following the race, "so I took a big hold of Papa Redbird. We all knew how fast he was—hell, he led every step of the way to win the Arlington Classic, also at 1¼ miles only the month before. I wanted him ready for Citation in the late going."

But there'd be no "late-going" surge by Citation against Papa Redbird, not this time around. Arcaro elected to tackle Papa Redbird early. "I figured we'd rock him good and early," Arcaro mused, "put him to sleep right away."

Baird couldn't believe his eyes. Cy and Eddie moved right alongside settling up the backstretch. Baird recalled: "So I roused Papa Redbird, stung him a few times with the whip, even let out a holler. I figured we'd leave Citation in our dust, at least for a sixteenth of a mile or so.

"God, here's Citation moving right with us, Eddie urging him, that big colt matching us stride for stride. They were out to bury us right then and now. And, by gosh, they did it!"

Cy breezed right by Papa Redbird, the latter dizzied by the ease with which Citation conquered speed with speed, and so early in the race; Papa Redbird had no other recourse—he simply threw in the towel.

"I neutralized Papa Redbird on purpose," Eddie said. "I wanted him out of the way early, and since I did ask or insist that Cy put him away, Cy's taking charge was deliberate. We weren't toying with him or the others, which meant to beat us they'd have to catch us. And Cy would never cotton to that."

Volcanic did try valiantly, storming to Citation's right flank under strong urging as the field straightened for home. Remember, this was Washington Park, home of America's longest homestretch—1,531 feet—so a lot of hard racing remained.

Citation shook off Volcanic as he would a pesky horsefly—and he was giving Volcanic eight pounds, too.

Eddie glanced back. Both Volcanic and Papa Redbird were kaput, and there was no immediate sign of Free America. "So I eased Cy back ever so slightly. There was no reason to push him. He had done his job and, as always, did it like a real pro."

It was during that momentary lapse into complacency that Free America detonated unannounced, uncoiling inexorably, like a runaway freight train—that powerful, that deadly!

"Free America literally caught us napping," Arcaro recounted. "He [Free America] was under no orders to let us win, and I'm sure he remembered getting beat by Citation by a mere head in last year's Futurity right here at Washington Park. It was as if he were bent on revenge. He was on a power roll—he had the momentum, too—when he breasted us with a full furlong yet to run."

Sportscaster Jack Drees called the race on the radio: "Here they come, curving into the stretch, better than a quarter mile to come . . . and Citation's drawing clear . . . Volcanic is finished . . . so is Papa Redbird . . . and big Cy looks home free. . . .

"But . . . hold on, racing fans, here comes Free America . . . and *he is flying* . . . and he's got Citation by the throat."

Yes, Free America had pulled within that same scant head by which almost a year ago to the day he failed to collar Citation behind Bewitch in their controversial 1-2-3 Washington Park Futurity finish.

This time, with a full eighth of a mile remaining to wreak revenge, a vindictive Free America made one serious mistake: he dared look Citation in the eye!

Awakened by the suddenness of the challenge, Citation glared back at Free America. One could only imagine what personal vibes resonated between Cy and Free America at this electric moment in time.

For certain, Washington Park's gargantuan homestretch was transformed into a tunnel of noise. The crowd emitted a frenzied delirium, an uproar that dazzled the stadium to its rafters.

Warren and Lucille Wright stood, cheered, and screamed without partiality. They loved Citation and the superstar he was, but if he had to lose, why not to his own stablemate? They could live with it.

"I can't believe it!" Arch Ward yowled in Ben Lindheimer's ears. The latter was paralyzed by the ambivalence created by the match race unfolding before their eyes. His heart, like those of track official Bob Henderson, Calumet general manager Paul Ebelhardt, and farm secretary Margaret Glass, belonged to Citation.

Sports writer Elmer Polzin worried not a whit. "I was watching Citation closely through my glasses, and I sincerely think I saw Free America charging before either Arcaro or Citation did. If Cy was the horse I knew him to be, he'd react like the great ones do."

Polzin was right. Arcaro later tried to find the right word to describe Cy's awesome response. "Maybe it's 'resilience,' or maybe call it 'conditioned reflex,' or maybe just the will-to-win 'instinct' he was blessed with at birth. It took him only two, maybe three, strides to accelerate and match Free America's closing surge—not on his life would he allow the other guy to head him!"

Drees excitedly concluded his radio call: "Citation's not finished, not yet . . . and he's fighting back under Eddie Arcaro . . . but Free America is full-out . . . he's under a full head of steam . . . they've got a hundred yards to come . . . and, would you believe Citation is *actually* starting to draw clear . . . yes, he's rolled with Free America's Sunday punch . . . and Citation's drawing away at the wire!"

"There's not a horse living, except Citation, that Free America wouldn't have passed that day," Jimmy Jones praised. "I know he must have been really frustrated. He was full of himself, had all that momentum going for him, and he all but caught Citation. To have Cy turn him away that easily had to be a real crusher."

Citation's official winning margin was one length "going away." He traveled the 1¼ miles in 2:01⅗, second fastest American Derby 'til then. And he quelled any lingering doubts as to his supremacy over Free America.

The Chicago crowd did ready obeisance to Mighty Cy as he cantered back before the stands head bowed, by now an accepted and expected hallmark of majesty and magnificence. Jimmy personally greeted Cy, while Ben formally congratulated Free America for his splendid effort.

Warren Wright took his customary place alongside Ben Lindheimer in the Winner's Circle to receive the shiny American Derby trophy emblematic of Citation's latest conquest—his ninth straight win since losing to Saggy in the Chesapeake Trial on April 12; his thirteenth victory in fourteen outings as a three-year-old; his twenty-first score in twenty-three career starts. His record was growing sensationally.

More importantly, Citation ruled the thoroughbred world as the sport's eighth Triple Crown champion. Unbelievably there would not be another Triple Crown hero during his lifetime, making the achievement all the more overwhelming.

Calumet farm secretary Margaret Glass kept comprehensive notes and records of all stable goings-on. This afforded her rare insight into what those records and notes meant and showed.

"First, Citation should have never lost a race—he should have been twenty-three for twenty-three at this stage," Glass stated. "He gave away that win to Bewitch as a two-year-old, then made mincemeat of her the next time they met on the square.

"Citation then whipped Armed and older horses like he was 'dancin' in the rain.' He destroyed unbeaten Coaltown in the Derby and won the Triple Crown easily. He came back from injury while beating older horses for the third time in the Stars & Stripes to thoroughly burst Free America's bubble in the American Derby. And, of course," Glass added, "he should have never lost to Saggy in Maryland."

Such was Citation's greatness as summer rolled to a close in Chicago. Leaving Chicago was "such sweet sorrow" for all who loved and admired the handsome bay colt. Many felt they'd never see him again; for a fact they knew they'd never see his likes again.

Chicago bid Citation a fond bon voyage amid a mixture of happy cheers and tears. He was off to New York's Belmont Park where he had conquered twice before: in the Belmont Futurity as a two-year-old, more recently in the Belmont Stakes to sweep the Triple Crown.

Cy left Chicago in the bloom of manhood and class. He was better, stronger than ever, for his American Derby effort. The Joneses and Eddie Arcaro were dedicated to putting the final stamp of invincibility on the greatest thoroughbred of all time.

They were off to the Big Apple.

Chapter Twelve

Invincibility

*H*aving caught his second wind following untoward injury in Chicago's Stars & Stripes Handicap, Citation arrived in New York bigger than life. And the welcome he received befitted his stature as possibly "the greatest thoroughbred of all time!"

Turf scribes Red Smith and Joe Palmer withheld no praise as Easterners turned out en masse to hail the conquering hero. It was as if Citation had been bred in the Empire State. New York's newest adopted son could do no wrong, and the city warmly embraced him as one of their own. Nary a hint of snobbery or provincialism—Cy had won 'em over with a regality of class, speed, hard work, and, most of all, an aura of invincibility that captivated even the most blasé observer.

Fact is, Calumet shipped the bulk of its star-studded stable to Belmont Park for full-time autumn action. Even Coaltown was again flashing mercurial heels, hinting he wanted, and deserved, another crack at his Kentucky Derby conqueror.

"Coaltown's still the fastest horse in America," Ben Jones repeated, "but not the greatest. He'd be Horse of the Year if it weren't for Citation. He's that good."

Case in point—Coaltown authenticated his genuineness with a return to victory, including the Swift Stakes and the Drexel and Jerome Handicaps, streaking the latter's mile in 1:36 flat—fastest Belmont Park time of the season for the distance.

Ben and Jimmy Jones always rated a horse by who he beat, how he beat 'em, how many times he'd beat 'em, finally time, the latter the least important criterion for evaluating that intangible element known as "class." They weren't minimizing Coaltown's forte, which was sheer speed; rather they were highlighting Citation's greatness to excel in all four classic standards of judgment.

Never shy, Cy was willing and eager to face Coaltown again, but to accommodate that clash a major schedule change was required. Cy's number one objective all along was the October 2 Jockey Club Gold Cup against older horses, the nation's supreme test of class and stamina—two full miles, a distance from which most thoroughbreds today would cower.

At two miles, the Jockey Club Gold Cup—its distance years later would be reduced to 1¼ miles—wasn't for the fainthearted. No timorous equine athlete would be caught dead in the starting field. It was only for the most stalwart, certainly not Coaltown's cup of tea. He'd try 1¼ miles, but no further, not on his life.

Still, the fans wanted to see Citation and Coaltown go at it again, even if it meant at a distance less than two miles.

Always accommodating, within reason, of course, and without endangering the animal, Calumet and the Jones boys concocted an incredible two-race package for Citation: Cy would start against three-year-old stablemate Coaltown—also against other top-quality older horses—in the Sysonby Mile on Wednesday, September 29; then return *only* three days later on Saturday, October 2, for the two-mile Jockey Club Gold Cup!

No horse—past, present, or future—ever tackled such a monumental task. In effect, three-year-old Cy would first face the fastest older horses in the world at one mile. Three days later, he would confront the world's greatest stayers at a grueling two miles!

Some—those of little faith—thought the Jones boys had gone off their rocker. Others—those convinced Citation truly was "the great one"— loved the idea.

"If Citation can accomplish such a feat, he'd do so as the unique colt everyone of us believe him to be," Warren Brown told Elmer Polzin, one sports scribe to another.

Others, including Joe Hirsch and Charlie Hatton of the *Daily Racing Form*, were from Missouri—they wanted to be shown!

In addition to Coaltown, who was fresh off his Jerome win at Belmont, giving him the advantage of a start and a win over the track, four older certified speedsters boldly stood in Citation's path in the Sysonby Mile. It was weight-for-age—Citation and Coaltown started with 119 pounds each; the older stars, including the top-drawer filly, First Flight, who got in with 123, at 126 pounds. The field also featured such speedballs as Spy Song, Natchez, and Star Reward. The latter had distinguished himself earlier at Arlington with a snappy 1:35⅗ mile score in the Sheridan Stakes. They were really primed.

For a three-year-old, taking on and whipping older horses was racing's touchstone of achievement. Many a sophomore failed in so noble an endeavor. No three-year-old, Man o'War included, ever accomplished what Citation did in early February at Hialeah when he knocked off older horses in successive races, particularly seasoned stars the caliber of Armed, Delegate, Faultless, and Kitchen Police.

Triple Crown king Count Fleet was felled by injury before he could strut his stuff. Both Whirlaway and Assault emerged with Horse of the Year recognition; both, however, suffered significant defeat as their three-year-old campaigns wore on.

Eddie Arcaro found himself the center of attention in press and radio interest as the Sysonby and Jockey Club Gold Cup approached. Next to Citation, Arcaro's name was the most recognizable in horse racing, and since Citation couldn't talk, though he loved posing for photographers, and Ben and Jimmy Jones preferred the background during these clamorous days, Eddie became the stable's unofficial spokesman.

"I told everybody who'd listen," Eddie volunteered, "that for your ordinary great horse the feat would be impossible, even foolhardy, but that Citation was one in a million. There was no limit to his class, certainly no limit to his speed or stamina.

"I reminded 'em all that I had never really let him run full out, and if the going got rough in either race, I'd just let out another notch. I bragged, 'he'll win, and he'll win big!'"

How big is "big"?

This big: Spy Song used his winged hooves to establish an open lengths lead as soon as the Sysonby field was dispatched. There were few horses, except maybe Coaltown, who could match his reckless abandon once given his head. Even Coaltown was content to lay third behind Natchez as Spy Song, without undue urging, ripped off the opening half in :45⅗. Citation, seemingly outrun, was fourth at this juncture, nearly six lengths off Spy Song, Natchez, and Coaltown.

"Now Belmont's racing surface in those days was a bit cuppy," Eddie recollected, "slower than, say, Churchill Downs, Pimlico, or Arlington and Washington. American or world speed records weren't all that common at Belmont in those days.

"I knew Spy Song, Natchez, and Coaltown were really winging it leaving the half-mile pole. Coaltown was especially full of run. Remember, he had the lead coming to the mile pole in the Kentucky Derby, and the Sysonby was only a mile race. I didn't want to wait until the final sixteenth to collar him. He might get to feeling pretty confident if I let him run free that long. So I asked Citation to pick 'em up, just a cluck, mind you."

Cy leapt into overdrive. His surge was monstrous. Eyes popped as did cameras as Cy galvanized the Belmont crowd with one of the most phenomenal moves ever—from six lengths back at the half to two lengths in front less than a quarter of a mile later!

Incredibly, Citation—presto!—picked up six lengths on the fastest horses in training within a furlong, offhandedly dashing clear by two lengths in the next furlong—all this from "one cluck" from Arcaro.

Eddie gathered Cy in for the final sixteenth, winning handily by three lengths in 1:36, equaling Coaltown's earlier Jerome clocking as the fastest mile of the Belmont season.

Again testimony as to how inscrutable are the vagaries of "time" in evaluating a horse's quality. Coaltown recently won the Jerome on the same oval in 1:36 for the mile. Citation had just conquered in identical time. This time, however, Coaltown, reeling in the aftermath of Cy's crushing surge, could do no better than third, losing second by a neck to First Flight, beaten over three lengths for it all.

"Try figuring 'time' out," Ben Jones would have shrugged, "and when you do, don't forget 'class.'"

American racing was alive with headlines and cheers for Citation's Sysonby achievement. Even *Daily Racing Form*'s Joe Hirsch acknowledged the performance as "outstanding." Joe Palmer echoed his laudatory Belmont commentary as to Citation's irrefutable superiority.

Back in Chicago, the printed accounts of Arch Ward, Warren Brown, Dave Feldman, John P. Carmichael, and Elmer Polzin, all of whom journeyed to Belmont to cover the latest episode in Cy's meteoric career, extolled the colt's proven invincibility.

Only question remaining: Could he come back—and succeed—in the two-mile Jockey Club Gold Cup with only three days' rest?

"We certainly didn't have much time to savor our victory," Arcaro said. "Before you knew it, he had to swing back into action, this time at two miles—and they were waiting for us."

The "they" were owners, trainers, and horses galore who had been pointing for the Gold Cup in the belief that Citation would renege on his racing coup pledge, or, even if he tried, he'd not be the super horse essential to pull it off.

Arcaro's faith in Citation was imperishable. Ben and Jimmy Jones likewise were unshakable in the belief that their colt could handle the pressing Gold Cup challenge. At least, they had no doubts as to Cy's physical and mental condition. He cooled out perfectly following the Sysonby, was on the track for long gallops Thursday and Friday mornings.

"If anything, he looked and acted stronger than ever," Jimmy Jones smiled.

The quantity and quality of his opposition swelled with each passing hour. It was as if the world of thoroughbred racing conspired to make one last supreme, all-out effort to test Cy's indestructibility.

"Either he is, or he ain't, the greatest horse who ever lived," said turf scribe Elmer Polzin. "On Saturday we'll have our answer, and I'm betting he passes the test with flying colors."

Blood-Horse Magazine writer Kent Hollingsworth wrote: "Next, he was sent two miles against a field of stayers, the quality of which Man o'War may not have met."

Not Man o'War, certainly not Seabiscuit, Equipoise, Phar Lap, Armed, Whirlaway, or Count Fleet, ever faced the kind of stout-hearted horseflesh which lined up against Citation at a testing two miles.

First, there was Phalanx, the greatest stayer of his day, now a powerhouse four-year-old, the 1947 reigning three-year-old champ, whose fiver-length Belmont Stakes victory at 1½ miles the season before remained a thing of beauty. Phalanx could run all day—he had won the 2⁄₁₆ miles Daingerfield Handicap. Distance was his strong card, a genius he wouldn't surrender without a fight.

Second, there was Miss Grillo, a Horatio Luro–trained import from Argentina. Among her victories were the New Castle 'Cap, the 2¼ miles New York 'Cap, and the 2½ miles Pimlico Cup in world record time. Two miles was right up her alley.

Third, there was the towering seventeen-hand mare Conniver, champion handicap mare of the year over no less a stalwart distaffer than

Gallorette. Conniver was an unconquerable female machine, sweeping the Vagrancy, Beldame, and Comely Handicap over her sex, also the Brooklyn Handicap against the boys.

Every member of the Jockey Club Gold Cup starting field improved with distance. They boasted an amalgam of speed and stamina expected to test Citation from the start—speed up to the mile, endurance to get 1¼ miles, heart to prevail at two miles.

Warren and Lucille Wright expected victory. That was their primary desire and concern. How Citation would win was left to him, and, of course, to Ben and Jimmy Jones, also his rider, Eddie Arcaro.

Cy was perky and upbeat Gold Cup morning at Belmont. He had galloped and eaten heartily the day before. He wouldn't eat the morning of the race, a practice he recognized; intuitively he knew Saturday was race day.

The Joneses and Arcaro huddled confidently at Citation's stall. Eddie was asked how he figured the race might be run?

"I think today's the day we blow 'em away," Eddie grinned. Later Eddie would have used the phrase "nuke 'em" as his response. He knew Cy had never been asked for his all, nor was Eddie suggesting same. "I'd just let him run at third-or-fourth gear speed from the get-go, that's all."

"You're the boss," Jimmy nodded.

"Whatever's right," Ben agreed.

Thus, the greatest horse-jockey team in racing annals went postward that afternoon. No trumpets, no brass, no ostentation, and no flashy showboating. Modestly—serious but not somber—Citation, his head bowed to the ovation which engulfed his appearance, entered the track from the paddock, trotted, then cantered, finally galloped to the starting gate located at the half-mile pole near the far turn. The field would negotiate the far turn a first time, then gallop past the stands, then, striding under the finish wire, would proceed to take another full lap around Belmont's sprawling 1½ miles oval to complete the exacting two miles, a full half mile farther than Cy ever attempted.

If only television were available to the masses as in Secretariat's day twenty-five years later, or just five years down the line (1953) when the sport's first Triple Crown races would receive extensive television coverage, making Native Dancer a household name when he won the Preakness and Belmont after losing the Derby in a photo finish. And yet, even without the major television coverage enjoyed by other athletes, Citation had unconditionally conquered the world of sports.

Jockey Club Gold Cup day was one of thoroughbred racing's magical moments, "and the beat went on" for Mighty Cy.

There had been countless memorable moments before—exciting hoof-to-hoof combat as with Broker's Tip and Head Play, Seabiscuit and War Admiral, or Alsab and Whirlaway; and unforgettable races with Assault, Stymie, and Armed—and there would be myriad more in generations to come.

Yes, racing awaited those encounters which would include Coaltown versus Capot and Ponder, Hill Prince versus Middleground, Nashua versus Swaps, Round Table and Bold Ruler, Affirmed and Alydar, Sunday Silence and Easy Goer, Alysheba and Bet Twice, Kelso and Gun Bow, not to forget singular spectacular events spotlighting Native Dancer, Tom Rolfe, Damascus, Tom Fool, Buckpasser, Dr. Fager, Secretariat, Spectacular Bid, John Henry, and Cigar.

Citation's Gold Cup may not have proved a competitive bonanza; it was certainly no white-knuckle affair. But it would become a race to remember, truly one for the books; not because Cy successfully repulsed his many worthy challengers, but because of the manner in which he certified his lofty reign. He was "cool" from start to finish, and from start to finish he was the personification of untapped power.

The crowd roared its approval when Cy and Arcaro took the lead with total authority as soon as the starter's bell sounded. He packed his scale weight of 117 as opposed to 124 on older giants like Phalanx. Weight wasn't the big factor here; it was the two-mile distance which each of his courageous rivals craved.

"It was one of the few times I asked him to run early," Eddie recalled. "He could catch any horse he could see, and he could fall down, get up, and still win any race. Besides, once he took a purposeful lead, there wasn't a horse around who could come close to catching him.

"I hand-rode him the whole way. The track was deep, didn't favor speed, but he neither knew it nor cared. If they wanted us—and they did, especially Phalanx—I dared 'em to come get us."

Along with both Derbies—Kentucky and American—also the Belmont Stakes, "The Jockey Club Gold Cup became one of the races fondly tucked away in the memories of my mind," Eddie confessed.

"Citation was in manly full bloom. Hell, he had already stamped himself as special in the Derby, when he ran down Coaltown after spotting him a six-length advantage leaving the half-mile pole.

"He then proved his stamina with that cakewalk in the Belmont," Eddie recalled. "And he won the Stars & Stripes against older horses, coming from behind despite having wrenched his hip and sprained his ankle. He clobbered Free America in the American Derby, then overpowered the nation's fastest horses to win the Sysonby Mile galloping. And that was only three days earlier."

Eddie diagnosed the Gold Cup perfectly. Miss Grillo and Conniver were long-distance superstars. They intended to make Citation hustle from the opening bell. Another Gold Cup entrant, Beauchef, had both a measure of speed and endurance. He'd be among Cy's stalkers. Phalanx, of course, packed a late run second to none; he would save his vaunted coup de grâce for the final quarter mile. Hopefully, by then Cy would have been softened up for the kill.

Citation bounced along on a three-length lead when Conniver went into overdrive. She got within a length, shook her head in dismay, then embarrassingly retreated. Cy dashed clear again, this time lancing to a five-length command.

Beauchef, who feared no man's horse, male or female, stormed audaciously to test the leader after the first mile. He gamely whittled away, slashing Cy's lead in half. Then flamed out.

"Cy was wired as never before," Arcaro added. "'Superhuman' is the best word I can use to describe what he had become. Sure, he was a horse, but his stride was pistonlike. Now, he wasn't an angry or hateful horse; once in a race he was merciless, but never like he was that day. Every time someone challenged him, he simply broke their heart by grinding their challenge into the dirt."

Both Conniver and Beauchef tried valiantly, were still trying when Phalanx unleashed his awesome late kick three furlongs from home. Phalanx shifted into top gear, exploding as his people and fans expected, passing Beauchef as if he were walking, uncorking an electrifying move that elicited a cascade of "oh's and ah's" from Belmont's packed house.

The Jockey Club Gold Cup race was afoot!

Phalanx stretched low, lengthening a stride that knew no bounds. His courage undiminished, his stamina unquestioned, four-year-old Phalanx drew dead aim on his younger, more illustrious foe—pulled the trigger, and fired point blank!

He pared Citation's commanding lead to five lengths with a quarter mile remaining; his rider repeatedly stung him with the whip. Phalanx boiled imperiously; his move had "upset" written all over it.

Arcaro craned only once, saw Phalanx closing "like the wind." Much like Eddie did in the Belmont, so eloquently described by Joe Palmer, he dropped his hands imperceptibly, letting out the slightest notch. No whip, not even a spur.

And Cy's lead mushroomed to eight widening lengths!

His bubble burst, Phalanx kept up the hunt, running his heart out despite the shocking truth that he couldn't even get Citation to break a gallop. Citation won "eased up" under Eddie Arcaro by seven lengths in 3:21⅗ for the two-mile marathon. Phalanx was a leg-weary second, twelve full lengths before Beauchef, the others on their way to the showers.

Cy's proud return to his "second home"—the Winner's Circle—was bathed in warm affection and hearty ovation.

Years later when Hall of Fame trainer Woody Stephens—who had saddled a record five-straight Belmont Stakes winners—was asked if he could recall any event that might equal Secretariat's thirty-one-length world record romp in the 1973 Belmont, he responded without hesitation: "I sure do—what Citation did those four days in the Sysonby and Jockey Club Gold Cup. What a feat!"

There was talk and rumor aplenty—but not from Calumet's camp—that Citation was considering retirement following his four-day Belmont glory sweep. There was no Breeders' Cup in those days, no so-called official championship event.

Citation had achieved invincibility. He proved himself unbeatable no matter track, distance, opponent, or condition. He not only won the Triple Crown as only a world-beater could, but he had mastered older horses in five encounters.

Retirement not only was the furthest thing from Calumet's mind, but Calumet publicly decreed that Citation would definitely start back in 1949 as a four-year-old, should the best laid plans of mice and men not go awry.

"Retire him now, hell no," chorused Wright and the Jones boys, to which Arcaro added a hearty "amen."

Hindsight would have told them to pack up their tents and steal away until 1949. In all fairness, however, Citation was sound as the day he was foaled. He had whipped all challengers without taking a deep breath. In all minds, he certainly wasn't over-raced; fact is, he required racing to remain fit. It was his lot in life. His calling.

Besides, Warren Wright knew his arithmetic. He needn't be a financial genius to know that if Citation kept on winning—and there was no earthly reason to think otherwise—he could be the first thoroughbred in racing history to pass the million-dollar mark in earnings. Wright loved money and the prestige breaking that record would bring, and the colt was closing in on the elusive mark with each victory. If all went well, Cy would easily set the record as a four-year-old. His stud career would have to be put on hold for another season, that's all. For that matter, even Whirlaway raced as a four-year-old six years earlier, racking up a second straight Horse of the Year crown in the process.

Thus, invincible Cy craved new worlds to conquer.

That "new world" was the Empire City Gold Cup, a 1⅝ miles route race at weight-for-age, which, according to historian William H. P. Robertson, was created by track entrepreneur James Butler in the hope that the race would become an international championship event.

Endowing the Empire City Gold Cup with a $100,000 purse didn't hurt a bit; that alone attracted Warren Wright's financial eye. Citation, therefore, had his next race. The date in two weeks: October 16.

There was some international interest. Nathoo, hero of the Irish St. Leger, boldly accepted the challenge, as did Belgian champion Bayeux. Both were stayers of first-water quality, and, on paper, feared not Citation's prowess or reputation.

Phalanx, undaunted despite his recent thumping, also wanted another crack at Cy, as did stout-hearted Miss Grillo. Their people reasoned the shorter distance—three furlongs less than the Jockey Club Gold Cup—may turn fortunes their way. Travers hero Ace Admiral also wanted a piece of Citation.

Experts, however, saw the Empire City Gold Cup as simply another feather in Citation's cap. One diverting note: going against Citation also would be Ben Whitaker's four-year-old filly, Carolyn A., winner over colts in the 1947 Louisiana Derby; she was named for Eddie Arcaro's daughter. The Master, however, was no sentimentalist.

Unconquerable at two miles, Cy ostensibly should have no trouble at 1⅝ miles. "I figured only to use a second or third gear this time," Arcaro remembered. "No need to destroy 'em this time."

Cy actually took his time early, after resting his mighty frame against the stall wall prior to the start. He was racing fluidly in third after the opening quarter, three lengths off the leaders.

"No need to dawdle," Eddie felt, "so I chirped to him, and within a hundred yards, he went by the leaders, dashing clear by about two or three lengths. Carolyn A. tried, got to give her credit, and Phalanx unleashed his expected late surge."

But, same old story, Citation won in a breeze.

Phalanx bravely tested Citation approaching the furlong pole, a full eighth of a mile from home, closing boldly to within two lengths of the high-flying leader. Cy sensed the challenge before Eddie did, and, responding on competitive instinct, broke open a four-length lead, making a statement Phalanx could no longer deny. Phalanx's bid sputtered, but he deserved an "A" for effort.

Arcaro eased Cy to the wire with two lengths to spare in 2:42⅖, which clocking, similar to the 3:21⅗ turned in two weeks earlier at two miles, was the fastest of the year for those rarely contested distances. Again, time wasn't the factor; who Cy beat, and particularly how he beat 'em, was.

Elmer Polzin to this day marvels at Citation's "two weeks in another town," that "town," of course, being New York. "In a period of just eighteen days," Polzin explained, "Citation scaled down from the 1¼ miles of Chicago's American Derby to the mile of the Sysonby, then stretched out to the demanding two miles in the Jockey Club, before coming back to 1⅝ miles of the Empire City—and against the best older horses in training, and he did it like Superman!"

He was no longer being compared with Man o'War. Cy by now was incomparable. He had become the absolute against whom future stars would be judged. His greatness was incontestable. With the Empire City Gold Cup, Cy posted his twelfth straight win, his sixteenth in seventeen starts as a three-year-old, and his twenty-fourth in twenty-six career outings, which included eight for nine as America's champion juvenile the season before.

"Citation's invincible," announcer Clem McCarthy shared with his radio listeners. "No longer can he be compared with any other horse. He's in a class by himself!" That said it all.

Chapter Thirteen

Immortality

$\mathcal{S}$o what does the world of sports do with a horse already acclaimed as "invincible"?

First, it does him happy, ready obeisance, scattering flower petals, as it were, before his very feet, rolling out the red carpet amid thunderous voice and sound, duly paying homage to a dark bay four-legged athlete who in less than a year and a half had become a household name among sports fans of all ages.

Second, it hangs out as lure a stakes race for three-year-olds and up, adorned with a daring "winner take all" proviso. That's just what the Pimlico Special did on October 29, brainchild event of Pimlico Race Track in Baltimore, Maryland, site of Citation's easy Preakness victory only five months earlier.

In those days the 1 3/16 miles Pimlico Special was designed as a "by invitation only" battleground for *all* the good horses in training, the object being to help crown the season's Horse of the Year. It was yesterday's nearest thing to today's Breeders' Cup Classic.

There was a so-so 1970 movie curiously titled *Suppose They Gave a War and Nobody Came?* For the thoroughbred set, it would be "suppose they gave a title race and nobody came, except, that is, the champion?"

That's exactly what happened. Citation literally frightened away all opposition. Not one horse invited to participate was entered against him. It was total concession to his invincibility. No horse in the world wanted to "cross swords" with "the great one."

"First of all," Chicago *Tribune* sports editor Arch Ward told Chicago race track officials Ben Lindheimer and Bob Henderson, "no one ever thought Citation would still be racing strong and sound after such a unsparing campaign against all odds, and against all comers.

"Then for Citation to totally demolish and demoralize horses of all ages and sex automatically transformed him into some 'other-worldly' being. Even owners and trainers who had the courage, the money, and the tenacity to try him over and over again had come to realize it was hopeless and thankless to take him on.

"To run the Pimlico Special as a walkover was the ultimate compliment," Ward said. "No one owner or horse had the temerity to face him. So-called grit and lionheartedness had run its course."

A racing rarity, a "walkover"—most recently achieved by Spectacular Bid as a four-year-old in 1980—is created when scratches, or lack of entries, as in Cy's case, necessitates a race in which there is only "one starter," and that one starter is obliged to gallop the required distance to officially "win" the race and pocket the gold. There's no actual race, no real competition.

"I'll never forget that day at Pimlico," Arcaro ruminated. "It was as if they were running the Preakness all over again. The crowd was big, happy, noisy. You have to remember—it was not a televised event, and there was, of course, no betting. In reality it was simply an exhibition—Citation running against himself.

"God, the paddock was crammed with people. Yet there was no one but us—the Wrights, friends, Citation, the Joneses, and me—in the center of it all, but the way the crowed raved and ranted you'd think we were getting ready for the race of the century."

It wasn't as if the fans were forsaking Man o'War, Colin, Sysonby, Seabiscuit, Equipoise, Whirlaway, or Count Fleet. Those noble steeds had left their indelible mark on the sport. But "the greatest of 'em all" was now in their midst. And sport fans did him honor and praise.

Wearing saddle cloth number one—which numeral said it all—Citation walked proudly through the throng jamming the gap leading to the track; then, head bowed as was his majestic wont, cantered to the gate at the top of the Pimlico homestretch.

"I've had greater, more competitive and exciting races, before and since," Eddie fondly recalled, "but none as gratifying as with Cy's walkover. I was prouder than he—I honestly believe that."

The crowd's roar was deafening when the gate was sprung, the track coming alive with excited, appreciative humanity. "We had no opposition," Eddie smiled, "and Cy was no dummy. He knew all that screaming and noise was for him. And he came away running, not at top speed, of course. I made sure. I had a stranglehold on him."

The sound of cheers and awe grew louder with each powerful stride. Cy raced well off the rail into the first turn, angling out farther as he and Eddie settled up the backstretch. By the time they reached the far turn with less than a half mile remaining, they again reached earshot of the jammed stands. The noise swelled as Cy entered the stretch at the point where he started. Eddie, still sitting well back in the saddle, gave his friend one solid birdlike chirp.

Citation reached out, lengthening his "workout" stride just a bit. The throng thundered. "The crowd loved it, so did Cy, and, have to admit it, so did I," Eddie confessed. "I'll never forget the feeling, not until I die."

Despite Eddie doing everything in his power to keep Cy in check, the colt reeled off the distance in 1:59⅘. Eddie's arms were sore.

"It was the greatest public workout in racing history," said Plain Ben Jones.

Victory number twenty-five in twenty-seven lifetime starts, accomplished without opposition, all rivals choosing the safety and comfort of their stalls rather than match strides with the greatest thoroughbred who ever lived.

Citation was now cloaked in "immortality" as a racehorse. He could have—probably should have—retired right then. He was racing's all-time undisputed best.

"He's done it all—nothing more to prove!" Jimmy Jones cheered. Ben agreed.

But Warren Wright still wasn't satisfied.

"At first, Ben and Jimmy thought to retire Citation for good following the walkover," stable manager Paul Ebelhardt told Chicago track official Bob Henderson, "but old man Wright had already gotten it into his head that Citation would become the first thoroughbred in history to top a million dollars in earnings. That meant Cy would keep on racing as a four-year-old, which at the time seemed okay."

The Joneses preferred to rest Citation—who had just ripped off eighteen races in nine months—and point him for the Santa Anita Maturity early in 1949, a race restricted to four-year-olds, which for Cy, racing against his own age, would be like taking candy from a baby.

Years later it was rumored that Jimmy Jones second-guessed himself, wishing he had stopped Cy following the Triple Crown. Not so. First of all, except for his Stars & Stripes injury, Citation was like a bull; his machismo demanded action, and all subsequent wins up to Pimlico were accomplished with little or no exertion at all.

Arcaro also felt Citation deserved a break following the Pimlico Special. "The walkover was the frosting on the cake," Eddie said. "Yes, talk about him becoming racing's first millionaire would prevent him from entering stud duty as a four-year-old in 1949, but the way he was going it really wouldn't have taken him that long to break the earnings record, probably in early 1949.

Again Warren Wright threw a monkey wrench into Cy's plans. Ebelhardt always considered Wright bossy and ambitious, and at times a mite capricious, not the benevolent dictator he'd like people to think.

"Just like back in January when he wanted Jimmy Jones to get Citation ready early to whip Eddie Moore's Relic," Ebelhardt told Henderson, "it was a personal thing, to have his own way, or to make a point. Same thing happened after Cy won the Pimlico Special."

Scuttlebutt was that Wright had a close buddy with financial interest in Tanforan Race Track in California; that as a personal favor he'd ship America's sweetheart colt all the way by rail from Baltimore to San Francisco to run in the Tanforan Handicap.

"Putting Citation in a boxcar, even though it was his own private car, and shipping him thousands of miles from Maryland to California after so strenuous a campaign was criminal and inexcusable," Elmer Polzin told everybody who'd listen. "It was not only stupid and crazy, but heartless. But—wanta know something?—Citation did it, he made it, without complaining, without complications, far as we know."

Still, horse lovers wondered how much the arduous journey took out of Cy. Physically, he didn't appear any the worse for wear upon arrival in San Francisco. A day later he was on the track at Tanforan, stretching his legs and getting a feel for the track. He felt fine.

Unfortunately, the track was neither inviting nor suitable. Horsemen later criticized it as either concrete hard or quagmire deep. Whatever its condition, true or false, why subject America's finest equine to any questionable field of battle?

Wright, however, insisted. His personal sights were affixed not only on Cy becoming racing's first millionaire, but also to answer the more immediate challenge of a pair of older handicap aces named On Trust and Shannon II. Both were reluctant to become Cy's latest victims, but they calmly awaited two events: first, Citation's stakes prep, a six furlongs overnighter on December 3; then what weights would be assigned all three combatants for the December 11 Tanforan 'Cap.

The first event was the old automatic: Citation hauled top weight of 126 pounds to an easy victory in the prep over three-year-olds Bud Gallant and Barsard, conceding them fourteen and seventeen pounds, respectively.

The second—weights for the Tanforan 'Cap—was a bit more complicated. Tanforan management, salivating over Citation's presence, kindly assigned him 123 for the 1¼ miles Tanforan 'Cap. Older horses Shannon II and On Trust were given 127 and 124, respectively. Both horses were withdrawn by their people in protest.

No matter, Citation gave older runner-up Stepfather thirteen actual pounds, waltzed home by five lengths, setting a new track record of 2:02⅖ over a track fit neither for man nor beast.

And the track wasn't even "fast." It was labeled "good," which meant somewhere between "fast" and "slow," probably damp and drying out, certainly not conducive to speed. Incidentally, the track surface was "muddy" for Cy's initial Tanforan outing eight days earlier.

"Those two races at Tanforan—and they were races that should *never* have been—those two races probably took their toll," Arcaro sighed. "He made twenty starts as a three-year-old in less than eleven months and he won nineteen—and if it weren't for me being so tentative the very first time we got together in April, he would have won twenty straight!

"Even without the last two, Cy would have won eighteen in a row, and he'd be rested and freshened—better still, he'd be sound—for another banner season as a 1949 four-year-old. No man's horse could have touched him."

Sadly, Citation came out of his Tanforan escapade gimpy. His tendons were aching; he was limping noticeably. Then he "popped" an osselet, a hard leg nodule, sore and painful, a calcium buildup that rendered him a virtual cripple. He was sent home to Lexington.

Arcaro sympathized: "It's amazing he went that long before being struck down by serious injury. Everybody said he was racing's 'iron horse,' which he was. But even the strongest, most perfect machine will eventually break down or wear out. And when he did—let nobody say differently—he did so as the greatest thoroughbred who ever lived, at least the greatest I've ever seen or ridden. Now I never saw Man o'War, but I saw and rode Kelso and I saw Secretariat."

That wasn't just one man's opinion. Horsemen and media alike praised Citation as, if not superior to Man o'War, at least the greatest since "Big Red," for certain "the best" until Secretariat arrived in all his glory a quarter century later.

One fact remains: Had Citation stayed "retired" following the end of a three-year-old career, a campaign not even Secretariat could match, his achieved fame as racing's all-time "greatest thoroughbred" would have stood the test of time.

Chapter Fourteen

The Missing Year—Reflections

*I*f it's true that into every life a little rain must fall, then it was a deluge that hit Citation in 1949.

The transition from the "best" of years, 1948, to the "worst" of years, 1949, was a painful journey for Bull Lea's most famous son. By the time Cy officially turned four on January 1, he was a physical wreck.

Citation concluded 1948 as the most celebrated thoroughbred of the first half century. His career record read twenty-seven wins and two "excusable" seconds in twenty-nine starts with earnings of $865,150, of which an incredible one-season record of $709,470 was gleaned as a three-year-old of nineteen wins in twenty starts! By year's end he was just $50,000 shy of Stymie as the world's richest thoroughbred of all time.

And those were the days—no million-dollar races, no four-million-dollar Breeders' Classic, no five-million-dollar Triple Crown bonus, and no six-million-dollar race abroad—when money was money.

Catching Stymie, however, wasn't Warren Wright's true passion. He wanted to make Citation the first horse to surpass the million-dollar mark in earnings. He wanted to do it in 1949, and "as soon as possible, as soon as Citation was sound enough to resume racing."

Meanwhile, there was a pause at the end of 1948 to crown Mighty Cy with unprecedented honor and glory. He was three-year-old champion, handicap kingpin, and, of course, Horse of the Year by landslide vote! Inexplicably, he finished second to Coaltown as champion sprinter. The two colts met twice—the Kentucky Derby and Sysonby Mile—and Citation won both with consummate ease. Go figure.

Coaltown surely deserved recognition for his exceptional speed and courage, particularly as harbinger of what he'd accomplish in 1949. But he couldn't beat Citation doing anything; to edge Cy as Sprinter of the Year was an inexcusable impropriety by turf experts who sought to applaud Coaltown for his heroism in defeat.

"That's all true, but old Coaltown came back like gangbusters as a four-year-old," said jockey Steve Brooks, who by the spring of 1949, what with Citation out of commission, had ascended to number one status as Calumet's first-string reinsman. Arcaro, who'd continue to freelance, would, of course, be reunited with Cy if and when he'd return in 1949.

Despite near-crippling injury, Citation remained cheerful and upbeat at least the first three or four months of 1949. "Not since he started racing in April of 1947 was he ever laid low," farm manager Paul Ebelhardt said. "At first, he probably thought he'd be back in training in just a few weeks, much like it was in Chicago after he hurt himself in the Stars & Stripes.

"Not this time, though," Ebelhardt commiserated. "His lameness refused to go away. By May he was getting a bit depressed, I think. I could see it in his eyes. He had such great intelligence. He knew things weren't right. By July, however, even though he couldn't train or anything like that, I believe he was happy to be pain-free.

"The old glow was back, so was the look in his eyes. He was starting to adjust to retirement. I do believe he was pretty satisfied with his lot in life."

Not Warren Wright—neither adjusted nor satisfied. He wanted Citation back on the track. He wanted that Million Dollar Mark only Citation could deliver. He wasn't so cruel as to expect Citation to covet that goal as a certifiable cripple. But if the colt could come back fairly sound, so be it!

Wright gave the orders: Do anything, everything possible to restore Cy to racing soundness. He wanted to see Citation become racing's first millionaire before he died.

Apparently there was no actual "death wish" on Wright's part, "far from it," secretary Margaret Glass assured. But the old man's health was failing. He was seventy-four, was fighting early cancer, and his heart was losing ground. He had lost considerable weight. Never a big man, he looked even more diminutive and frail as 1949 unfolded.

There was some arcane criticism that he became inordinately obsessed with Citation becoming the first thoroughbred millionaire in racing history. No horse had ever surpassed the million mark. For Citation to do so became the old man's personal goal; he was frantically devoted to that accomplishment while he lived. More significantly, it was said he knew he was at death's door; he wanted Cy to score that elusive goal before he'd meet his maker.

"No such thing," exclaimed Margaret Glass, who for more than forty years, starting in 1940 when Whirlaway was but a two-year-old, had faithfully served Warren and Lucille Wright, particularly the latter after she was widowed and became Mrs. Gene Markey with her September 27, 1952, wedding to Commodore, later Admiral, Gene Markey.

"Mr. Wright never acknowledged he was as gravely ill as his doctors implied during his final two years," Glass confirmed. "His dream, or demand—you can call it anything you want—that Citation become the first horse to win a million dollars in my opinion had nothing to do with his health. Like most of us, Mr. Wright rarely thought of dying. He loved life, loved racing, and he had the whole world in his hands. Giving up on life was the last thing he thought of."

Glass said Wright hired "every reputable veterinarian in sight" to hasten Citation's rehab. "Again he called in the team of Charles Hagyard, Art Davidson, and Bill McGee. They and their assistants were at Citation's daily beck and call. And Mr. Wright sought other opinions. Like most of us, he was astounded, actually, shocked, that Citation had been injured so severely. We all sorta figured Citation was unbreakable, a true iron horse," Glass sighed.

They were all wrong. Citation was "human" after all. He wasn't unbreakable or indestructible. Age four was a thoroughbred's most mature year—and age four had passed him by.

Not that he couldn't come back as a crackerjack racehorse as a five- or a six-year-old. Others had done it, mostly with mixed results. Many of racing's "comeback kids" did win important events. They also lost. In many minds, however, Citation transcended such mundane considerations and conjecture. Such as:

What if Man o'War made a comeback as a four-year-old?

Years later, what if Secretariat dared to return to racing as a five-year-old after a year's layup at the farm of his birth?

Most experts concur: The best Man o'War or Secretariat could do would be to tarnish, not enhance, their reputations.

There was no need for Citation to ever make a "comeback." He had achieved both invincibility and immortality; as a three-year-old he compiled a record as none before or since. In 1948 he won at distances from six furlongs to two miles. He tackled every racing surface: fast, good, sloppy, muddy, and heavy. He was ridden by three different riders at nine different tracks and in seven different states. And he performed flawlessly.

Citation outgunned the world's fastest sprinters at their own game; he humbled the greatest stayers as their favorite distances; he raced on the lead or from off the pace; *seven* times he took on older horses, giving them weight, too, and *seven* times he emerged victorious—such was Citation's towering greatness! No thoroughbred past or present boasted such credentials. And that's not counting his Pimlico "walkover" in which no older horse dared face him!

Wright, though, was insistent. Citation would return, he promised, sooner or later; and the sooner the better. But all the king's horses and all the king's men couldn't put Cy back together again, at least not in 1949.

Meantime, life went on as usual. Especially was there ample opportunity for media and fan alike to bemoan Citation's absence, at the same time extol his fast-growing legacy.

Admittedly, comparing horses is futile. But horsemen like Sunny Jim Fitzsimmons, Max Hirsch, and Ben Jones had fanned the flames, particularly among a post-war public eager for another super sports hero. Folks weren't so far removed from America's horse-and-buggy days that they didn't appreciate a charismatic equine of uncommon grace whose level of talent knew no bounds. Citation was their horse.

Back in Chicagotown—Easterners Joe Palmer and Red Smith had already dusted off every conceivable adjective of adulation—baseball sports announcer Jack Brickhouse, who enjoyed betting a bob or two on his favorite horse when not busy at the mike, publicly marveled at Citation's accomplishments. He called Cy "racing's own Babe Ruth!"

Baseball's Lou Boudreau (who passed away in early August 2001), eventual Hall of Famer who in 1948 led his Cleveland Indians to their last series title, was a closet race track pundit. Born and raised in Harvey, Illinois, just a stone's throw from now defunct Washington Park on Chicago's great South Side, Lou always stated that concomitant with Cleveland's 1948 series conquest, Citation's emergence that same year as racing's newest and greatest icon "was a wonderful coincidence" he'd "never forget to my dying day."

Most sports writers, realizing that Citation was "hobbled and seriously more troubled physically than originally diagnosed," frankly felt he'd never make it back to the races by his five-year-old season of 1950, if ever. So they unashamedly sought what they considered inevitable comparisons with the sport's original great one, Man o'War.

Unlike Ben Jones who evaluated a horse by who he beat, how he beat 'em, how many times he beat 'em, and then, least of all, time, a few experts felt that "time" was still the best yardstick, failing to gauge how deceptive "running time" might be, considering the huge gap of some twenty-eight years between Man o'War and Citation.

Ben didn't originate one of racing's most popular axioms—"time only counts when you're in jail"—but he believed it. "Tracks differ everywhere," he said, "with different surfaces within one state, like Florida, Kentucky, New York, or Illinois. Then there's weather factors, not to mention track conditions. And don't you never forget about the horses you face. They can make you run faster than you can, or have to, or they can make you throw in the towel."

Racing historian William H. P. Robertson devoted some hours trying to match Citation with Man o'War. His conclusion: "Running time . . . offers no basis for valid comparison. Man o'War ran with steel horseshoes over tracks that were in general slower than surfaces Citation negotiated with aluminum plates. Man o'War shattered a number of records, Citation shaved a few—but they were horses of different types. 'Big Red' was a gay, ebullient giant who squandered the energy with which he had been so copiously endowed; Citation was a slick, relentless running machine, of calm, efficient disposition, evidently content just with getting the job done."

The two colts' weight-carrying ability elicited more than just a few comments. Man o'War toted on the average several more pounds than Citation when they were two- and three-year-olds. But weight assessments differed in both eras. Man o'War packed on poundage as a three-year-old going against other three-year-olds often carrying equally high weight, whereas Citation's lighter package as a three-year-old came about by the fact that he was often meeting older horses.

Whereas Citation "took on the world" by racing in seven different states from New York to California to Florida, "Big Red" raced in only two states, Maryland and New York, plus one restricted outing in Canada. Cy was far more well-traveled than his predecessor.

The aforementioned analyses were addressed again in 1973 by race historian Peter Winants as mighty Secretariat stood poised to become the first Triple Crown winner since Citation.

His opinion: "Man o'War versus Citation. Who knows? It's impossible to compare great athletes from different eras, to say nothing of great horses . . . weight-wise, Man o'War has the edge. He carried more of it, but so did his competitors. Competition-wise, the nod must go to Citation. By the time he was three . . . Man o'War's competitors rolled over and played dead. There were always good ones, though, taking a shot at Citation. . . .

"I don't mind sticking my neck out. I'll go with Citation. All in all, he shows me more. . . . Okay, Secretariat, you're next. What are you going to do about it?"

And Secretariat did plenty, no doubt about that, and he did it in a highly charged television arena hungry for his brand. Billy Reed, who wrote for *Sports Illustrated* from 1969 to 1997, stated: "Citation probably was under-appreciated . . . had you been able to put Secretariat in 1948, and Citation in 1973, I'm confident Citation today would be remembered as affectionately as Secretariat." Television is that powerful.

More so, opined horsemen who had seen both Cy and Secretariat. Sage old-timers Woody Stephens and Charles "The Bald Eagle" Whittingham were firm believers in judging horses first by whom they met and beat, rather than going gaga over purely fast running times. Running time, they felt, was like racing against the clock, "not against real opponents."

Secretariat never met the kind of "real opponent" Citation met and defeated. Sure, Secretariat hammered Sham in both the Derby and Preakness, then incurred deification with a thunderous thirty-one-length victory in the Belmont Stakes, in world record time, too.

That's a fact. It's also a fact that Sham was not the Sham of old in Belmont; the courageous colt broke down before the race was half over; the others in the race were mere window dressing; and Secretariat was loosed free on the pace to do as he pleased—in effect, he was racing against the clock—turning in a one-race performance that literally was second to none.

Perhaps it's cruel to quote the bromide, "One robin a spring doth not make," in appraising Secretariat's sensational three-year-old campaign. Also, I suppose, unfair, also somewhat untrue, but done only to counter the contemporary opinion of thoroughbred experts and observers who made an incredible "rush to judgment" to deify Secretariat primarily off two supreme efforts:

One, he won the Triple Crown, becoming the sport's ninth such champion, more importantly, the *first* in twenty-five long years since Citation.

Two, his thirty-one-length triumph in the Belmont Stakes in world record time was indeed unprecedented, truly a thing of beauty.

Few recall that he, like Citation, was defeated, and inexcusably, too, prior to his Kentucky Derby triumph; but, unlike Cy, he also lost following his Triple Crown sweep. This fact conveniently was omitted from his résumé as the new millennium dawned (2000)—four times as a 1973 three-year-old he was pitted against older horses: unaccountably, inexplicably, he lost *two* of them—two of four—to the likes of Onion and Prove Out! Those defeats are seemingly lost when evaluating Secretariat's waning season against what was considered the cream of his older crop in 1973.

Cy went into a limbolike state of retirement in 1949 with a reputation and record that was sterling by any yardstick. He atoned for his "gentlemanly" defeat by Bewitch, vanquishing her in the Belmont Futurity. He expiated his well-chronicled loss to Saggy with an unequivocal triumph in the Chesapeake Stakes a week later. He already had beaten older horses like Armed and Delegate while still an actual two-year-old. He won the Triple Crown more decisively than any colt before or since. He then crushed older horses another five times from one to two miles, never drawing a deep breath. He did things Man o'War never accomplished; he did things Secretariat could only dream of.

And had Cy not been forced to return to action a year later, in 1950, the aforementioned debate would have been purely academic.

Headed by trainers Sunny Jim Fitzsimmons, Max Hirsch, and Ben Jones, those horsemen who saw both Man o'War and Citation freely cast their ballots for Mighty Cy. And many who lived to see both Citation and Secretariat as two- and three-year-olds also voted in Cy's favor.

Turf scribes Warren Brown and John P. Carmichael were particularly impressed by Citation's "inability to lose," as "possibly the most determined racehorse ever."

Elmer Polzin also saw both Citation and Secretariat in person. "Except for Sham and Riva Ridge, go ahead, name any other top horse Secretariat beat. Yes, he beat Forego in the Derby, but Forego wasn't yet the Forego we'd get to know in later years," Polzin said.

"And when push came to shove against older horses," Polzin added, "Secretariat had nary an excuse losing two of four, and to ordinary horses like Onion and Prove Out. One he couldn't catch in late stretch, the other passed him in late stretch. You never saw that happen to Citation as a three-year-old.

"Let's be honest: Secretariat was a great horse, fast and flashy, and him winning the Triple Crown before nationwide television was Hollywood at its best. But 90 percent of his fame came off one race, the Belmont. That one race made him a superhero. But he beat nothing of substance—it was his running time and the huge margin that made him a star. And I'd never take that race away from him."

Citation fans, like Palmer, Winants, Robertson, Brown, and Polzin— and there were countless others—recall the drove of top horses, age three and older, he whipped in 1948. It began with Armed, Faultless, Delegate, and Kitchen Police before the Triple Crown, then included such fine three-year-olds as My Request, Better Self, Escadru, Papa Redbird, Coaltown, Free America, Billings, Vulcan's Forge, Bovard, Salmagundi, Ace Admiral, and Volcanic, stakes winners all.

Citation's unrelenting devastation of older horses, however, which started with Armed, Delegate, and Faultless, became his undying glory.

He thoroughly vanquished Phalanx, Conniver, Miss Grillo, Fervent, Colosal, Knockdown, Rampart, Carolyn A., Stepfather, Eternal Reward, Pellicle, and First Flight, among others.

"And he beat 'em all never full-out," Eddie Arcaro assured. "Imagine what he would have done if he were ever pressed, or if I let out all the gears in him. Just once I wish we could've gone all out with him as a three-year-old. But then, he was a smart cutie, too—he was determined never to lose, but he'd win only well within himself."

Now, there were skeptics. Two renowned *Daily Racing Form* columnists— Charles Hatton and Joe Hirsch—barely acknowledged Citation's greatness. Hatton refused to compare him with Man o'War and later called Native Dancer (1953) the greatest horse of all time, only to accord that honor to Secretariat in 1973.

Hirsch on July 4, 1997, in a series entitled "The Greatest Ever," did admit to Ben Jones and Eddie Arcaro as "the best trainer and jockey I've seen." And he hailed Secretariat as "perfection" in a thorough-bred, adding: "In forty-nine years . . . [which by his own calculation in-cluded 1948] I've seen a lot of great horses but none as brilliant as

Secretariat in his three-year-old season." He then saluted thorough-bred greats like Kelso, Forego, Tom Fool, Spectacular Bid, Nashua, Swaps, Native Dancer, Seattle Slew, Affirmed, and Cigar. But no Citation, not even a mention. Even if for some reason he failed to see Cy in action in 1948 before he officially retired in 1951—not even a mention?

Citation didn't need their recognition to stand alone atop his breed. And he was never entirely alone during his year on the farm at Calumet. Vets and handlers were at his side daily. He reportedly tried to breeze a short distance after his eighth month of recuperation, only to pull up a bit sore. He was given another month of rehab. Wright, however, still wanted him ready for racing at Santa Anita by early January.

Even without Citation, Calumet continued to excel at the races. Coaltown emerged from behind Cy's gigantic shadow to pummel oppo-nents with authority and aplomb. He was older, more seasoned as a 1949 four-year-old, and not having to deal with his more illustrious stablemate on a regular basis, Coaltown flourished, coming into his own to the de-light of Ben and Jimmy Jones.

Warren Wright also should have been elated with Coaltown's rebirth, which, of course, he was, but not to the exclusion of his obsession to re-turn Citation to the racing wars as soon as possible.

Coaltown "was a constant delight for all of us," said Margaret Glass, Calumet's loyal secretary. "I've always called Armed, Bewitch, and Citation the 'ABCs' of Calumet Farm. In a way we all overlooked Coaltown, but he wasn't going to let us forget him, not by a long shot."

Coaltown hit the track running, and winning, in his first 1949 outing, a six furlongs dash on February 5 at Hialeah. Known primarily as a sprinter, a title he landed at Cy's expense the year before, Coaltown tack-led a more exacting 1⅛ miles nine days later. It was only an allowance af-fair, but Bull Lea's quickest son rolled to an easy ten-length tally in 1:47⅗, equaling the world record!

Whether Coaltown's spectacular launch as a four-year-old made it eas-ier or harder to forget Citation's pain and misery back on the farm is prob-lematic. For sure, Coaltown had his own agenda, Cy or no Cy, and he went about it with his usual dispatch.

A week later, again at 1⅛ miles in the McLennan 'Cap, he went a bit slower—1:48⅖—beating stablemate Faultless and Shy Guy in a four-length gallop. This meant he would start back in the 1¼ miles Widener

Handicap under a light 123 pounds—handicappers still regarded him primarily as a sprinter—which he hauled to a handy two-length victory.

"It was amazing what he could do without having to worry about Citation," said trainer Jimmy Jones. "Now he was king of the hill."

Coaltown went on a victory binge that would have made his buddy Citation proud—or jealous.

"Nonsense," said Jimmy Jones. "Coaltown was only doing what he had done the year before as a three-year-old, and would have kept on doing if it weren't for Citation. He was an exceptional horse, faster than most, and had more than a touch of class. Except for Citation, there were few horses in America who could touch him."

Jimmy was a prophet. On March 19 in the Gulfstream Park 'Cap, Coaltown shouldered 128 pounds to a seven-length victory over Three Rings, to whom he gave ten pounds, and aging stablemate Armed who had 116. Again "speed" was his middle name, and Coaltown streaked the classic distance of 1¼ miles in 1:59⅘, matching another world record.

Once again, horsemen started comparing Coaltown with his sidelined entrymate, Citation. The latter, of course, was still in Calumet's recovery room; he couldn't answer his critics.

Coaltown successfully toted 130 pounds in Maryland, again packed 130 in New York to win the Gallant Fox Handicap by seven lengths over Vulcan's Forge in 1:56⅕ for 1 3/16 miles, giving the runner-up no fewer than eleven pounds. He then invaded Narragansett, romping to a twelve-length victory.

Coaltown then headed for Arlington Park in Chicago; his admirers called him the "new" Citation. He was perfectly primed for the coveted Equipoise Mile, in many minds his favorite distance; he proudly accepted top weight of 132 pounds.

He then did what Citation never did when right. He lost. He faced up to a blistering early challenge from a horse named Carrara Marble, hitting the half in :44⅖. Another classy one, With Pleasure, took command at six furlongs in a blazing 1:08⅗. Coaltown stalked, then collared them in midstretch, but was "empty" when long shot Star Reward, lightly rigged at 116 pounds, breezed on by, downing Coaltown by three open lengths in 1:35 flat. He was beaten fairly and squarely, but not disgraced.

Sports-race commentator Jack Drees, at that time serving as public relations consultant to Arlington-Washington's Ben Lindheimer, echoed the sentiments of numerous other race writers and historians: "Big difference between Citation and Coaltown was that Coaltown was virtually unbeatable as long as things went his own way. He couldn't hold off Citation any time, we know that. But he could handle most any other horse if he wasn't strongly pushed or challenged early.

"Citation, on the other hand, could be attacked from the outset going six furlongs or two miles, and still draw clear any time he wanted. His reserve was inexhaustible. Coaltown was next best, but there was always that certain something, a vulnerability, that separates the good horse from the great one."

True to Drees's observation, Coaltown bounced back a winner from his Equipoise Mile defeat, piling up victory after victory, including the Stars & Stripes in track record time, wreaking revenge on Star Reward. He followed that up with wins in the Arlington Handicap, the Whirlaway Stakes, and the Washington Park Handicap. In the latter he barely held on over teammate Armed in a torrid finish.

Following Citation's stakes pattern the year before, Coaltown then journeyed East. Unlike Cy, however, who dominated everything Easterners could throw at him, Coaltown would meet a young three-year-old colt who'd prove more than just a pesky nemesis. His name: Capot.

Speaking of Capot, American racing had another outstanding three-year-old who just happened to have been bred and owned by Calumet Farm. He was a son of Calumet's 1944 Kentucky Derby–Preakness champ Pensive; he was named Ponder, and he was the greatest stretch-runner of his day.

Both Ponder and Coaltown were entrusted to jockey Steve Brooks, the same young man who "pulled" Citation when the latter "failed" to catch the filly Bewitch in Cy's sole two-year-old loss, the Washington Park Futurity on August 16, 1947, the event that propelled Cy into national limelight. It was a one-ride privilege for Steve.

No jockey rode harder, or whipped mightier, than Steve Brooks. Steve was a tender ten-year-old when he first rode competitively; he nailed his first winner at seventeen. His dream was to ride "great horses for Calumet Farm," a dream he realized in 1949.

When Brooks set down a horse for the drive, that beast knew he'd have to give his best, or else! Steve never spared the "rod." Nobody, except Teddy Atkinson, owned the reputation as "the slasher." Eddie Arcaro could whip just as strongly; he simply didn't resort to the whip as often or as eagerly as Steve.

Steve loved Coaltown's natural speed. Likewise, he adored Ponder's late kick. "Greatest stretch-runner I ever rode," he bragged.

Like his running modus operandi, Ponder started slowly as a two-year-old in 1948, failing to win in four starts, picking up one second and a paltry $400 for Calumet coffers. He won his maiden victory in early January at Tropical Park in Florida, then won two more as Derby day approached. It wasn't until Derby week at Churchill Downs that Ponder edged stablemate De Luxe as the stable's number one candidate for the Roses Run.

Ponder was stretching out to one mile in the Derby Trial at Churchill Downs, and though he finished a so-so second to Fred W. Hooper's speedball favorite Olympia—the latter had Arcaro in the irons—he displayed finishing strength. Among those in his wake was the fancied Capot, who wound up five lengths further back in third.

Olympia, Ponder, and Capot all came back for the 1949 Derby. Olympia, however, at least on paper, seemed unbeatable, especially with Arcaro up. The fleet colt was an Eastern sensation, having won the Flamingo Stakes, the Experimental Free Handicap, and the Wood Memorial before humbling Ponder and Capot in the Trial.

Olympia, however, was cut from the same cloth as Coaltown. His forte was speed. Unlike Coaltown, however, Olympia never really excelled at distances approaching 1¼ miles. The Kentucky Derby was his Waterloo.

For Ponder the Derby was nirvana. Olympia sported his customary early lick, leading the pack to the mile. Ponder dawdled at the other end, trailing the field until they curved around the far turn, moving boldly into twelfth at that juncture. By the time Olympia turned for home on top, Ponder had powered to sixth.

With a quarter mile to go, it was obvious Olympia was in trouble despite energetic rousing from Arcaro. Brooks also went to work on Ponder—and his power surge was spectacular to behold!

Ponder cut loose in upper stretch, swung wide to steer clear of trouble and fading horses, sweeping on by with eye-popping ease. With a drive that would have made Whirlaway blush, Ponder dashed clear by three lengths over Capot with Palestinian closing somewhat to take third. A tired Olympia struggled home a well-beaten sixth.

Again, to show what value running time held, Ponder finished off 1¼ miles in a unremarkable 2:04⅗. But the manner in which he swamped his opponents was one for the books. The Derby chart showed Ponder some ten lengths off the pace at the head of the stretch, which made his closing kick all the more sensational.

What really shook up the racing world was that a Calumet Farm entrant trained by Ben and Jimmy Jones was allowed to go off at sixteen to one odds. That was a first, never to happen again for Calumet; also a first for Brooks, the hard-hitting rider bagging his first $100,000 race.

Olympia thereafter would stick to sprints. Ponder was now racing's newest three-year-old wonder colt, and along with his older stablemate Coaltown, the toast of the town.

But Ponder hadn't reckoned with Capot that seriously. The latter was the personification of speed, not as electric as, say, Olympia, and occasionally uncooperative with his rider, Ted Atkinson, if restrained early.

Most race followers figured Ponder would again clobber Capot even at the shorter Preakness distance of 1¾ miles. Shows how wrong a fellow can be.

J. H. Whitney's Capot was just reaching his peak, and the shorter Preakness was tailor-made for his style of going. He flashed winged heels to late stretch, then held on desperately to register a head score over Palestinian. Ponder had an even fiercer case of the slows that day; he didn't get untracked until too late, finishing fifth, but closing sharply in the final furlong.

"Ponder will murder Capot in the Belmont at 1½ miles," was the pardonable battle cry of railbirds, especially after the two rivals met in the Peter Pan at 1⅛ miles prior to racing's final leg of the Triple Crown. Ponder left no doubt, hiking his stock for the Belmont by storming from far back to defeat Colonel Mile and Old Rockport, as Capot faded away a weary seventh, beaten a good ten lengths by Ponder.

Brooks told the Jones boys Ponder had the Belmont "in his hip pocket," that "no horse in the world, save Citation, could withstand his closing kick." Capot, though, was on the improve, and he and his famous jockey, Ted Atkinson, turned in an Academy Award–winning effort.

Capot broke in front in the Belmont, and stayed there throughout the marathon 1½ miles. Ponder, as was his custom, was dead last as solid favorite after the mile. Brooks, unfortunately, didn't have Arcaro's "clock in his head," failing to sense Capot's snail-like 1:15⅕ for six furlongs or the mile in a slowpoke 1:39⅖.

"I waited too long," Brooks said afterward. "I just couldn't imagine Ponder not catching Capot at 1½ miles. By the time we reached the top of the stretch, with less than a quarter mile to go, we were ten lengths behind Capot. We slashed away all but a half-length by wire's end. It was a tough one to blow, but we did it, and it was all my fault."

The "turtle and the hare" parted company, winning some, losing some, before they'd meet again. Capot lost his next two starts; so did Ponder. So expectations ran high when Ponder and Capot met again for the last time that season. Occasion was the July 30 Arlington Classic at 1¼ miles, and Ponder was invincible, scoring from behind by three lengths as Capot floundered home some fourteen lengths back.

Al Gore probably would insist that all elections are not exactly kosher, and in the instance of Capot being voted in as both three-year-old champ and Horse of the Year over both Ponder and Coaltown, he'd have a good case. But that's the way it happened.

True, Capot beat Coaltown and one other rival in New York's Sysonby Mile in 1:35⅗ by 1¼ lengths. And after finishing third to Royal Governor and Three Rings in the Grey Lag 'Cap, Capot successfully coveted the Pimlico Special, the same race Citation won in a "walkover" the year before.

This time eighteen horses were invited, but only three—Capot, Coaltown, and Ponder—showed any interest in the outcome. Capot's trainer, John Gaver, shrewdly stated he would pit his colt against either Coaltown or Ponder, but not both, no way. A smart move.

Ponder, incidentally, following his crushing victory over Capot in Chicago's Arlington Classic, went on to finish a strong second to Coaltown in the Whirlaway Stakes, pulverized all comers with a track record win in the American Derby, then proudly sauntered off with the two-mile Jockey Club Gold Cup, which Capot, of course, declined.

Faced with trainer Gaver's ultimatum, Jimmy Jones tapped Coaltown as Capot's lone competition in the Pimlico Special. "Ponder would have smothered the both of 'em had he been allowed to race," Brooks opined. "As it was I thought Coaltown could beat Capot on his own but he wasn't exactly himself that day. Unbelievably, Capot beat us from the gate, and Coaltown gave it up early. We were hopelessly out of it so I eased him up in midstretch. I think Capot won by a dozen lengths, but it was a hollow victory, like when Armed beat Assault in their match race two years earlier. But then, that's racing."

Capot's selection as Horse of the Year over Coaltown was, at best, questionable. How the polls selected him over Ponder, however, was shocking, a mystery not even Sherlock Holmes could solve.

"You can't win 'em all," Ben Jones shrugged. "What's really bad is when it doesn't make any sense."

What did make sense, though, was that Coaltown was unanimously honored as Handicap Horse of the Year. Incidentally, Bewitch, whose 1948 three-year-old season was compromised by the same kind of leg injury—though not as serious—that felled Citation, came back marvelously as a 1949 four-year-old filly and was crowned the nation's queen of older females.

And Delegate, who ate Citation's exhaust in prior encounters, was named Sprinter of the Year. Poor Ponder received only lip service. The long-winded son of Pensive should have been three-year-old champ—he whipped Capot more times, and more decisively, than he lost, but for Capot to be acclaimed Horse of the Year meant he also had to capture his divisional title as three-year-old king. So went the vote.

Except for Capot, who made only three inconsequential starts as a 1950 four-year-old, the others all played a major role, past as well as future, in Citation's enduring career. For the record, Coaltown would race two more seasons (1950–51), eventually retiring with twenty-three wins in thirty-nine starts and earning $415,675. He disappointed at stud, after which he was sold to racing interests in France.

Ponder and Bewitch also would continue racing with marked success. Parenthetically, Calumet in 1949 also had a pair of three-year-old fillies, Two Lea and Wistful, who tied for their divisional title. Of the above quartet, Ponder, Bewitch, and Two Lea would play an active part in Citation's comeback years of 1950–51.

And Steve Brooks, whose love for Citation remained unabated since their sole "date" in the 1947 Washington Park Futurity, would realize his dream of a lifetime—to ride Mighty Cy again!

Chapter Fifteen

"Cy's Back—But Not All the Way Back"

$\mathcal{W}$ith those words, turf experts Kent Hollinsworth and Peter Winants aptly described Citation's dubious return to the racing wars.

The grand warrior was five years old, still harbored scars of injury. He convalesced ten months before Jimmy Jones finally acceded to Warren Wright's relentless obsession that Citation needed to go back to racing. His bankroll stood at $865,150 as American racing turned the corner into 1950.

Cy was returned to serious training in November 1949, then rushed to make his first "comeback" start on January 11 at Santa Anita.

"It was foolish on our part," Jimmy recollected. "He wasn't really right, nor perfectly sound, and he had been away a full year, a year which could have been his very best were he healthy. But the old man wanted that record so bad—he could taste it—and I was too young and too dumb to do or say otherwise—so I went along with him.

"Now that I can look back—I was always two, maybe three, weeks behind Cy in training, so I never really had him up to what we were asking of him as a five-year-old."

Ben Jones always felt that Cy wasn't totally sound. "He was not really that fit to race big time. He should have stayed on the farm with the mares as the next logical stage of his life—as sire."

"And his record should have read twenty-nine for twenty-nine," added Jimmy. "Hell, Twilight Tear won eleven straight. I think Man o'War won fourteen in a row, and a great horse called Colin was unbeaten in fifteen races. Cy in his three-year-old season already had won fifteen straight, and nineteen of twenty. And he won eight of nine as a two-year-old. Throw out those two silly losses—and they really never counted—and he'd be remembered for twenty-nine straight wins in an unbeaten career, with a reputation, also a legacy, no horse before or since would ever approach."

Tommy Trotter, one of the nation's most respected racing officials having served at tracks in New York, Illinois, and Florida since the late 1940s, concurred with the Jones boys in praising Citation as "the greatest thoroughbred who ever lived."

"Especially when Citation was a three-year-old," Trotter emphasized. "No colt ever did what he did. And I agree, he should have won all twenty of his races that season. No horse before or since could have touched him at age three."

Trotter's favorite "older horse" was the golden gelding, Kelso, who swept five straight Horse of the Year titles (1960–64). But when it came to appraising three-year-olds, Tommy cedes that "Citation was in a league of his own."

America's sports media fell in love with Citation all over again. He had been sorely missed. His fame undiminished, Cy's glowing presence at Santa Anita, especially his morning trials, evoked avid press coverage. He was the nearest thing to the Michael Jordan of his sport.

Eddie Arcaro also kept tabs on Citation's status and progress. The Master was in Florida, thousands of miles away. His return to Cy's saddle was expected and promised; the five-year-old's major goal was the famed Santa Anita Handicap in late February.

Steve Brooks, of course, was now Calumet's primary jockey, and his work aboard both Ponder and Coaltown impressed the Jones boys. Steve also had been sharing Citation's training workouts, and since "the big horse's" first start in some thirteen months was a simple $5,000 six furlongs allowance sprint, Jimmy Jones assigned Brooks the riding privilege, for which Steve virtually begged. Arcaro agreed, much as he did when N. L. Pierson deputized for Eddie in that allowance prep for the American Derby back in August of 1948.

Both Brooks and Cy's regular exercise rider Freeman McMillan saw nothing changed in Cy's mien. "He had that same professional look in his eye," Brooks beamed. "Sure, he was a year older, and was coming off a long layoff, but the old spirit was still there. He was still smarter than any horse around, and still the most determined and most focused dude I've ever seen or ridden."

Brooks hadn't been aboard Cy in an actual race since the colt was a two-year-old, but McMillan knew him like the back of his hand. "Cy was strong, the perfect racing machine," McMillan said, "but as much as he tried, and he gave it his best shot every time I rode him, he just didn't seem as fluid or as flowing as before. He was a bit more rigid. Remember, he had suffered several major physical problems. So he wasn't as supple as before. 'Supple' is the word I heard the vets use when talking about his condition and comeback from sore tendons.

"But he was ready mentally, that I'm sure of," McMillan assured.

There was one thing, though, that troubled both Brooks and McMillan. And it was a concern also voiced by track clockers, those eagle-eyed men who, with personal stop watch in hand, timed each and every horse they could identify in the early bright.

"Nobody could miss Citation," Brooks shook his head, "or any of the Calumet band, who came out every morning decked out in the devil's red and blue with Ben and Jimmy Jones at the helm.

"The Jones boys had a reputation of not babying their horses," Brooks continued, "but they never abused 'em either. But if they were sound, and could stand up, they were worked hard, to their limit, but within reason."

Brooks and McMillan agreed with Santa Anita's clocking corps—Citation was strenuously trained. He was on the track every morning, galloped, breezed, seriously pushed, and carefully pressed. Every observer concurred: No horse shouldered a heavier work schedule than Citation leading up to his scheduled January 11 racing return.

"But, you know something?" Brooks always recounted, "'Big Cy' took it like a man, all in stride. Still, it made a guy wonder. Sure, he's an 'iron horse' and all that—he had to be to be put through what he endured—but any other horse might've caved in or something. Mr. Wright wanted him ready, and he wanted him to win the Santa Anita Handicap—it was a personal thing again. But man, they moved Cy along big time, yes, they sure did."

In his comeback bow, Citation caught a track other than fast for the tenth time in thirty starts. There was slop and goo everywhere, and a dreary day to boot. And one of Cy's challengers that day was Rex C. Ellsworth's speedy Roman In, who'd later set a world record of 1:08⅗ for six furlongs. He could run, and he liked slop, too. Cy would carry top weight of 124 pounds; Roman In got in with 116.

"I was more nervous than Cy," Brooks shuddered. "I was just hoping he was a semblance of what he once was. It would have killed me to screw up and get him beat."

No one—not Calumet Farm, Ben or Jimmy Jones, Steve Brooks, Citation, nor the media—was aware that on that day, January 11, 1950, thoroughbred racing history was made.

Citation registered his sixteenth straight victory, a modern-day miracle, unassailable for forty-six years until equaled, but not surpassed, by the amazing Cigar, the latter fast approaching the pinnacle as the number one money-winning horse of all time. Cigar's 1996 feat at Arlington Park in a special event named the Citation Challenge, while admirable and worthy of acclaim, didn't come close to Citation's, which was remarkably achieved in Triple Crown competition and major league action against the best older horses in training.

"It wasn't until much later that we realized what Citation had achieved," said trainer Jimmy Jones. "Pardon me if I've said all this before, it should have been thirty straight, not sixteen."

Nevertheless, Cy's sixteenth straight was recorded in 1:11⅖ over a sloppy course, rallying from off the pace, third at the head of the stretch, to splash home by 1½ lengths over Bold Gallant with the nimble-footed Roman In another neck back in third.

Steve Brooks was ecstatic. In his own mind, he had atoned for his part "in getting Citation beat" in the colt's only loss behind Bewitch as a two-year-old in 1947.

"Citation was absolutely marvelous that day," Brooks loved to recall. "I know we didn't beat the likes of Coaltown or Phalanx—I had no delusions about who we beat—but he was poetry in motion. Yes, he relaxed at the gate just like he used to do, and, yes, he paraded to the gate and back to the Winner's Circle with his neck arched like he always did. He didn't forget any of that, not for me he didn't."

But was he the old Citation?

"I don't think so," Steve shared privately. "He was all business, and his great heart was intact. He still was that well-oiled machine, but something—physically—was missing."

Brooks and Jimmy Jones reasoned logically that it would probably take a race or two before Citation "would be his old self again." Actually, they were more hopeful than optimistic in view of what agonies he had gone through the past year.

Arcaro took pleasure in Cy's successful return. "Sixteen straight's gonna be one helluva record to match," Eddie told Brooks. "I see no reason why he can't keep the string alive."

With Jones's permission, Arcaro decided not to fly out to Santa Anita until the February 11 San Antonio Handicap, Cy's final major prep for the Santa Anita 'Cap two weeks hence, February 25.

Jones, however, wanted to give Cy one more tightener between his comeback win and the San Antonio. He entered him in the La Sorpresa Handicap two weeks after his winning seasonal bow, on January 26. Arcaro, after discussion with Jones, agreed to let Brooks ride Cy again, and again at six furlongs. This time Cy's weight would be personally assigned by the racing secretary.

Which brings us to Santa Anita's racing secretary, Webb Everett, an ambitious man who cleverly worked his way through the ranks; he started out as a jockey's valet, then moved into the racing office, and was the racing secretary-handicapper of record during Seabiscuit's heyday.

Everett loved to assign weights that would attract attention. He was loud, gregarious, witty, and flamboyant, usually all at the same time. He knew the sport, and he knew the people who ran it. Among his more novel moves was to court and marry Marjorie Lindheimer, adopted daughter of Arlington-Washington impresario Ben Lindheimer. With Lindheimer's death on June 5, 1960, Marje Lindheimer Everett assumed control, her older hubby, Webb, at her side.

For Citation's second comeback start, Everett piled on the weight: 130 pounds for the champion and only 114 for the rugged South American Miche, who already owned a victory over a horse name Noor. Miche was a genuine foe.

In the La Sorpresa 'Cap, Citation did what he had never done before when at the top of his game: he lost, and he lost fair and square!

Brooks was heartsick. "He tried every step of the way. He was sluggish at the start, struggling still to find his best stride after a year on the farm," Steve sighed. "But he got going pretty good around the turn, then grabbed Miche by the throat in midstretch. I thought Cy was just playing with him. I was wrong. He simply couldn't catch him, and we got beat in a photo, a short neck."

"Oh, how the mighty have fallen!" ridiculers might chide.

"We had no real excuse," Brooks verified. "The time, over a fast track, was 1:10⅘, but we did give Miche sixteen pounds, and that may have been a bit much, since it was only Cy's second start in fourteen months. None of that really mattered, though, and wouldn't have been a factor at all if he was himself. Not only that, but he acted somewhat tired while pulling up, something he had never been before. God, how I hated to see him lose. I know he didn't like it either."

Therefore, Jimmy Jones, painfully aware of how badly Warren Wright wanted to add the Santa Anita 'Cap trophy to his myriad awards, turned up another notch on Cy's training schedule. He felt—later admitted he was mistaken—that all Citation really needed was extra work to get him shipshape for the big race.

Besides, Eddie Arcaro would be coming from Florida for the upcoming San Antonio. Everybody hoped reuniting Arcaro with Citation would prove the magic elixir—the answer to Cy's fans' prayers.

Most media folk were willing to forgive Cy his first defeat in seventeen starts. There were many extenuating circumstances. Every sports fan in the nation appreciated the injury Cy had suffered to his left foreleg at the end of 1948. What they didn't know at the time was that Cy was also nursing a tender ankle, probably the same one he sprained in Chicago a few months earlier in 1948. Real trouble in that ankle wouldn't surface for another month or so.

Though dismayed by Citation's defeat, narrow or not, Arcaro was brimming with high hopes, anxious and impatient to rejoin his "favorite horse" in the longer 1⅛ miles San Antonio Handicap. "I galloped him the day before the race, and he seemed okay to me," Eddie recalled, frowning.

"But I couldn't read his mind, and he doesn't talk. During 1948, however, we 'forged a mutual rapport,' as one Chicago turf writer put it, and except for when he hurt himself in the Stars & Stripes at Arlington, I never knew him to take an unsound step. He was strong as a bull, and, in a competitive sense, just as mean.

"So I had to wonder privately," Eddie confided, "why he couldn't catch Miche the race before? Ben Jones tried to make me believe Cy was a little stale from the long layoff, that he needed the race. But I also remember it was Ben who once told me, 'any horse Citation can see, he can catch!'"

Brooks tried to blame himself for the loss to Miche, but Arcaro wasn't buying. Both closely reviewed the film of the race; Brooks did nothing wrong; Citation simply got beat. No excuse.

Once again Webb Everett honored Citation with top weight for the San Antonio, keeping him at 130. Rated only two pounds behind at 128 was Cy's younger stablemate, now four, the stretch-running Ponder. The

Jones boys decided to send out both Citation and Ponder just in case some other horse might harbor a notion of upset.

Ponder also was a favorite of Brooks, the jockey's hard-riding-hard-hitting style fitting the colt to a T. "If Cy's not himself, Ponder could win it all," Steve informed Eddie. "So he'll be close by, just in case."

The San Antonio boasted a ton of speed, particularly the quick-starting Bolero, whose presence suited Cy perfectly. "We'll just let Bolero set all the pace he wants," Eddie smiled. "He'll give us something to shoot at."

Bolero leapt to the lead as the field left the starting gate. Eddie, aboard Cy for the first time since they teamed up to win the Tanforan Handicap fourteen months ago to the day in 1948, moved to fourth from fifth as they sped toward the far turn. Ponder and Noor were far back.

"Citation seemed okay," Arcaro said later, "striding out strongly, and was running easily. I felt much of the old competitive fire, and he wanted to 'go get' Bolero. So I clucked to him—and he took off like a shot!"

Cy rolled into second circling the far turn, now two lengths off the high-flying Bolero. Eddie stole a backward glance; Ponder also was accelerating. Bolero hung tough when Citation collared him a furlong out, then gave way, as so many front-runners before had done.

No sooner had Citation grabbed command—here comes Ponder turning up the heat. Again the improbable happened. Just over a year ago, once Citation took a purposeful lead, it was all over; he'd never allow another horse to collar him from behind.

Shockingly, Ponder caught, and passed, Citation, dashing clear by a slender length. Now, Eddie never pressured Cy when his stablemate moved alongside fifty yards from pay dirt; Eddie sensed Cy's tank at that late juncture "was almost empty," adding: "Calumet had its sights trained on the big Santa Anita 'Cap, and if he couldn't win this prep like in the old days, I wasn't going to push him unduly."

What really bothered Eddie was Cy's "lack of desire" to "instinctively" repulse the bid as he had done when collared by Free America the summer of 1948 in the American Derby at Washington Park.

Eddie's only conclusion: "Citation is *not* the Citation of old, not now anyway. Either the long layoff had taken a bigger toll than everyone expected, or he was hurting somewhere, someplace."

Eddie broached the delicate subject of Cy's present physical condition with Jimmy, who grudgingly was forced, if not to agree, at least to admit that "something's wrong."

Fact is, Calumet's inner sanctum was fraught with a puzzling mix of dread and anxiety. Owner Wright impatiently sought the million-dollar mark, wouldn't take "no" for an answer. In his mind there was no viable reason Citation wasn't the wonder horse of yesteryear.

Though Jimmy Jones insisted he had "no valid reason"—he couldn't find anything physically wrong with Citation—to dissuade or divert Wright from his avowed goal, he did privately admit to Arcaro, later for public consumption, "that we should have skipped the Santa Anita Handicap for the good of the horse, for the good of all concerned," explaining: "Yes, we were out here in California to win the big Handicap. If I had been a little older, more sure of myself, I might have said, 'Let's skip this one, he's not quite ready for it.' But Mr. Wright was determined to win the Santa Anita Handicap, and I suppose I felt he could win the thing even if he wasn't at his best. See, at three, Citation could fall down at the eighth pole, and still get up and beat any horse in the world."

Arcaro agreed, but still expressed disappointment and concern over Citation's San Antonio loss. Cy gave Ponder two pounds, which wouldn't have mattered a whit in the past, still lost by a length. Yet, he was good enough to give Noor sixteen pounds and managed to save second over the latter.

Eddie shrugged: "But Citation was tired and losing ground at the finish. As always he was all business, and he looked great physically, at least to the eye. Inside, he still had the great heart and will to win. But whatever the reason, he couldn't put the two together. I told Jimmy they shouldn't have gone this far so fast. His comeback win was fine, but when he lost to Miche in his next start at six furlongs, the red flag went up.

"And getting beat in the San Antonio simply meant, far as I was concerned, that Cy should be rested, even sent back to the farm. Better still—retired for good."

Had the Arcaro-Jones discussion—which came awfully close to "bombs away" except for cooler heads prevailing—been leaked to the media, the latter would have had a field day. One could only guess the maelstrom of controversy it would have caused on the sports pages.

Jimmy acquiesced to Wright; Arcaro also agreed to return for the ride—Citation would start back in the 1¼ miles Santa Anita Handicap on February 25 as originally planned. Bravely, Citation accepted 132 pounds, this time having to give Ponder eight pounds, a switch of six pounds in Ponder's favor since their first clash, which Ponder won.

Webb Everett's weight allotments again came under scrutiny among horsemen and the media. This time, however, he had an out. The Santa Anita weights had been announced far in advance, prior to the San Antonio in which Cy failed to stave off Ponder, giving the latter two pounds, also sixteen pounds to third-place Noor, no mean feat.

Noor was about to explode on the American racing scene. He was a dark brown son of Nasrullah, tall and leggy, built similar to Whirlaway, a suggestion that the Charles S. Howard steed—he was purchased in a $175,000 deal that included Irish Derby winner Nathoo—exuded "classic" potential, the breeding, and the looks to run all day.

Noor had won once in six starts as a four-year-old in 1949, was improving quickly, however, and had finished second recently. He was still looking for his first American stakes win as the big 'Cap loomed.

Arcaro thought Citation's top impost of 132—heaviest he ever carried—was "somewhat excessive, especially compared with the 124 given Ponder." Eddie didn't know much about Noor, who, in receipt of sixteen pounds, was breathing down Citation's neck in the recent San Antonio. For the big Handicap, Cy was now asked to give Noor twenty-three pounds, seven additional pounds. Everett rated Noor at a lowly 109; his jockey, the cagey Johnny Longden, rode light, but not that light, and was one pound overweight—Noor went postward at a feathery 110.

But something else also rankled Arcaro.

Calumet Farm's penchant for running two- or three-horse entries in major stakes was becoming a bit much. Eddie thought the stable's insatiable appetite for success occasionally exceeded normal limits and common sense. He always reasoned that, unless absolutely essential, either for strategic purposes, like sending out a "rabbit" to ensure a realistic early pace, why clutter up the field?

"Two big horses, like Citation and Coaltown, or Citation and Ponder, I could see. But adding a third horse just confuses the issue, especially when all eyes are on 'Big Cy.'"

Chicago turf scribe Elmer Polzin probably came closest to Calumet's problem: "Warren Wright wanted to win everything in sight, and he had the guns to nearly do it. Ben and Jimmy knew it, too. Calumet was geared to sweeping everything in sight. They loved to run 1-2-3 every time, if possible. This time, in the Santa Anita 'Cap they made a big mistake."

Arcaro's protestations notwithstanding, Jimmy also entered the four-year-old filly Two Lea along with Citation and Ponder, looking to make it a powerhouse, unbeatable Calumet entry. The nation's top three-year-old filly the year before, Two Lea toted 113 pounds.

Among other 'Cap starters was Cy's old compatriot as a 1948 three-year-old, My Request, a multiple stakes hero, at 122. Pegged at 118 was Solidarity, while On Trust packed 117. Rated at 111 was the fine mare, But Why Not. Noor, of course, jogged postward under 110 pounds, four less than he toted in finishing third behind Ponder and Cy last out. Citation, to repeat, would give Noor twenty-two pounds.

Arcaro warned Steve Brooks on Ponder and Johnny Gilbert on Two Lea to "stay out of my way out there. I don't want you messing me up."

Jimmy Jones later confessed he'd have done better leaving Two Lea in her stall.

Chapter Sixteen

One Partnership Ends—
Another Begins

*E*ddie Arcaro's comment that "two's company but three's a crowd" unwittingly precipitated the beginning of the end of the most exciting and
successful partnership in thoroughbred history—the greatest horse and
the greatest jockey team ever!

Of course, other factors were involved, but fact that Citation went into
the Santa Anita Handicap having just lost two races in a row for the first
time would play a major role in a mutual decision by Calumet and Arcaro
that the Citation-Arcaro duo had run its course.

Plus, Calumet's insistence on starting the three-ply entry of Citation,
Ponder, and Two Lea also played a big part in the race's outcome. Jimmy
described it best: "Citation went into the first turn with only one horse
beaten—Ponder, I think it was—and when Arcaro started moving up
with Citation, Ralph Neves on Solidarity slammed into him. Neves got
the meeting for it." (The jockey was suspended for the balance of the
Santa Anita meeting for the blatant infraction.)

"Anyways, Arcaro went on with Citation," Jimmy continued. "We had
Two Lea out there to set the pace for him, and Arcaro figured for sure
Johnny Gilbert would move the filly out a little bit and let him through,
but Gilbert stayed right on the rail, and Arcaro had to take up and go
around her, so he lost momentum there.

"And there was where Noor just rushed right by him. At the eighth
pole, Two Lea still had the lead by a head, but Noor was taking her, and
Citation was two lengths back and getting a little rubbery; but he came

on again, and got beat only 1¼ lengths, giving Noor twenty-two pounds, and him breaking the track record. Two Lea hung in there pretty good, beat Ponder a neck for third." Jimmy's voice betrayed his frustration and anguish. Cy had lost his third race in a row.

There were more explanations, excuses, justification, and reasons to rationalize Cy's defeat than snowflakes in a blustery winter storm. To begin with, Citation turned in a courageous effort under a heavy impost.

Racing's rule of thumb is that five pounds equals one length at distances one mile or more; thus, Cy was at least three lengths "better" than Noor, according to that yardstick, which, of course, is only a generalization, and not a proven one at that.

Arcaro easily could have blamed the defeat on two things: first, the glaring misdeed by Solidarity that all but knocked Cy down; second, being denied racing room by his own stablemate, Two Lea, at a most crucial stage of the race, which allowed Noor to surge into a commanding lead, forcing Cy to play "catch-up," which he almost pulled off.

Moreover, Cy did manage to avenge his San Antonio loss to Ponder when he gave his entrymate two pounds at the shorter distance of 1⅛ miles. This time he gave him eight pounds and whipped him decisively, and at Ponder's favorite 1¼ miles distance.

Jimmy ceded he should have "skipped the Anita 'Cap," and later admitted Citation, after suffering barefaced interference and an inexcusable lack of cooperation from teammate Two Lea, was a bit 'rubbery' in late stretch, yet still was managing to close ground on Noor, the latter noted for his love of distance.

"In the past," Arcaro told Jimmy, "none of what happened to Cy would have stopped him. Yes, Two Lea screwed us royally by blocking our path, which allowed Noor to sweep on by, and, you're right, Cy was 'rubbery' in late stretch, but if he were the Citation I knew he would have gone right up there and finished Noor off.

"He's giving it his all, and he's not short on conditioning or training. He's just not Citation. Jimmy, he's only a shell of his former self. We can't go on this way. Something's gotta give."

What "gived," unfortunately, was the wondrous partnership of Citation and Arcaro.

Even Jimmy again confessed: "I really should have stopped on Citation right then"; instead he cranked Cy up for the San Juan Capistrano just one week away.

Then, why *didn't* Jimmy stop right then and there with Citation?

"The weights shifted for the next big one, the San Juan Capistrano at 1¾ miles, and they shifted in our favor," he justified.

What happened behind closed doors between Jimmy and Arcaro was never fully disclosed. In 1996, Eddie declined further comment on the sensational estrangement of rider and horse, saying he'd not give additional info "as long as Jimmy's alive," not realizing he was at death's door himself. Arcaro passed away on November 14, 1997, three months shy of his eighty-second birthday, February 19, 1998. Jimmy was still alive and fairly active when the world ushered in the new millennium.

Eddie called the weight shift "negligible." Webb Everett dropped two pounds off Citation to 130, increased Noor seven pounds to 117. The spread went down from twenty-two pounds to thirteen, a shift of nine pounds that Jimmy opined he "could live with."

Arcaro countered with his final argument: Citation was not the Citation of old, and he was tired and tailing off while Noor was on the improve and just coming into his own.

"Arcaro gave up on Calumet and Citation too soon," said sportscaster Jack Drees.

Elmer Polzin put it a little more succinctly: "Arcaro gave up on Citation too soon—*one* race too soon."

And that race—the San Juan Capistrano at 1¾ miles—was memorable; more than memorable—unforgettable.

Thousands of race followers praised the 1950 San Juan Capistrano as "one of the great races of all time!" Jimmy Jones agreed, "except, of course, we got beat."

March 4 at Santa Anita was a weekday. No matter—sixty thousand thoroughbred lovers jammed the Arcadia track for what some still regard as "the race of the century." Eight horses contested the 1¾ miles marathon, but only two horses really mattered.

Steve Brooks was returned to Cy's back, and there he'd remain, except for two future engagements. Ageless Johnny Longden, who'd eventually rate Noor "second only to Count Fleet [1943 Triple Crown champ] as the best horse I ever rode," was aboard Cy's newest nemesis.

Noble Citation gave Noor thirteen precious pounds and the race of his life in the most thrilling and awesome racing spectacle of modern times! Fans may have stood on their seats and cheered wildly as Secretariat rolled to his incredible thirty-one-length 1973 Belmont Stakes victory.

But on this day twenty-three years earlier, they went ballistic at the sight of two great horses—head to head, nostril to nostril—racing inseparably for a full half mile in a race too close to call at wire's end!

"Greatest race I ever saw!" racing secretary Webb Everett cheered, obviously satisfied his weight spread brought the two gallant horses noses apart right down to the finish.

Cy had stalked the leaders early, then was sent by Brooks to take charge at the first mile run in a leisurely 1:38. Two years earlier, Cy taking command would have meant: "That's all she wrote!"

But Longden shifted Noor into top gear some four lengths behind Citation. Noor and Citation locked horns as they swung around the far turn. They were stride for stride, heads bobbing, and the sixty-thousand on hand went wild—yells, screams, programs, and hats sawn asunder—as Citation and Noor hit the wire together in world record time of 2:52⅗!

The third finisher, Mocopo, was thirteen lengths back.

Steve Brooks masterfully rode Citation, though the margin of defeat, scant as it was, was of little solace. "It was a head bob, pure and simple," Brooks groaned. "Cy and Noor were locked stride for stride for nearly three furlongs. Neither gave an inch. Except for the head bob in Noor's favor, Citation would have redeemed himself for all time."

The San Juan Capistrano race film confirmed Steve's analysis. After a protracted drive, Citation was giving Noor thirteen pounds—or 2½ lengths if racing's rule-of-thumb weight yardstick that five pounds equals one length had any warrant—and lost by a whisker. Cy's nose was in front the stride before the wire, and in front the stride after the wire. But the head bob put Noor's nose ahead *at* the wire—where it counted.

Race observers second-guessed the outcome as would be expected. No one faulted Brooks's ride, but the general feeling was, had Eddie Arcaro been aboard, he'd never allow Citation to lose at the wire. Especially because Arcaro was at his very best in torrid one-on-one combat in close finishes.

Arcaro had authored the famous triple-negative race-riding axiom by which he lived: "*Don't never* get beat *no* noses!"

"Like I said," Polzin reminded, "Arcaro gave up on Citation too soon— one race too soon!"

The San Juan Capistrano both galvanized and polarized the racing world. Many thought that Citation ran "a winning race" under the circumstances of his comeback and the thirteen pounds he gave Noor. Still others felt despite the narrowest of margins that up'n'coming Noor had Cy's number and may have taken the heart right out of Calumet's favorite son.

Sounding more than ever like a broken record, Jimmy Jones again publicly stated: "We probably shouldn't have kept going with him. We really never gave him enough time." Then, unconsciously, certainly unwittingly, Jimmy confessed what others, including Eddie Arcaro, suspected all along: "You know, you have to give a cripple more time to come back, and I was always pushing him . . . and Noor kept improving."

"A cripple"? Citation, "*a cripple*"? Yes, Jimmy uttered the word no one dared to speak. He probably didn't realize what he said or implied, but its meaning was undeniable. Cy was physically deprived while competing, yet mentally sound, emotionally strong, spiritually still unconquerable. He simply couldn't get his body do what his heart thought it could still do.

So Jimmy, doubtless with Warren Wright's prodding and blessing, again compromised his own good sense. "We were after Stymie's money record [$918,485], and after the Capistrano race we needed only $10,000. And that put us even closer to 'The Million-Dollar Mark.' Besides, even though Citation was running second, he never really was beaten bad."

So Jimmy convinced Wright to compromise. He'd give Citation a much-needed rest—not a layoff, say, back at the farm; simply a rest from race activity on the track. Thus, Cy was given a ten-week respite, which he needed, given his chronic tendon soreness and a quietly developing ankle problem.

Arcaro empathized with Citation's frustrating ordeal. "My leaving Cy was heart-breaking, and maybe I should have waited a little longer. But he wasn't totally all right. So I chose to remember the good old days."

Besides, Arcaro was busy with a young three-year-old colt named Hill Prince, a husky son of Princequillo owned and bred by Christopher T. Chenery, a strong favorite for the 1950 Kentucky Derby. Eddie found solace in Hill Prince's burgeoning greatness, winning the Preakness after finishing a strong second to Middleground in the Derby; he also lost the Belmont to Middleground before becoming the darling of American racing.

Hill Prince and Arcaro thereafter won everything in sight, nailing down both the 1950 three-year-old title, also honors as undisputed Horse of the Year. Arcaro, as usual, kept busy in the saddle.

Therefore, Steve Brooks became Citation's official jockey. "I was overwhelmed at having Cy," Steve admitted. "I had no idea how many steps slower he was from his glory days, and, frankly, I didn't care. Naturally I wished he were the Citation of old, even the Citation I rode once as a two-year-old, but having him was my greatest pleasure."

Brooks spent every free moment with Cy around the Calumet barn, first at Santa Anita, then at Golden Gate Fields, while Cy took advantage of his much-deserved break. "He was all horse," Steve marveled, "always cheerful, but businesslike at the same time.

"One bad thing—I'd give my right arm to change the San Juan Capistrano result. He did everything but win, and he and Noor broke a track record that had stood for five years. He could have won it as easily as he lost it—just a head bob," Brooks shook his head.

"And he still wasn't back at the top of the game. That's why Jimmy freshened him up. Fact is, Cy galloped back to the Winner's Circle in the Capistrano head bowed, thinking he had won it. I never told him differently," Steve smiled.

Steve again in 1950 rode with uncommon success for Ben and Jimmy Jones. Just as Doug Dodson's ties with Calumet made him the world's number one winning rider in 1947 in money earned with $1,429,949; and Arcaro in 1948 with $1,686,230; Brooks had finished out 1949—thanks mostly to Ponder, Coaltown, and Two Lea—with $1,316,817, a seasonal, personal high. Had Citation managed to win a few more races, 1950 would have been another record-topper for Steve. As it was he was right near the top behind Arcaro.

Citation apparently enjoyed and benefited from his ten-week rest. "However, he seemed to relax a little too much by the seventh or eight week," Brooks recalled, "as if he were getting used to things nice and easy. So Jimmy moved him back to strong gallops and wind sprints to make sure he'd be at his best—whatever 'best' was for him at that stage of his career—for yet another comeback."

Citation's younger buddy Ponder continued his winning ways in 1950. He wouldn't test Cy again, but he did win the Santa Anita Maturity, also several other "name" stakes, including a summer foray to Chicago when he uncoiled from far back to win the Arlington Handicap. The cyclonic son of Pensive retired after one start in 1951 with fourteen major wins in forty-one starts and earnings of $541,275.

"He didn't have Coaltown's speed or Citation's class," Brooks exulted, "but his late kick was second to none."

Citation, meantime, in early May 1950, was scratching along toward his second comeback victory. He had won his five-year-old bow, his sixteenth straight, then finished second four straight times, Noor becoming the first horse ever to beat him twice.

Noor was ailing slightly in early May, so Citation's first start off that long layoff would be without his adversary—a $4,000 allowance six furlongs dash at Golden Gate Fields, a prep for the then-famous Golden Gate Mile two weeks hence.

Hard-riding Brooks rode once "too hard" in an earlier race, incurring the stewards' ire, and was unavailable for Citation's May 17 return, that honor falling to youthful Gordon Glisson, who the year before led all jockeys in races won with 270.

Cy shared top weight of 120 pounds with speed ball Roman In, the latter quick on the draw as any horse in America. He finished a well-beaten third in Citation's only win back in January at Santa Anita, but had developed into a "speed tiger" during Cy's layoff.

Citation again finished second, failing to catch Roman In by less than a length. And again it took a world record performance to deny Cy his second win of the year—Roman In whistled the six furlongs in 1:08⅗, tying the world standard.

"Citation tried," Glisson commented upon dismounting, "and he'll improve off the effort, I'm sure. He was certainly going strongest at the end, but Jimmy Jones told me not to push him all that hard."

Brooks, watching Citation's defeat from the stands, couldn't help wondering when the grand old campaigner would "catch a break." It was bad enough the game champion was racing on "only three legs, but, worse still, he was losing to world-beaters at all distances."

Then there was good and bad news. The good—Roman In, for all his speed, didn't want Citation at the Golden Gate Mile distance. The bad news—a week before the Golden Gate Mile, Abe Hirschberg's equally rapid Bolero lowered the six furlongs world record to 1:08⅕. And Bolero's next stop would be the Golden Gate Mile.

Jimmy and Steve were stunned. "Dumbstruck" actually was a better word. "It seems the only way Cy can win again—and his next start's the Golden Gate Mile—is win and run in world-record time himself," Jimmy philosophized.

Brooks nodded: "I just hope he's up to it."

Finally, Citation was up to it, and more. He accepted top weight of 128 pounds for the Mile stakes, giving five pounds to lightninglike Bolero, and twelve pounds to the multiple stakes winner On Trust.

A sideline note: were Citation to win the Golden Gate Mile, and he had to win it to turn the trick, he'd displace Stymie as the world's all-time money-winning champion. Brooks rejoined his partner for the supreme effort, and as they proudly jogged postward, something, an inner feel, and the way Citation was striding out, hinted that he was virtually pain-free. Maybe even close to the Citation of old?

He'd have to be, because Bolero's winged heels waited for no man's horse. The world-record holder at six furlongs was so fast he even smashed his old mark with six furlongs in 1:07⅗. Cy, however, was equal to the test, and he moved boldly and confidently to Bolero in midstretch. Brooks asked Citation for his best, and on this day, he got it—a going-away almost one-length victory in world-record time of 1:33⅗! And the title of world-record money-earner with $924,630 in the bank to boot!

That should have done it. In one fell swoop, Citation attained the summit, capping his comeback with two unprecedented achievements— he was now the fastest thoroughbred in the world, and the world's all-time greatest money winner!

Who could ask for anything more?

Besides, Brooks sensed Citation was a bit "ouchy" following his world-record mile. "I think his ankle was starting to hurt. Jimmy said, 'he'll get over it in a day or two.' But Cy had come back, and he could now go out a winner without question, if he liked."

Warren Wright, however, "didn't like." Now that Citation appeared more like his old self again, on the surface anyway, it was imperative that he again focus on becoming the sport's first thoroughbred millionaire. Unfortunately, Wright was ailing again, hardly realizing he had just six months of life remaining in his seventy-five-year-old body. But he wanted that million-dollar title. He shared that dream with wife Lucille; she became a willing cohort.

In the final analysis, most everyone acquiesced to Calumet's million-dollar quest for Citation; that is, except Noor. But then nobody asked Noor. And he was strong and healthy again, still on the improve, bent on adding to Calumet's misery and frustration.

"Cy was hurtin' slightly following his world-record mile," Brooks stated, "but within a week he seemed whole again. So Jimmy pointed him for the following week's Forty-Niners Handicap at 1⅛ miles on June 17. All this with no real break for racing's struggling iron horse.

"I loved being around Citation," Brooks said, ambivalently. "One day he seemed hale and hearty, the next a bit gimpy. If we all loved him in the right way, he'd be back on the farm, resting on his laurels. But it always seemed we had to get just one more race out of him. Worst thing of all, he never complained. Hurtin' or not, he'd prance and give his best. He was all heart. He had 'true grit,' horsemen would say."

Weights favored Cy for his Forty-Niners bout with Noor—128 to 123, Cy, of course, again top-weighted, but this time conceding only five pounds to his arch rival, a shift of eight pounds in his favor following their last meeting in the San Juan Capistrano.

Brooks, though "ridin' high" following the world-record Golden Gate Mile and expecting another superb effort from his amazing partner, harbored concerns about Cy's tender legs and sore ankles. "I honestly could feel he wasn't right physically. Sure, he had the all the smarts and his will to win, but his physical equipment wasn't all there. And he was being tested to the limit. In our last three starts we went from 1¼ miles, to six furlongs, then to one mile, and, now, 1⅛ miles. No sound horse was ever asked to do what he had to do—and he wasn't exactly sound, not by a long shot."

But Citation as always tried. He ran down the swift Roman In, to whom he was giving seventeen pounds, only to succumb to Noor's imperious late surge, losing by a neck in a photo—but again in world record time, 1⅛ miles in 1:46⅗! Cy's usual proud bowed-head canter after the race belied painful heartache, Brooks reasoned.

But the foolishness wasn't over yet. The media was shocked to learn that Cy and Noor would actually go at it again just one week later, this time at 1¼ miles in the Golden Gate Handicap. Brooks was nonplused; Eddie Arcaro in New York speechless. Informed fans everywhere were convinced that this time Calumet had finally gone "one race too far."

"Back in Chicago," Elmer Polzin recalled, "we thought Calumet Farm and the Jones boys—actually it really was Warren Wright's fault—had gone bonkers. They were racing Citation like there's no tomorrow. Fifty years later, they'd all be hauled off to jail."

Citation ran on pure guts and courage. Calumet's "magnificent cripple" had finally gotten a break in weights—Noor at 127 gave Cy one pound—nevertheless he would race that June 24, 1950, for the first time since his 1947 juvenile season, *not* as the favorite.

"Listen, the fans aren't dummies," said sportscaster Jack Drees. "They knew the score, that Citation, despite his record win in the Golden Gate Mile—and that was a tremendous race—he wasn't the old Citation, and that Noor, who was still improving, had his number. So they made Noor the favorite, and they were right, too."

On Trust carried his feathery 103-pound assignment to a long lead in the Golden Gate 'Cap, ripping off nifty fractions, with Citation and Brooks staying within range, some thirteen or fourteen lengths back. Steve admits he was keeping one eye on On Trust, the other on Noor, who was even farther back at the field headed for the final quarter mile.

The field passed the mile in a searing 1:34, On Trust still seven lengths ahead of Citation. Noor, meanwhile, was rolling, and he and Cy took up the chase in tandem. This time Citation "had nothing, no response, no kick at all," Steve all but cried afterward. Noor flashed on by, whipped Citation by three lengths, biggest margin by which he was ever beaten, but in world-record time of 1:58⅗, shaving 1⅗ seconds off Coaltown's prior speed mark.

"It was a devastating defeat," reported Chicago sports columnist Warren Brown, who attended Golden Gate that day. "Citation was just what Jimmy called him, 'a cripple.' And all his physical problems finally ganged up on him. It would be insane to race him again."

Calumet, Wright, and the Joneses had run out of options. They ceded his "physical tailspin," and sent him back to the farm, ruing their dumb mistake of not having done so following his world-record Golden Gate Mile triumph only three weeks earlier.

That did not mean, however, that Citation was retired for good. No way. Jimmy might have really considered it, but he hated the thought of Cy going out a loser. Brooks himself had mixed emotions; but not Warren Wright. The master of Calumet Farm, as sick as he was, still wanted that million-dollar mark.

Therefore, Cy went back to Lexington a physical mess, but not to the life of luxury he deserved.

Chapter Seventeen

"The Spirit Is Willing, But the Flesh Is Weak"

*M*ighty Cy had no voice in the matter, but like so many sports champions before and after he just couldn't make retirement stick.

Maybe it's the love of grease paint, or the limelight, or the crowd's roar—just one more bow. Or an inability to grapple with those pesky personal questions: If and when to retire? Have I stayed too long? Can I ever reclaim those glory days? Should I venture a comeback? How long to stay this time? And will I ever admit to an athlete's most feared enemy—age and the passage of time?

So many great ones tempted destiny and defied the ravages of declining skills: Babe Ruth, Joe Louis, Jim Thorpe, Magic Johnson, Muhammad Ali, Johnny Unitas, Sugar Ray Robinson, Jerry Rice, Gayle Sayers, George Foreman, George Blanda, Earl Sande, George Woolf, and, most recently, Michael Jordan. Great ones all, and for the most part they had certain things in common.

A few suffered embarrassment in comebacks, others serious injury. A few did enjoy a gratifying renaissance moment or two, even among those who never really wanted to call it quits; they simply didn't know when to hang up their cleats. Regardless, each remains a treasured "one of a kind" sports icon to this day. We salute, if not their good sense, definitely their heroism and indomitable spirit.

Citation fits in there someplace. Hard really to say, since he never spoke, and nobody ever asked him. And, unlike his human counterparts, who age slowly, as a horse Cy's aging was extremely rapid. Yes, horses have been known to live twenty-five years or more. Their best racing year, however, is age three; they're totally mature at four; they're past their prime at five; and they're on the decline by six. Of course, there are exceptions, mostly among geldings who have fewer distractions; for them there's no exciting "call of the stud barn."

Citation's first comeback had considerably diminished his 1947–48 record of twenty-seven wins and two seconds in twenty-nine starts. He went into his "second retirement" with twenty-nine wins and nine seconds in thirty-eight starts, never having finished worse than second, and earnings of $938,630. He still needed $61,370 to become racing's first equine millionaire.

His heart—and his human friends and connections—said *yes*. His body kept saying *no*.

"There was nothing wrong with his attitude or spirit," track manager Bob Henderson reported back to Ben Lindheimer following his regular fall visit to Calumet Farm in Lexington.

"If he could race on class and spirit alone," Henderson added, "nothing could have stopped him. But his body, especially those tendons and ankles, betrayed him. One vet there—and Cy had vets all over the place—said Cy might just make it back, but only if given time to heal completely. But time obviously was running out, if not already."

Moreover, Cy was hearing that distant "call of the stud barn." Not that he was becoming studish, though he couldn't be faulted for wondering, "What's going on over there in that barn with all those mares?" His hormones weren't boiling, but he was of age as a stallion, when any other horse of his stature would already have embarked on an eagerly awaited career as thoroughbred sire. He'd have to wait.

Citation's placid, businesslike mien made him the perfect patient; he just needed more time, time that Warren Wright knew was trickling inexorably like sand through his own personal hourglass. As the winter holidays approached, Wright, just like Citation, was but a shell of his former self.

Meantime, Cy's arch foe Noor kept winning in California, adding the American Handicap to his roster of conquests, this time without a tired Citation to kick around. Cy's people couldn't help but wonder whether vastly improved Noor simply loved California's pasteboard strips—which had helped do Cy in—or could also excel out East?

Noor failed to do what Citation did at his prime—win anywhere and everywhere. He ventured East with an array of starry triumphs in

California, particularly his heralded San Juan Capistrano photo victory over Citation in a race not soon to be forgotten.

Noor caught a cold after shipping to Belmont Park; he was idle for nearly two months. His first start on September 18, less than three months after his last win over Citation on June 24, found him losing to a hard-hitting son of Shut Out named One Hitter. Noor now knew first-hand what impact weight wielded—he carried 128 to One Hitter's 107.

Noor and One Hitter clashed again four days later in the 1½ miles Manhattan Handicap, which, weight notwithstanding, was tailor-made for Noor's affinity for distance. Lo and behold, One Hitter, this time carrying 110 to Noor's 128, won again. The margin of victory was only a neck, but somewhat revealing since Noor at one stage had actually overhauled One Hitter, simply unable to sustain his drive.

What happened next was a happy secret conversation between Eddie Arcaro and Steve Brooks. Eddie had forever given up Citation to Steve; they both were devastated by Citation's inability to dominate Noor over the "concrete-hard" racing surfaces at Santa Anita and Golden Gate Fields.

"Noor's a great one, but not that great," Arcaro told Brooks, "and, unlike Cy in his heyday, he's finding Belmont's slower going a little tough to handle. I think he's one of those 'horses for courses.' Watch what we do to him in the two-mile Jockey Club Gold Cup."

The "we" of which he spoke was the team of Eddie and eventual Horse of the Year and champion three-year-old Hill Prince; and that team rented the veil of invincibility Noor wore so proudly in his Eastern invasion. Hill Prince vanquished Noor by four lengths!

Noor's feelings were hurt, but he would gain more than a measure of revenge that winter when returned to the West Coast and his type of hard race course. He returned to his winning ways and remained a credit to his breed.

Citation's world at the farm of his birth continued unsettled. Word got around that Wright kept the pressure on, not to retire Cy to stud duty, but to "get on with him so he can come back" and break the million-dollar bank.

Bob Henderson's "inside" farm connections told of Cy's frustration, trying to regain racing trim while undergoing rehab as age six approached. "From what I heard," Henderson revealed, "he maintained his usual upbeat spirit, did what he was told, and seemed to get around pretty good when not unduly pushed.

"He flashed a couple good weeks in November of 1950," said Henderson, "and this buoyed up Wright's spirits, but then got a little gimpy again in mid-December; and they had to let up on his training."

Citation was feeling and looking much improved by the end of December when the unexpected occurred—Warren Wright, whose health had been on the wane for nearly a year, was felled by a massive heart attack. The man who two decades earlier had started and ran the world's greatest thoroughbred racing-breeding empire of all time died on December 28, 1950.

"Mr. Wright's death, while not totally unexpected, still came as a great shock to all of us, especially Mrs. Wright," said farm secretary Margaret Glass. "I suppose we all just thought he'd weather this storm like he did all the others."

According to Glass, Mr. Wright was buried in Chicago, and his widow, Lucille, "was named life tenant of the farm, which was held in trust by the Warren Wright Trust. She could run it, or she could sell it, but if she sold it, the proceeds were to go back into the trust."

Lucille Wright, perhaps in devotion and tribute to her late husband, chose to run it, which she did successfully until her death on July 24, 1982. For the record, Lucille Wright married Rear Admiral Gene Markey on September 27, 1952; they stayed together until his death on May 1, 1980.

Margaret Glass liked and enjoyed working for Lucille Wright, or, as she was later known, Mrs. Lucille Wright Markey, or Mrs. Gene Markey. "She was a kind, gentle woman, always gracious, occasionally generous, but a woman who, as the saying goes, liked 'to play it close to the vest.' Rather than making a practice of automatic pay raises for the help, she'd shower you with expensive gifts usually acquired abroad or in her travels. Let's just say she was 'frugal'—that's the best word I know to describe her."

In assuming the reins at Calumet, Lucille Wright's first and most pressing question was, "What to do with Citation?"

Dignity and a sense for the fitness of things among those people involved seemingly would dictate that the gallant champion be officially retired to stud duty. Understandably, Ben and Jimmy Jones hated for Citation to go out on a losing note. But his recent comeback, while ill-advised after a year's absence, did include a flash or two of his former greatness before slowed by injury.

Mrs. Wright answered "the Citation question" the only way she knew, the only way her late husband would have wanted: "We're going to make Citation racing's first millionaire horse. It was my husband's dream—and we'll see it through if at all possible."

Only really positive thing Jimmy Jones did "the second time around" for his aging warrior was "not to rush him, nor ask more of him in his races than he could deliver."

Brooks explained: "Jimmy told me not to use the whip, never to put him into an all-out drive, one that could make him overexert, to let him run on his own power without aggravating his sore tendon or tender ankle. If he could win, fine, if not, that's okay, too, as long as he stays sound.

"In a way it was sad. We were asking the greatest horse who ever lived, but who was no longer that same 'greatest horse,' to work and strive in public just to fulfill an old man's dying wish."

Back in Chicagotown, Wright's longtime friend, track magnate Ben Lindheimer, was somewhat miffed that Calumet hadn't saved Arlington or Washington Park as stamping ground for Citation's 1950 and 1951 comeback quests. When Lindheimer heard Cy was being primed for yet another return to the races, he all but begged Mrs. Wright and the Jones boys to hold off until July or August when the Windy City's summer season was in full force. He felt Chicago deserved the honor. Probably right, too.

Mrs. Wright dutifully deferred to Jimmy Jones as to when and where Cy would resume his quest to become racing's first millionaire.

Surprisingly, Cy—he had been away some ten months—was returned to the races at California's Bay Meadows on April 18, 1951, in an insignificant six furlongs sprint worth a paltry $3,250 in purse money.

"Apparently Calumet was going to nickel-and-dime Citation to that million-dollar mark," Jack Drees deplored.

"It was a disgrace what they were doing to Citation," Eddie Arcaro later shared with anyone who'd listen. Some argued he was still smarting over his fall-out with Citation when the horse needed him most.

"Not true," the noted rider replied. "Cy and I parted company for many reasons. But I loved that guy. He was the greatest horse as a three-year-old that I've ever seen or ridden. What they were asking him to do, and what they were doing to him was downright criminal."

Mighty Cy had never complained before; he wouldn't now. Obediently he took the track at Bay Meadows on April 18, two weeks or so before the

1951 Kentucky Derby, and unhappily proceeded to do what he had never done before—he finished third—finishing worse than second for the first time in his life!

"He actually raced fairly well," said jockey Steve Brooks, "and, like I was told, I never used him. We were fourth soon after the start, maybe six or seven lengths off the lead. We actually moved up a notch to third, maybe three lengths behind the leaders, A Lark and Pancho Supreme, a furlong out. Yes, he was third, but beaten just one length for it all. And he showed some punch near the end."

Running time, which often seemed overrated those years over California's infamously hard strips, again was headlined: this time a scintillating 1:09⅗ six furlongs by the winner, A Lark, just a tick off Bolero's track standard.

What bothered Mrs. Wright more than this latest episode in Cy's luckless "second" comeback—bad enough he failed to finish among the first two in thirty-nine starts—was that the winner, A Lark, who was owned at the time by Mrs. N. G. Phillips, actually had been bred by Calumet Farm. That was bitter wine indeed.

Brooks noticed a few differences in Citation between his five- and six-year-old attitudes. "He had smartened up a bit, like a wise old owl. I think he started to realize he no longer could do the things as a six-year-old that he had done when a youngster at three. He was so intelligent, he started to give himself some slack—he was still the most determined racehorse I've ever seen, but now he seemed to deliberately hold back a bit, so as not to strain or hurt himself for no good reason."

Jimmy also eased Cy's training schedule. "I didn't work him much between races. There was no reason to make it any tougher on him than it was. I felt he was starting to feel better physically, so rather than work him, we'd race him into shape."

A week later, therefore, Cy was back in action, again at six furlongs, again against his conquerors, A Lark and Pancho Supreme. Weight, like time, really wasn't a factor at that distance. Whereas Cy gave A Lark eleven pounds and was equally weighted at 120 with Pancho Supreme in their first encounter, this time Cy gave 'em both only two pounds, 120 to 118.

Again, the same result, at least for Cy. On April 26, he finished third for the second straight time, closing ground from fifth, beaten nearly three lengths. This time Pancho Supreme turned the tables on A Lark, defeating the latter by one length in identical time as in their first clash. So much for time and weight.

Jimmy Jones then informed Hollywood, "Here we come!" Hollywood Park was one of the few major tracks in the United States Citation had not raced over. Fact is, Hollywood Park in Los Angeles would be the thirteenth different track he'd compete at since his racing debut as a tender two-year-old at Havre de Grace in Maryland almost four years ago to the day.

And who would have "thot it"—Hollywood Park would prove Citation's lucky thirteenth! Hooray for Hollywood!

But not right off the bat. Two weeks after his second third-place finish at Bay Meadows, Cy was entered in the May 11 Hollywood Premiere 'Cap, another six furlongs dash. The Hollywood park handicapper treated Citation kindly, giving him only 120 against nine intrepid opponents, nine horses who no longer cowered at the very mention of the name Citation.

The 1951 Kentucky Derby was already history without help from Calumet. Count Turf, a long shot son of 1943 Triple Crown champ Count Fleet, and owned by New York restaurateur Jack Amiel, pummeled favorite Battle Morn (Arcaro up), the latter along with other fancied colts, including Repetoire and Mameluke, among the also-rans. Calumet, though reeling from Warren Wright's death, was far from dead in the water. The stable would come back with a vengeance in 1952.

Citation's comeback, however, occupied the nation's spotlight the spring and summer of 1951. Hope that the aging wonder horse would rebound in the Hollywood Premiere crashed at the outset. Citation was slammed hard at the break, knocked back to last, was still next-to-last turning for home. He had been virtually eliminated from contention.

"He recovered nicely with no real urging from me," Brooks exclaimed, "and he started picking up horses late, but the six furlongs was just too short to make amends."

And another inglorious first for Citation: he finished a strong fifth—beaten by less than three lengths—first time in his life he would ever finish out of the money! A horse named Special Touch won the race.

Thus, the dark cloud hovering over Cy's head was growing, if not bleaker and more ominous, surely thicker with gloom and frustration. Both Bewitch and Coaltown—Cy's same-age stablemates in days of yore—were back; their giant presence was a guarantee that Citation's quest to reach and surpass the million-dollar mark would be difficult at best, particularly if he were forced to race against them in upcoming stakes as in past seasons.

By now media practitioners everywhere were in accord—whether contemporaries like Joe Palmer, Red Smith, Arch Ward, Warren Brown, Jack Drees, Clem McCarthy, Elmer Polzin, Dave Feldman, Bill Boniface, Joe Kelly, Tom Gilcoyne, Dr. Alex Harthill, Charlie Hatton, J. J. Murphy, Joe Hirsch, Leon Rasmussen, or Kent Hollingsworth; or latter-day experts and observers like Tom Hammond, John McEvoy, Jim McKay, Haywood Hale Brown, Frank Wright, William Nack, or Jack Whitaker—Citation was *not* the Citation of old, nor would he ever be again. He just might reach the million mark if kept glued together, but it would take nothing short of a miracle for him to excel in big league stakes company, and, importantly, with dignity and head held high.

"That was a tall order," Brooks groaned, "especially to do so with head erect. He had just lost his third straight of the year, and though it was a promising fifth, it was still 'out of the money,' a real slap in the face for Big Cy."

But the "miracle" everybody thought virtually impossible was gathering. Citation again girded for battle, this time for Hollywood's May 30 Argonaut Handicap at the middle-distance of 1¹⁄₁₆ miles. As he paraded postward—head bowed, neck arched—he was still a mere shadow of his former self, but—voilà!—if you looked closely, the "shadow" was starting to take on shape and substance.

Chapter Eighteen

Greatness Revisited

$\mathcal{B}$y Memorial Day 1951 fabled Calumet Farm was in a state of flux with Citation smack-dab in the eye of the storm.

Warren Wright was dead. His widow was running the show. Ben and Jimmy were doing their usual yeoman best with the horseflesh given them. The stable's greatest stars—Citation, Coaltown, Bewitch, Two Lea, and Ponder—weren't getting any younger.

Calumet hadn't topped the owners' money-winning list since 1949, its fourth straight title and seventh in nine years—financial frosting on an incredible dynasty, perhaps the greatest in all sports.

Like any profit-motivated endeavor, racing included, when the blush of the rose fades, answers and solutions are sought, sometimes irrationally, oftentimes merely for the sake of change. Calumet Farm's many marriage and divorces with contract jockeys rivaled those of Mickey Rooney and Artie Shaw, not to mention Elizabeth Taylor.

When Steve Brooks and Calumet got together in 1949 there was no stopping the devil's red and blue express—Ponder, Coaltown, and Two Lea saw to that. Citation's heroic but somewhat lackluster comeback in 1950 wasn't enough to retain the stable's annual bloom of success.

Mrs. Dodge Sloane's Brookmeade Stable and Payson-Whitney's Greentree Stable would top the standings in 1950 and 1951, respectively, each with around $650,000 in earnings, half the usual gold Wright's Calumet Farm was expected to mine each season. Calumet was a close second each year, but the stable was unaccustomed to "second best" status.

George Steinbrenner years later would blame his New York Yankees managers. With Calumet the logical thing was to blame, then fire, or change, jockeys in an effort to stem the tide of failure and disappointment. Brooks all along was Warren Wright's and the Jones boys' choice, but not necessarily that of Wright's widow.

Lucille Wright was often seen in the company of husband-to-be Gene Markey throughout 1951. Though they wouldn't marry until September of 1952, he had her ear during those early formative months she ran Calumet following her husband's passing.

There were other outside influences, too, including Arlington-Washington executive director Ben Lindheimer. He was still mildly irritated Calumet chose California over his Illinois tracks for Citation's two comebacks in 1950 and 1951.

By the time Citation was being readied for the Memorial Day (1951) Argonaut 'Cap at Hollywood, Lindheimer was scheming up a rare Chicago racing bonanza for the following year.

"What was the greatest combination in all thoroughbred racing?" general manager Bob Henderson proffered with a grin. "The answer, of course, is Calumet in general, Citation in particular, with master jockey Eddie Arcaro. Ben [Lindheimer] wanted that more than anything else for 1952."

No one expected Citation to still be around in 1952 as a seven-year-old, but Calumet was enjoying another formidable 1951 two-year-old crop which conceivably could rival the 1947 array of Citation, Bewitch, Coaltown, and Free America.

In fact, the stable's two-year-old sensation of 1951 was another son of Bull Lea named Hill Gail, with whom Brooks won that summer's Arlington Futurity when Steve was still Calumet Farm's first-string rider.

Lindheimer's coup, which would ensure Calumet Farm's presence in 1952–53, centered upon securing the season-long riding services of Eddie Arcaro, convincing the great jockey that riding full-time at Arlington and Washington Parks would serve him well financially.

Though never confirmed, Lindheimer reportedly paid Arcaro an up-front $25,000 annual fee to ride at Arlington and Washington. Mrs. Wright loved the idea of again having Eddie Arcaro as Calumet's number one jockey.

For the record, Lindheimer's plan to reunite Calumet and Arcaro in 1952 was a resounding success. Fact is, 1952 was an even greater year in money won for Calumet than 1948, second only to its 1947 record high when two-year-olds Citation and Bewitch shared the limelight with Horse of the Year Armed.

Arcaro teamed up with Calumet's leggy speedster Hill Gail to capture yet another Kentucky Derby for the world's premiere racing and breeding empire. Ironically, the horse Hill Gail trimmed to win the 1952 Derby was Dixiana's Sub Fleet in rein to riding expatriate Steve Brooks.

And when Hill Gail went lame following the Derby, Calumet called in "one even better" from its deep bench, Mark-Ye-Well, who, teaming up with Eddie Arcaro per Lindheimer's cabal, proceeded to win both the Arlington Classic and American Derby that summer in Chicago.

Parenthetically, Eddie Arcaro's favorite all-time filly, Real Delight, also was unveiled in 1952. Yes, like Hill Gail, Real Delight was an offspring of Bull Lea, Citation's daddy. She won eleven of twelve that year, including what was then renowned as the Filly Triple Crown, comprising the Kentucky Oaks at Churchill Downs (day before Hill Gail's Derby score), the Black-Eyed Susan at Pimlico, and the Coaching Club American Oaks at Belmont.

Incredibly, Real Delight and Arcaro combined to win eight consecutive 1952 stakes, including a sweep of Chicago affairs—Cleopatra, Arlington Matron, Modesty, and Beverly Handicaps.

Sire Bull Lea was all smiles. Thanks to Real Delight, Hill Gail, and Mark-Ye-Well, he topped the nation in 1952 as leading sire for a fourth time, breaking his own record, his progeny, which included no fewer than eleven stakes winners, earning $1,630,655. Warren Wright would have been proud, perhaps a bit green with envy, of the job his widow, now Mrs. Gene Markey, had done.

Returning to Memorial Day, 1951, few observers entertained any hope or expectation that the 1 1/16 miles Argonaut at Hollywood Park was about to become the opening stanza to "The Citation Miracle!"

For Calumet in many ways the Argonaut was like "the good old days." Jimmy Jones fired a typical three-ply shot—aging six-year-olds Citation, Coaltown, and Bewitch. Still unsure and bewildered by Citation's three straight defeats—Brooks was the regular rider for all three starters—Jones turned Big Cy over to veteran jockey F. A. "Freddie" Smith, best-known as the rider of Bimelech, winner of both the 1940 Preakness and Belmont Stakes.

Jimmy sought yet another opinion as to what ailed Cy, as if the world didn't know. Stable opinion was that in view of Cy's recent losses to horses like A Lark, Pancho Supreme, and most recently Special Touch in the Hollywood Premiere, he certainly didn't figure to handle either Coaltown or Bewitch, both of whom were still pretty special.

Citation carried 121 in the Argonaut. Freddie Smith jumped at the privilege to ride racing's erstwhile "greatest thoroughbred of all time." As with Brooks before, Smith was told to "go easy" on the old guy, what with all his ailments.

"Smith told me Cy galloped postward 'sound as a bell, kickin' and whinnyin' like a two-year-old,'" Brooks recounted, "that 'he never took not even one bad step,' that as far as he knew there's nothing wrong with this horse, by the time they reached the starting gate."

Citation that day did everything right but win. "He even rested against the side of the stall, like I was told he used to do as a three-year-old," Smith told Brooks. In fact, Smith said the old veteran was acting pretty confident by the time the gate opened.

One of the Argonaut big guns, certainly the one to catch, was A. J. Crevolin's Be Fleet, already victorious that year in the San Juan Capistrano and the San Francisco Handicaps. He packed 118 to Citation's 121. "I think we could have caught Be Fleet if you had given me the okay to push Citation," Smith later informed Jimmy Jones.

Cy broke from the gate in midpack, was steadied for a stride or two before settling into fifth, about ten lengths off the leaders, as they moved up the backstretch. "I never asked him for more than he was giving me on his own," Smith confided in Brooks. "And he was running smoothly."

Suddenly, to everyone's surprise, Citation "fired!" He moved authoritatively, passing both Bewitch and Coaltown as if they were on a treadmill. Be Fleet, meanwhile, lanced to what appeared an insurmountable lead, bounded along nearly five lengths in front as the Argonaut field approached the eighth pole.

Cy rallied from fifth to second, his wide-eyed jockey merely hand-riding to the wire; Cy closed gamely, beaten three lengths in second by Be Fleet. Amazingly, Coaltown and Bewitch couldn't keep up, winding up among the also-rans. A "sturdy" campaigner named Sturdy One saved third behind Be Fleet and Citation.

Word spread like wildfire!

Mighty Cy was back! Well, if not totally back, at least close to it. His move was genuine, brimming with vitality and energy, straining at the bit, finishing "full of run," a striking departure from recent events in which he appeared to be favoring an aching leg or tender ankle.

Brooks wanted back on Citation. Jimmy gave him the nod. Maybe, just maybe, the old guy was starting to feel good again? He guardedly was "cooled out" following his strong Argonaut second. Both Ben and Jimmy were at his side. No once-over exam for Cy; stable vets scrutinized him head to foot. And he passed every test with flying colors. His eyes were crystal clear. Nary a hint of pain or distress.

Could it be? Were his physical ailments now a thing of the past? Dare anyone hope that Citation was getting good again?

"Could be possible," Jimmy Jones glowed, "but we can't get ahead of ourselves. This time we really have to take it easy, one step, one race at a time."

Chicago's Ben Lindheimer, with *Tribune* sports editor Arch Ward listening in, immediately phoned Jimmy Jones; first, to congratulate Citation on his vastly improved effort; second, to encourage and invite Calumet to include Arlington and Washington Park on its summer racing calendar. If Big Cy was truly "coming back," Chicago racing wanted him.

Both Jimmy and Ben promised Lindheimer they'd be in Chicago with Citation—assuming the horse was still race-worthy—as soon as Hollywood Park closed in late July. Ben personally outlined Cy's race schedule for Lindheimer: "We plan to keep his next few races about two weeks apart if we can. First, there's a $15,000 handicap at one mile on June 14. Second, the American Handicap at 1⅛ miles on July 4. Third, the Hollywood Gold Cup at 1¼ miles on July 14." The latter race especially fitted Cy's purpose—its winner was guaranteed $100,000, a good piece of change.

"If Cy can stay sound," Ben continued, "and if he starts to winning again, he should bust the million-dollar mark by the Hollywood Gold Cup—and second money is $20,000. If not, or if he does, and he's still sound, you'll see him at Arlington. That much I promise," Ben vowed.

Lindheimer as always took Ben on his word. Citation in Chicago was as sure as tomorrow, as long as the six-year-old stayed healthy.

By beating both Coaltown and Bewitch, Citation served notice that, at least for the Argonaut, he was "in the pink" again. His army of vets could only guess how much he was hurting that day, if at all.

"There was no heat in his legs or ankles," Jimmy stated for the media, "and that's always a good sign. Vets tell us that muscle, tendon, ligament— any kind of soft tissue injury—requires not only more time to heal than a hairline fracture or bone break, but is more painful, for humans anyhow. Well, they say, why not for horses, too?

"Our real concern was whether or not Cy's big race in the Argonaut was a true indicator? Or was it just a one-shot deal? Did we just catch him on a good day?"

Brooks sensed his days with Calumet were numbered. Racing logic demanded changes when a stable was in a slump. The rugged jockey had enjoyed phenomenal success in 1949 with Coaltown, Ponder, and Two Lea. His reputation, like that of Doug Dodson and Al Snider of the not-so-distant past, was made, and his skills would be in demand.

He just wanted to make parting amicable, not inimical as with Dodson the winter of 1948. Old man Wright was gone, and Gene Markey was hitting it off with Mrs. Wright. And he heard the unconfirmed rumor that Ben Lindheimer was plotting a return marriage between Calumet and Eddie Arcaro for next year. Like Eddie Arcaro, Brooks acknowledged it was time to widen out.

"The 'writing was on the wall,'" Steve realized, "but Jimmy gave Citation back to me, at least for the Hollywood Park meeting, and I kinda felt that maybe the two of us could go out in a blaze of glory together. I wanted only the best for him—how I loved that horse!"

Cy's next start was an overnight mile affair on June 14, the Century Handicap, latest in a series of preps pointing to the Hollywood Gold Cup. Again he was pitted against super-speedy Be Fleet. A weight shift was in order, since Be Fleet had beaten Citation by three lengths in the Argonaut while in receipt of three pounds. And there were many folks who felt Citation's strong second was freakish in nature, not all that genuine. Plus, the shorter one mile suited Be Fleet perfectly.

Not too surprisingly, Cy dropped one pound off his prior loss in the Argonaut, 120 from 121, while Be Fleet was asked to pick up five pounds, 123 from 118, a six-pound weight switch in Citation's favor due mainly to the shorter mile distance. Moreover, Be Fleet was riding the crest of a string of impressive stakes scores, and his connections confidently felt that their speedster had Citation's number.

Brooks conferred privately with Cy's regular exercise rider, Freeman McMillan. "I didn't ride him in the Argonaut," Brooks explained, "but Freddie Smith insists Cy raced brilliantly on his own courage, and showed no sign of trouble. How's he feelin' to you?"

McMillan replied candidly: "I honestly think he's okay again, I don't mean he's the colt he was in 1948. Heck, he's three years older, and spent a whole year on the farm with bad wheels.

"But—and I don't know if it's for real or if I'm just imagining it—he's galloping and breezing full-out, more smoothly than before, and he's not favoring his ankle. Maybe the damned thing's finally healed, but I'm still afraid to ask him for everything. He could easily injure that leg all over again. All I can say, Steve, is you have to go careful with him."

McMillan's word to the wise was sufficient.

Steve Brooks handled his comrade-in-arms with kid gloves. He recognized Be Fleet as legitimate, a quality foe no matter who was giving whom weight. He respected Sturdy One for his consistency. The one mile of the Century 'Cap was of no real concern; Cy already held the world record for the mile. Of genuine concern—not to punish or spur Cy unduly. Steve had to walk that thin line between honest effort and effort that would cause his friend to overexert and race beyond his present physical condition and capability.

The fans jammed the rail for a closer look at Citation as the horses walked, then jogged postward. Steve patted Cy's cocked neck, already damp with sweat, and whispered words only his mount could hear: "Take it easy, big fellow. It's only a mile. You've been twice that far before, so we've got nothing to worry about. But I'm not going to push you at all— let's just do it, easy does it, okay?"

Brooks later swore Citation understood. "At least that's the way he handled himself from the moment we were loaded into the gate. I figured to have one eye on Be Fleet, the other on Sturdy One. I also figured they'd be out there wingin', so we'd let them do it, but not for too long. Didn't want them to control the race. And if Cy was anything like he used to be, he'd kindly follow directions without balking. And guess what? That's just the way it went."

Two lengths behind Be Fleet and Sturdy One as they flew into the far turn, Citation, responding to Steve's command, gunned three deep to wrest command. It was a three-horse match race as Citation, Be Fleet, and Sturdy One straightened out for the run to the wire.

Steve sheathed his whip early; he'd only hand-ride Cy, who clung to a short but decisive half-length advantage. The riders aboard Be Fleet and Sturdy One were all out, as if waiting for Cy to crack.

"That was one helluva race," Ben Jones told Ben Lindheimer that evening by phone. "The three of 'em remained within a length of each other right to the wire, and it was right there, at the wire, that Big Cy looked like he was ready to skip clear."

Citation won it by that same half-length margin he enjoyed a furlong out; Be Fleet was second, less than a length ahead of Sturdy One in 1:35⅘ for the mile. The drought was broken—Cy was back where he belonged, the Winner's Circle, his first win after four losses in 1951, and his first in six tries since he broke the world record for the mile at Golden Gate Fields almost a year ago to the week.

Hollywood Park racing fans enthusiastically showered Mighty Cy with a joyful shout reserved only for bona fide heroes. Some had prematurely given up on the grand champion; most, however, were unabashed in their jubilation, a show of sweet delirium; cheers, perhaps a few tears, of exultation, as if justice had finally triumphed.

Only Calumet and its people held back ever so slightly, tranquilizing the moment of high glee, tempering its ecstasy, reserving final judgment until positive Cy had emerged unscathed. Only if he came out of the race in fine fettle, unruffled and uninjured, only then would merriment be allowed.

Cy wasn't even breathing hard. And he jogged back to the Winner's Circle without a hitch in stride, not a hint of a limp. The Jones boys scrutinized him perfunctorily; the horse's real head-to-toe inspection would come later at the barn.

At exactly eight that evening, Citation was pronounced A-OK!

Now everybody could celebrate. Citation had returned to his winning ways, did so in a major overnight handicap, had taken a giant step closer to that coveted million-dollar mark. No damage either.

"I told you so," McMillan festively punched Steve Brooks's arm to commemorate the occasion. "He's back, and if he is, take it from me, this is just the beginning!"

"I can't help it, Freeman," Brooks responded, "but I just gotta wait until he gets on the track tomorrow or the next day. I want to believe it, sure, but how come, all of a sudden, how come he's feelin' good again?"

"Hey," McMillan sucked on a beer, "he was bound to heal. We just never gave him enough time before. I'm telling you—if not now, he'll be his old self again, you'll see, and soon!"

July 4 seemed the perfect time for all of Calumet to celebrate. The race of the day in California—it was the Stars & Stripes in Chicago, the same race Cy won over older horses as a three-year-old three years earlier—was the American Handicap, final tune-up for the Hollywood Gold Cup.

Coincidentally, that July 4, 1951, the same day Citation would seek his second straight comeback victory in the American Handicap, Cy's former jockey, Eddie Arcaro, would ride Royal Governor to a popular victory in the Stars & Stripes, now a grass fixture, at Arlington Park, which track anxiously awaited news of Cy's performance in California.

Citation would start with Bewitch as entrymate—Citation duly honored with second top weight of 123 pounds—Moonrush got 125—his girlfriend Bewitch allowed a feathery 106. And Be Fleet took on the challenge of added distance—1⅛ miles—with 122 on his back. Sturdy One shouldered 112.

Citation was packing weight again, sure sign the word was out—"the great one" was back!

A "sound-again" Citation guaranteed he'd become the first thoroughbred in racing history to break the coveted million-dollar mark. "At the moment," Jimmy Jones recalled, "becoming the game's first millionaire seemed like a big thing, and to achieve it was worth what we were putting Cy through. Now we know, a million was a piddling compared to the inflation of the coming decade, and in years to come."

Jimmy later compared it to breaking the four-minute mile, or the guy pitching baseball's first no-hitter—sports comparisons were limitless—with the feat often forgotten with the passage of time. It's the athlete's overall class, of which Cy had plenty to burn, that immortalizes the performer, not money won, especially in a sport where purses tend to spiral upward as the dollar devaluates and inflation skyrockets.

Case in point—the present-day annual Breeders' Cup Thoroughbred Championship Series, in which the cheapest winning pot is $600,000 for one race, on up to between two and three million going to the Classic winner. A horse winning one big race in some Arab land can easily "triple" what would take Citation thirty-two winning races to achieve!

But in 1951 hope that Citation would become the sport's first millionaire was colossal news. More significantly, Cy appeared capable of doing it with panache, taking on major league competition in blue ribbon stakes, in the style to which he was accustomed.

The Fourth of July holiday greeted Citation with a smile. The aptly named American Handicap was the perfect springboard to the lucrative Hollywood Gold Cup ten days hence. The plant was jammed with horse-lovers, and Citation was their choice, both sentimentally and at the betting windows.

Realizing this race could very easily be his last, what with his age and physical equipment riding on his every stride, media coverage doubled. Even with victory—and that was no sure thing—could not this be his farewell, depending upon how he endured the 1⅛ miles challenge?

Cy endured just fine. Sporting his old verve and focus, he bided his time early. Brooks handled him cautiously, but not as cautiously as before. "I just felt he was no longer hurting," Steve was all smiles afterward. "His stride was more sure, almost effortless, like he was when I rode him when he was only a two-year-old.

"We moved into fifth after the first quarter, maybe five lengths off the lead, and I felt he could blast off whenever I asked."

Steve had to ask Cy for speed as the field bunched up around the last turn. Be Fleet unaccountably retreated, but Sturdy One was pushing unusually hard. Bewitch also was in a running mood, so to avoid traffic congestion, Steve urged Cy to take command inside the final eighth.

From that point to the wire, Citation was in front, first a head, then a neck, then by a half-length as Bewitch, discovering new courage and relishing the added distance, tried to make a race of it.

"Not today," Brooks chortled, "nobody beats Cy today, and maybe never again!"

Citation stuck gamely to his task, beating Bewitch by that same half-length margin, giving her seventeen pounds. Sturdy One was another three lengths back in third. Be Fleet threw in a clunker, was unplaced.

Hollywood Park came alive, aglow with the spirit of Citation's second straight victory. The whole sports world took note: for the first time since December of 1948, Cy had won two races in a row. His reputation reaffirmed, his prowess restored despite age, he now was within $15,000 of becoming thoroughbred racing's first equine millionaire.

And he was getting better with each race. Just like the good old days!

Chapter Nineteen

Citation's Last Goodbye

C itation was a mite tired following the American Handicap.

"That's good," Jimmy Jones approved, "it'll make him even fitter for the Gold Cup. Pretty soon, and I'm betting on it, he'll be as good as new—all the signs are there."

Jimmy said it, but dare he believe it? Was Citation really "getting good again"? Two straight wins was nothing to sneeze at. Many great horses even in their prime often failed to notch back-to-back major wins, so he was progressing; and his achievement was doubly impressive since he showed no signs of injury or lethargy.

Only way to accurately judge Cy's condition was to race him. If he actually "was back," then he'd do what he used to do naturally—he'd keep on winning, which meant the $100,000 Hollywood Gold Cup, and the crown of racing's first thoroughbred millionaire.

Citation's money quest overshadowed most everything else in American thoroughbred racing. Count Turf, ridden by former Calumet Farm reinsman Conn McCreary, had won the Kentucky Derby; Brookmeade Stable's lightninglike Bold spread-eagled his field to score an easy seven-length victory in the Preakness under Cy's former rider, Eddie Arcaro; C. V. Whitney's Counterpoint, Dave Gorman up, who finished eleventh in the twenty-horse Derby field and second in the Preakness, scintillated with a four-length victory in the Belmont Stakes and eventual selection as 1951 Horse of the Year.

Most media attention, however, was riveted on Citation's Hollywood Gold Cup, and, win or lose, what his plans would be after that. Remember, Ben Jones promised Ben Lindheimer Cy would return to Chicago's Arlington Park come what may.

The Gold Cup followed the American Handicap by exactly ten days, more than enough time now that Citation again was perky, spry, sound, and apparently pain-free. McMillan informed Brooks that "Cy's even stronger than before he won the American 'Cap. He's closer to his old self now than he's ever been the past two years."

The Joneses reminded Mrs. Wright that Citation would reach the million-dollar mark even if he finished second. All three, however, subscribed to Joe Palmer's 1948 assessment of Citation either "barely winning or barely losing" the Belmont Stakes as "unsatisfactory"; they applied that same analogy to Cy's current quest—hitting the million mark with a second-place finish was "unacceptable." He had to win; "second" wouldn't do.

Jimmy Jones apprised Mrs. Wright that were it true—that Citation was again approaching the Citation of old—he should be given the chance to atone for "all those races he should never have lost" the past two season when but a shell of himself. And that Chicago and New York would lovingly welcome Big Cy at a moment's notice.

She liked the idea, said she'd think it over, but not until Citation won the Hollywood Gold Cup.

Jimmy Jones and Steve Brooks quietly concurred on Gold Cup eve that they'd "let Citation run his race, not full-out, but give him his head to win with authority, let the world know he's getting good again, and make 'em all beg to want to see more."

The media swarmed all over Hollywood Park. The press box was jammed with writers and photographers from every major sector of the country. Once unthinkable, the fact that Cy might be crowned the sport's first equine millionaire was headline news.

"And no horse—not Man o'War, Equipoise, Seabiscuit, Phar Lap, Whirlaway, or Count Fleet—deserved and warranted that honor more than Mighty Cy," said Chicago sports authority Elmer Polzin, adding: "It's only fitting that the best horse who ever lived should be the first to break the million-dollar barrier!"

Never the showman, Citation nevertheless on July 14 put his talents on display in a performance which would have made Man o'War and

Secretariat proud, and would have drawn rave reviews from the likes of Kelso, Spectacular Bid, Seattle Slew, Affirmed, Cigar, even Point Given.

Of course, he was on stage at Hollywood Park, whose proximity if by name only assured an aura of ostentation and glitter. To say the dark bay six-year-old got caught up in Hollywood's showy spotlight was the understatement of the year.

The script seemed already written—an exciting, glamorous, and dramatic climax—cinema's wonderland of fulfilled dreams, and its handsome hero, brimming with machismo and derring-do, dressed to steal the show before the final curtain.

The weights for the Gold Cup were assigned earlier in the season. Citation packed 120 to Be Fleet's 122. Again, Cy's favorite female running mate was Bewitch, lightly rigged at 108, and less than $20,000 shy of becoming the world's leading money-winner of her sex.

It didn't take an Einstein to calculate that if Citation and Bewitch could pull off one of their patented 1-2 finishes, they'd reign unopposed as the world's richest male and female thoroughbreds of all time. Steve Brooks knew it; so did jockey Glenn Lasswell, signed to pilot Bewitch.

The Gold Cup marked Cy's forty-fifth lifetime start, and, should he triumph, his thirty-second victory and twenty-second stakes score. Victory would vault him well over the million-dollar mark—$1,085,760 to be exact—a "one in a million" achievement.

Lasswell on Bewitch conferred with Steve Brooks prior to the race. Last thing he wanted to do was upstage Citation, if such a feat were possible.

"Needn't worry," Brooks mollified, "Bewitch couldn't beat Cy on his worst day, and today, well, he's gonna be at his best, at least as best as he can be under the hell we've put him through."

Attendance at Hollywood Park had increased proportionally for each of Citation's appearances during his five-race stand, which started May 11 with that close-up fifth in the Hollywood Premiere Handicap, first time he ever finished out of the money. Interest swelled in subsequent starts, particularly his two recent victories—the June 14 Century 'Cap and the holiday fireworks surrounding his Fourth of July triumph in the American Handicap.

Racing fans were wild in jubilant anticipation of history in the making. 'Twas a real shame the event couldn't be shown on nationwide television. But pioneer television moguls weren't dim-witted; they took note of

Citation's magnetism and the national press coverage his million-dollar quest generated.

One year later, 1952, would mark the first year the Kentucky Derby was broadcast to a major television market, chronicling Calumet's Hill Gail victory with Eddie Arcaro nailing his fifth Derby win; the following year, 1953, the entire Triple Crown was so honored, making Native Dancer a household name and racing's first television matinee idol. Even the slowest thinking mind could appreciate the sporting interest Citation would have commanded were television coverage available to the masses.

With or without television, July 14 was perfect in every respect. The sun was bright and warm and the track was fast. Ten horses paraded postward, but the crowd only had eyes for one, reserving a deafening ovation for a six-year-old stallion whose courage under fire had already achieved legendary status.

Railbirds lined the fence with cheers and tears of genuine devotion. And Citation returned their affection in kind the only way he knew— neck proudly arched and head regally bowed—in what many felt might be a mutual farewell to the greatest love affair between man and animal to that time. Cy was Secretariat without television.

"For Citation not to win, and not win big, would be criminal, an insult to the greatest moments in sports history," said Chicago race-sports announcer Jack Drees. "He just had to come through."

"No need to spare the horses today," Jimmy Jones said moments earlier when he hoisted Steve Brooks into the saddle. "Today's his day, and if it's to be his last, give him his head, let him make it special!"

Steve smiled, said nothing, merely patted Citation's neck, and with a tender brushing motion smoothed out the hair atop Cy's handsome head. Citation never looked more resplendent.

"Hey, Big Cy, you look like a million bucks," one fan shouted as horse and rider left their stall. Others chimed in: "Yeah, you look like a million!" One cheered: "Cy, you're worth two million!"

History—much of it dimmed by years of time—was made in spectacular fashion that day. The horse with the mammoth heart, and the speed, stamina, and class to match, left nothing to chance. He sprang from the gate fourth in the field of ten, then drilled along the rail into third following the opening quarter in the 1¼ miles test.

Be Fleet was quick afoot as usual, sprinting clear early. Cy was three lengths back in third settling up the backstretch, but pulling on the bit.

"Ah, the heck with it," Steve said aloud, "no reason to wait, go get 'em, big guy!"

Citation took off like a shot, leaving Be Fleet in his wake. Ears pricking, head held high, and eyes forward, Cy never looked back. He was racing's Iron Horse all over again. Maybe not the colt he was as the 1948 three-year-old who single-handedly galvanized the world of thoroughbred racing—but close enough!

Striding clear with speed to burn, Citation carried Steve Brooks to an electrifying four-length victory in 2:01 flat, and, with hooves flashing, ran into racing history!

He literally waltzed back to the Winner's Circle, showing off, as it were, with that proud, trademark neck-arched prance a true racing fan would almost "kill" for. He was back—this no one could deny—and he was back, whole-hearted, whole-souled, and whole-bodied.

"He may not be Citation of three years ago," Jimmy verified, "but he's getting good again—watch out world!"

And the world was indeed watching. Especially Chicago and Ben Lindheimer's Arlington-Washington combine, Calumet's annual summer home away from home. Also, the rest of the world's racing community— all eyes glued on Citation and what he'd do next.

Incidentally, Bewitch did manage to garner second money on the heels of an explosive stretch charge that nipped Be Fleet at the wire in the Gold Cup. She was a distant second—Citation was "home free" like the Citation of old—but the $20,000 she banked hiked her career earnings to $462,605 to reign as the richest thoroughbred filly or mare of all time. Victory and success all around.

Citation cooled out perfectly. No sign of pain, nary a bad step, sound as a bell—finally. Thanks to three straight major wins, Cy's record was forty-five starts, thirty-two wins, ten seconds, two thirds, once unplaced, and a world-record shattering bankroll of $1,085,760.

"It's not what it should have been." Jimmy chose his words carefully. "Twenty-seven wins and two seconds in twenty-nine starts, or twenty-nine straight if we knew what we were doing, would have been a whole lot better, but it's a great achievement for a six-year-old cripple who never knew the meaning of the word 'quit.'"

Mrs. Wright and Calumet were deluged with congratulatory notes, calls, and effusive handshakes. The long-awaited celebration seemed endless. Sad he wasn't directly involved in the festivity and tasteful revelry of

Citation's grand feat, Eddie Arcaro respectfully called Mrs. Wright and the Jones boys with proper and sincere expression of pleasure and delight. The Master also rejoiced, albeit long-distance, with Steve Brooks.

"You stuck with Cy, Steve," Arcaro praised, "and you deserve big credit. I'm proud of you, the both of you."

Brooks thanked Eddie, adding: "The privilege was all mine, he's the greatest horse I've ever seen or ridden. I could only imagine what he was like when you rode him at his best. My only concern right now is, where do we go from here?"

"That's up to the boss, or bosses," Arcaro replied, "who probably will be Jimmy or Ben Jones now that the old man is dead. For my part, I'd like to see him go out on top. Just a shame they put him through all those unnecessary races these past two seasons."

Brooks agreed, but reluctantly. He had just recently tasted what "the real Citation" was like, and he would have liked to treat his palate one last time, maybe even a time or two more.

California would have loved to keep Citation there; but Chicago also was calling. New York also expressed interest in the sport's first millionaire and the sports-page following he elicited.

"The Calumet board of directors, those in charge of racing strategy, put their heads together," Margaret Glass recalled with a smile, "but, instead, they bumped heads, as if caught between the devil and the deep blue sea. Both choices had drawbacks."

If Mrs. Wright and the Jones boys kept Citation in training there'd always be a chance for injury or mishap. To retire him now would deprive racing of its most cherished icon. What to do?

"I wanted to run him again," was Jimmy's vote. "He was just getting good, and I could see him improving with every start from then on in. Besides, we promised Arlington we'd be on our way to Chicago."

Ben gave his son's choice tacit approval. Jockey Steve Brooks said he would do whatever was best for Cy; in his heart, however, he'd love to ride Citation—"just one more time."

Mrs. Wright, of course, was not only "the court of last resort," but judge and jury as well. She opted for retirement, offering only this terse explanation: "Because that's the way Mr. Wright would have wanted it."

With those words, the racing bridle was removed for the third and final time from Citation's head; his racing shoes were hung up for good. There was no rebuttal from the Joneses; nor would any have prevailed. Now that it was over, it was over!

Well, not quite.

California and Hollywood Park had no quarrel with Mrs. Wright's decision to retire her superstar. His presence and amazing series of comeback victories had served the track and industry well. But all hell broke loose in Chicago at Ben Lindheimer's Arlington Park. The commotion flared, but only privately between Calumet and the Chicago tracks' majordomo.

Jack Drees was privy to the turmoil swirling behind the scenes. As forceful and intractable as Lindheimer could be, he relented, acknowledging Citation's retirement as "the wise choice."

But he sought—as did Mrs. Wright and Ben and Jimmy Jones—some suitable compromise to soften Chicago's disappointment, which, under the circumstances, seemed like the fair thing to do.

"How 'bout a Chicago farewell appearance?" Ben Jones volunteered. "We'll have Citation under tack gallop before the fans at Arlington Park in a final salute before he goes on to stud duty at the farm in Lexington."

Ben Lindheimer loved the idea. "We'll stage it on a Saturday and Arlington will make it an appearance fans will never forget."

So it was—but not until Calumet sneaked in a furtive "final Citation gallop" at Hollywood Park—that the magnificent stallion, not yet totally unwound from racing trim, bowed out before cheering thousands at Arlington Park in late July 1951.

Oh, yes, there was one other slightly controversial wrinkle which required ironing out before Cy said his last goodbye. Who would ride him?

Al Snider was dead, and Doug Dodson was out of the question. Eddie Arcaro, who teamed up with Citation to make unforgettable history during the colt's three-year-old glamour season, was the first choice. But what about Steve Brooks, who rode him in twelve of his last sixteen starts, including his last three wins, capped by the Hollywood Gold Cup?

Decisions, decisions.

A politically correct compromise was struck. Brooks would still be riding for Calumet that summer and fall. Arcaro would be returning as "first-call" rider for Mrs. Wright—who would by then be Mrs. Gene Markey—in 1952. No need to make matters worse.

Thus, regular exercise rider Freeman McMillan got the nod, unanimously. Everyone was happy; and Freeman was ecstatic, singularly honored. He would don the devil's red and blue in Arlington's picturesque outdoor paddock where horses were saddled under huge trees bearing their saddle-cloth number, then stroll through the tunnel under the stands, emerging in full view of thousands of cheering fans, and proceed to gallop to the top of the stretch, then turn and gallop to the Winner's Circle where he last appeared following victory in the Stars & Stripes Handicap on July 5, 1948.

Frank Ashley was Arlington's regular track announcer, no Orson Welles he, but a southern gentleman who called a pretty good horse race. But on special occasions as this, public relations consultant and radio race announcer Jack Drees was called upon to address the huge throng in bidding adieu to Mighty Cy.

One might call that afternoon Citation's "fifteen minutes of fame"— that's about how long the ceremony lasted. But the bay stallion already had gloried in racing's spotlight for some four years, ever since his first start and victory at Havre de Grace in Maryland on April 22, 1947.

Everything Drees said over the public address system had been said before: a recounting of Cy's matchless career, especially his three-year-old campaign, in which he won nineteen of twenty, including the Triple Crown, his earlier two wins in Florida over older horses, plus five more against elders, punctuated by his walkover in the Pimlico Special.

Drees then recalled Citation's comeback as a five-year-old after missing his 1949 four-year-old season, his courage in spite of injury, and, of course, most of all, his heroic determination in the face of repeated adversity.

Even an adept wordsmith like Drees could not do justice to the aura of love and affection that radiated throughout Arlington that afternoon. The applause was constant, at times deafening. Fans everywhere were on their feet hailing the sport's all-time conquering hero.

One had to be there, and, if you were so privileged, branded in your mind and heart for all time was that last-time familiar scene—this gallant, muscular dark bay stallion galloping up and down the homestretch, neck arched and head bowed, graciously accepting admiration from all his fans and friends, an adoration earned by no thoroughbred before or since. "Race, Cy, just one more time!" would be their cry.

The debate over whether Citation was the sport's greatest equine continues unabated to this day, skewed somewhat by the passage of time, dimmed by the truism that because of passing years, "the memory of them is soon forgotten."

Ed Schuyler Jr. of Associated Press, in a television appearance on an ESPN-TV special saluting Citation's legendary greatness as the new millennium dawned, put it in proper perspective: "When someone says Citation might have been the greatest horse that ever lived, they have a legitimate argument—he (just) might have been the 'greatest horse who ever lived!'"

Amen to that.

Epilogue

$\mathcal{L}$est we forget, though denied the right to go out sooner as undisputed champion, Citation still went out as a hero—he was named in one poll as 1951 Handicap Horse of the Year off his Hollywood season. Had he not retired, who knows what other fame he might have achieved?

And the noblest of all thoroughbreds wasn't half bad as a sire either. Knowledgeable horsemen predicted that "the greatest horse who ever lived" would find it impossible "reproducing himself." Like so many great ones past and present, he was one of a kind, "his own kind," but he still took pride in producing a bevy of outstanding thoroughbreds as a sire.

Big Cy's first foals raced in 1955 as two-year-olds. Included among them was a swift youngster called Fabius, who, just like the Roman general for whom he was named, "loved a fight." Fabius was a classic winner just like his daddy, might even have won a Triple Crown if it weren't for a stretch-flyer named Needles, who, incidentally, just happened to be a son of Calumet Farm's late-kick champion Ponder.

Keeping it "all in the family," so to speak, Needles caught Fabius at the shadow of the wire to win the 1956 Kentucky Derby. Citation's favorite son, however, trimmed Needles by two lengths in the Preakness Stakes. Needles came back to win the Belmont; Fabius was a close-up third. Fabius banked $331,384, later becoming a fairly productive sire on his own.

Another of Cy's finest progeny was the 1959 three-year-old filly champion in two of three polls, Silver Spoon. She whipped colts, including eventual Preakness winner Royal Orbit, in the Santa Anita Derby, later was a strong fifth behind Tomy Lee and Sword Dancer in the Kentucky Derby. In 1978, she was inducted into the National Museum of Racing Hall of Fame at Saratoga.

There she joined five other Calumet Farm greats—Whirlaway, Armed, Bewitch, Twilight Tear, and her own daddy himself, Citation. Like father, like daughter. A very classy collection of horseflesh.

And Cy had other $100,000 winners among his offspring, including Get Around, Guadalcanal, and Manteau, each of whom enjoyed success at stud. And the win percentage of Citation's sons and daughters remained impressive.

While Citation luxuriated at the farm where he first saw the light of day, while he "made love," ate, drank, and frolicked like the king he was, things were happening fast and furious in the world of thoroughbred racing.

Bull Lea had his second Kentucky Derby winner in 1952 when Calumet Farm's Hill Gail, Eddie Arcaro up, whipped Dixiana's Sub Fleet, ridden by Steve Brooks, by two lengths. Hill Gail wasn't as sound as his paternal half brother Citation, wound up on the shelf, bypassing both the Preakness and Belmont, though both races bore some kinship to Calumet—Conn McCreary, he of Pensive fame, rode Blue Man to victory in the Preakness, while Arcaro switched over to guide One Count home on top in the Belmont.

And before season's end, Ben and Jimmy Jones pulled from their hat more than just an able three-year-old replacement: he was another of Bull Lea's fabulous sons, Mark-Ye-Well, who sparkled all summer and fall, winning both the Arlington Classic and American Derby for Chicago's Ben Lindheimer, later annexed New York's Lawrence Realization, adding $286,745 to Mrs. Wright's coffers, helping Calumet rack up its fourth million-dollar season and eighth financial title. Mark-Ye-Well raced brilliantly as a four-year-old, winning both the rich Maturity and Handicap at Santa Anita, eventually retiring with earnings of $581,910.

And incredible Bull Lea continued to scintillate. The world's finest sire won his fourth crown, breaking his own record as his progeny earned $1,630,655 in 1952 alone.

And yes, Lindheimer succeeded in pulling off the racing coup of the 1950s—Eddie Arcaro had become Calumet Farm's first-string jockey, particularly in 1952; together they seemingly won everything in sight, especially at Arlington and Washington Parks in Chicago.

Not only were Mark-Ye-Well and Hill Gail two of the nation's top three-year-olds—the third was Mrs. Walter M. Jeffords' One Count, regularly ridden by Arcaro—but Real Delight, the undisputed three-year-old queen of American filly and mare racing, also was a daughter of Bull Lea. Eddie Arcaro was a regular rider for all the above.

"In the space of four or five years, I had the pleasure to ride two of the greatest horses of all time," Arcaro would later relate. "In Citation I rode the greatest horse who ever lived, and that was as a 1948 three-year-old. And Real Delight—and I won eleven races with her in 1952, including eight stakes in a row—she was the finest filly I've ever ridden. Just like Cy, Real Delight would clobber older horses—she whipped the best older fillies and mares around in 1952."

So awesome was the Arcaro-Calumet combine the year after Citation retired, Eddie's mounts earned an all-time record $1,859,591, of which Mrs. Lucille Wright Markey's Calumet Farm banked $1,283,197.

During those memorable days of wine and roses, at one stage during the summer of 1952, Arcaro, riding both Mark-Ye-Well and Real Delight, won seven of nine Saturday stakes at Arlington and Washington. Citation, of course, had retired; otherwise, imagine what he might have accomplished in the handicap division with all those additional greenbacks just for the taking. Calumet would have broken the bank.

In 1957, one year following's Fabius's hard-luck loss to Needles in the Kentucky Derby, Cy's daddy, Bull Lea, sired an unprecedented *third* Derby winner—Iron Liege, ridden by the stable's newest contract rider, the fiery, indomitable Bill Hartack.

Other thoroughbred greats emerged in the 1950s and 1960s—Tom Fool and Native Dancer in 1953–54; Nashua and Swaps in 1955; Needles, Fabius, and Swoon's Son in 1956; Bold Ruler, Gallant Man, Round Table, Iron Liege, and Gen. Duke in 1957; and Calumet Farm's 1958 Kentucky Derby–Preakness star Tim Tam, a son of Tom Fool.

The 1960s unveiled five-time Horse of the Year Kelso; also Carry Back, Northern Dancer, Tom Rolfe, Buckpasser, Dr. Fager, Arts and Letters, Damascus; also Calumet's last Derby hero, Forward Pass, who several years later was awarded first money in the 1968 Derby when the winner Dancer's Image was disqualified for using a then-illegal pain-killing drug. It was Calumet Farm's record eighth winner of the Run for the Roses.

But in all of the above, did you detect that one unforgivable "sin of omission"?

Yes, through it all, no horse was good, or great, enough to win the Triple Crown. And no three-year-old would sweep the Kentucky Derby, Preakness, and Belmont Stakes while Mighty Cy lived and breathed.

Jimmy Jones called it "poetic justice," that as long as Big Cy walked this planet, no horse was "great enough" to follow in his hoofprints. "And there were some mighty fine colts around in the decades following his Triple Crown—just not great enough to turn the trick, that's all." And no one won sixteen straight races either.

The Triple Crown drought enhanced Citation's legend. If one believed such things, it seemed only providential that no horse would equal his feat while he lived. Oh, inflation and the proliferation of racing made his million-dollar mark inconsequential, but not the manner in which he accomplished it, nor his fabled durability.

While Cy reveled in his past glories as a sire in Kentucky, those who actually saw both him and Man o'War were slowly fading from the scene, as were those who were privileged to see Citation during his 1947–48 heyday, also his courageous comebacks in 1950–51.

By the time the great Secretariat exploded as the ninth Triple Crown champion in 1973—and first in twenty-five years since Mighty Cy— many of the renowned media turf writers, sports columnists, and radio commentators who had witnessed firsthand Citation's matchless talents were also gone.

The few who remained, those privileged to have seen both Citation and Secretariat do their thing, knew and recognized the thin line between the "fastest" and the "greatest" three-year-old horse of all time. Unless those who were mesmerized by Secretariat's greatness were also old enough to have seen Big Cy in person, no just comparison was possible.

Again, it's the difference of opinion that makes horse racing.

Ben Jones retired from active duty as Calumet's Racing Stable General Manager in 1960. At one of many visits with the also aging Citation, Ben marveled at the stallion's "high spirits. He was still hale and hearty, still looked like he could take to the track at the drop of a hat—and beat 'em all!"

Ben Jones died in June 1961. Son Jimmy was by himself; he retired as trainer three years later, became an executive of Monmouth Race Track, from which he also since retired. Jimmy was ninety-four when he passed away in September 2001.

Other Calumet trainers came and went—George T. Poole II, Henry Forrest, Frank Bonsal, Reggie Cornell, the latter succeeded by the youngest of all Calumet trainers, John M. Veitch, at age 30, in 1976.

In 1977, Arlington Park celebrated its fiftieth anniversary by opening the Arlington Park Hall of Fame, which included four Calumet equines—Citation, Twilight Tear, Armed, and Coaltown—and the fa-ther-son duo of Ben and Jimmy Jones as one of four honored trainers, and Calumet Farm as one of three stables. Jockey Eddie Arcaro, of course, headed the track's Hall of Fame jockey colony.

In 1981, the *Daily Racing Form* released its Twentieth Century Equine Hall of Fame, listing the fourteen greatest thoroughbreds of all time. Curiously, because the greatest horses of all time were announced in al-phabetical order, it was only proper that Citation topped the roster—fol-lowed by Colin, Count Fleet, Equipoise, Exterminator, Forego, Kelso, Man o'War, Nashua, Native Dancer, Secretariat, Swaps, Sysonby, and Tom Fool.

Sadly, Citation's "girlfriend" Bewitch was barren except for one foal, a filly, named Quizzical, by old friend Ponder. The baby was injured before she could race. Bewitch, once the world's leading money-winning mare, died September 12, 1962.

The 1947 Horse of the Year and the gelding who helped spotlight Citation's early three-year-old career, the hard-knocking Armed, died in May 1964.

Wonderful Coaltown, who would have been a veritable world-beater if not for Cy, passed away in June 1965. Ponder, racing's ultimate stretch-runner, died in October 1958. Cy's father, Bull Lea, died in June 1964; his mother, Hydroplane II, in February 1958.

All of Citation's regular jockeys—Eddie Arcaro, Al Snider, Doug Dodson, and Steve Brooks—are also gone.

Big Cy remained robust and vigorous until the very end. His last baby, or foal, arrived in early spring of 1970. Appropriately, that baby was named Cy's Last Sigh. Just like daddy, the youngster was a winner.

And Cy literally breathed out his "last sigh" August 8, 1970. Citation was twenty-five years old. His remains are among forty-seven of Calumet Farm's greatest champions, male and female alike, at the stable's perma-nent graveyard in Kentucky, only one exactly of its kind.

The graveyard's centerpiece is a Kentucky Derby monument com-memorating Calumet's eight Derby heroes. Right with it is a statue of Bull

Lea with forty-seven graves of past equine greats fanning out in a semi-circle, a nostalgic, picturesque setting nestled among plantings, flowers, and trees. You're not a true racing fan unless you've visited Calumet Farm's Graveyard of Champions.

And when you do, station yourself, and a loved one if possible, directly in front of Citation's headstone. Listen if you will, listen carefully, and see if you can't hear the distant roar of when thousands cheered during those glorious days of yesteryear when the name *Citation* was precious and dear to the hearts of all sports fans young and old alike.

Citation was indeed proud to display his wares and strut his stuff as a world-renowned athlete during a time when the word "class" said it all. And if you can picture in your mind's eye his signet canter—neck arched and head bowed—you'd be also proud to be numbered among that myriad of sports fans who still hail Citation as "The Greatest Thoroughbred Who Ever Lived!"

THE END
(Well, not quite—read on for outtakes.)

Outtakes

$\mathcal{A}$ long with this writer, among those few remaining ones who saw Citation in all his glory was former Calumet farm secretary Margaret Glass. She's alive and well in Lexington, Kentucky, near her beloved Calumet Farm where she toiled devotedly for Warren Wright and Lucille Wright Markey for forty years, retiring in 1980. And she remains a fountain of lively information.

Like all humans involved in goings-on at Calumet, she knew Citation well; but then she was closely involved with all Calumet greats—she's the one who coined the expression: "Armed, Bewitch, and Citation were the ABC's of Calumet Farm." She kept meticulous files and statistics, chronicling Bull Lea's matchless record as sire, plus the remarkable exploits of his hundreds of sons and daughters, as well as family-related feats of other stable stars who were offspring of mares sired by Bull Lea.

For example, Tim Tam, winner of the 1958 Derby, was a son of Tom Fool out of Two Lea, the latter a daughter of Bull Lea. Also, though not owned by Calumet, the 1976 Derby winner Bold Forbes was out of a daughter of Commodore M., who was by Bull Lea.

In addition to owning and breeding two Triple Crown winners— Whirlaway (1941) and Citation (1948)—Calumet produced *eight* winners of the Kentucky Derby, and Margaret Glass's financial research is eye-opening: total purse winnings for those eight Derby winners by way of victory in the Churchill Downs classic—$744,200, a drop in the bucket by today's inflationary standards.

Speaking of inflation, did you know that Bull Lea, the greatest sire of his day, stood for a "bargain-basement" fee of $750 his first year at stud (1940)? That fee was reduced as a wartime concession in 1943 to a low of $250; gradually rose again when his services were available to outside breeders, but only a trade basis for outside bloodlines needed for Calumet mares. Glass said the understood value of those trades was $10,000.

Bull Lea was leading sire five times—1947, 1948, 1949, 1952, and 1953. And his twenty-fourth and last crop of seven foals arrived in 1964. The great progenitor died on June 16, 1964.

Citation's hallmark head bowed, arched neck canter was neither taught nor practiced. "He came by it naturally," confirmed Glass. "Others could be taught and coaxed to do it if deemed necessary, or if they'd cooperate. And the only other horse I know to whom that stance also came naturally was our own Alydar. The two of 'em—Citation and Alydar—would have made a super entry."

As reported, Citation soared to the top as world's leading money-winning thoroughbred ($924,620) with his "comeback" victory in the 1950 Golden Gate Mile, in which he also set a new world speed mark. He retired as racing's first thoroughbred millionaire with earnings of $1,085,760 and remained number one until passed by Nashua in the Camden Handicap on May 19, 1956. Citation's hard-achieved million status lost luster as inflation ballooned and purses swelled.

Affirmed became racing's first *two-million*-dollar winner in 1979, capturing the same Hollywood Gold Cup that pushed Citation over the million-dollar mark twenty-eight years earlier. Citation earned $100,000; Affirmed banked $275,000 with his victory. Subsequent money-earning champs included Spectacular Bid, John Henry, Alysheba, and the sport's current leader, Cigar. Money won isn't such a big deal anymore.

Recent happenings appear to confirm rather than dispute the oft-heard claim that "they don't make thoroughbreds like they used to"—great ones who emit class, speed, power, and durability in one special package. Cigar may have been one of few who came close. Point Given might have proved another.

Winning streaks and career-race longevity—Citation scoring sixteen straight, Colin fifteen, Man o'War fourteen, and Round Table eleven—including brilliant win streaks by Native Dancer, Spectacular Bid, Real Delight, Secretariat, Seattle Slew, Twilight Tear, Forego, Tom Fool, Affirmed, Swaps, and Alydar, in addition to Cigar, have now become few and far between. Cigar's equaling Citation's sixteen-straight wins in 1996 was achieved against mediocre competition, and, conspicuously, did not include the colt's three-year-old campaign and the prestigious Triple Crown.

Where have all the great ones gone?

Fusaichi Pegasus fell apart after winning the 2000 Kentucky Derby as the race's first favorite since Spectacular Bid in 1979, dashing hopes of superstar status. Silver Charm, Real Quiet, and game Charismatic failed consecutively in their Triple Crown quests. More recently, Monarchos incurred injury following his sterling victory in the 2001 Kentucky Derby. And Point Given, who sparkled in the 2001 Preakness and Belmont, plus the Haskell and the Travers, to rate potential "great-horse" ranking, also was felled by injury. Unlike Cy, Point Given's connections never thought twice about *not* returning him to active competition. Wise choice.

Citation's two-year (1947–48) record of twenty-seven wins and two seconds in twenty-nine starts, which included nineteen of twenty as a three-year-old of which seven were recorded against his elders, speaks for itself.

In April of 1968, Gulfstream Park staged a "Computer Race of the Century," designed to crown the greatest horse of all time to that date. It was a welcomed promotional event.

The complete records of all the great horses of the twentieth century 'til that time were fed into the machine—a "computerized" 1¼ miles title bout race on dirt—which then spit out the results—Citation won with Man o'War second!

Hawthorne Race Course in 1981 staged a "human-computerized" race, similar but not identical. This race included Secretariat, Seattle Slew, Affirmed, Forego, and Spectacular Bid, all of whom raced after the initial 1968 joust. The "human" aspect involved "polling" thirty-five turf experts in and around the Midwest area, in which each writer, author, or radio-television commentator would submit his 1-2-3 choices—five points to the number one selection, three to number two, and two to number three.

Citation won again; this time Secretariat edged Man o'War and Kelso for second. The result was a mite controversial, stirred some lively debate, especially among the younger horsey set, whose minds and hearts were still filled with Secretariat's 1973 Triple Crown.

Hawthorne celebrated its hundredth anniversary as America's fifth oldest racing establishment with the 1991 Race of the Century sponsored by Amoco. Two young computer-savvy racing fans spearheaded the formidable project—in their animated race Secretariat nosed out Citation with Man o'War a close-up third.

So much for computers and surveys.

However, your author welcomes the intimidating task of one final "fantasy race" involving twenty of the greatest thoroughbreds of all time (this author's opinion, of course). Once before we concocted a similar race— the "2000 Kentucky Derby Dream Race," which was published in the January–February 2000 *Backstretch Magazine*, a quality read for horsemen and fans of the thoroughbred sport.

That race, while intriguing, spotlighted *only* Kentucky Derby winners. As a result, it lacked Man o'War, Kelso, Phar Lap, Seabiscuit, Forego, Nashua, Equipoise—even Dr. Fager, Cigar, and John Henry were conspicuously absent.

With apologies to such wondrous fillies and mares as Real Delight, Ruffian, Regret, Personal Ensign, Gallorette, Twilight Tear, Bewitch, Top

Flight, Busher, Genuine Risk, and Lady's Secret—they truly rate a Fantasy Race all their own—here's the field for our all-time title bout (listed alphabetically and in post position order):

1. Affirmed
2. Bold Ruler
3. Buckpasser
4. Citation
5. Count Fleet
6. Exterminator
7. Forego
8. John Henry
9. Kelso
10. Man o'War
11. Nashua
12. Native Dancer
13. Phar Lap
14. Round Table
15. Seabiscuit
16. Seattle Slew
17. Secretariat
18. Spectacular Bid
19. Swaps
20. Whirlaway

All carry 126 pounds. Distance: 1¼ miles. Track: Fast.

Apologies again are in order, this time to a bevy of outstanding male horseflesh, any of whom could have made the cut into the above field: Graustark, Colin, Sysonby, Coaltown, Meadowlake, Armed, Alysheba, Easy Goer, Assault, Gallant Fox, War Admiral, Sunday Silence, Cigar, Dr. Fager, Equipoise, Silver Charm, Thunder Gulch, and Point Given. Any others?

Our fantasy race is loaded with speed—Affirmed, Bold Ruler, Count Fleet, Seattle Slew, and Swaps.

And stalkers: Buckpasser, Citation, Exterminator, Kelso, Man o'War, Nashua, Native Dancer, Round Table, Secretariat, and Spectacular Bid.

Finally, the whirlwind finish of Forego, John Henry, Phar Lap, Seabiscuit, and Whirlaway.

All set for a mesmeric, once-in-a-lifetime confrontation, truly racing's seventh heaven:

"And they're off!"

"And to a beautiful start too, as twenty of the greatest horses of all time burst from the gate virtually in line . . . but it's Bold Ruler on the inside taking the lead . . . Citation is right there between horses second, but on the outside Swaps is also full of run . . . so is Seattle Slew, and, from between horses, Count Fleet and Man o'War also have their running shoes on today. . . .

"Here's the charge down the stretch for the first time, and Swaps joins Bold Ruler . . . they're both full of themselves, each under a snug hold, with Man o'War dropping in behind them third . . . Count Fleet moves between horses fourth . . . Citation now back to fifth . . . Affirmed scoots through along the rail sixth . . . Seattle Slew is steadied a bit seventh . . . Native Dancer is also in close quarters eighth . . . followed by Buckpasser ninth . . . then a gap of two . . . Kelso hugs the rail tenth, with Round Table alongside eleventh . . . Phar Lap races strongly twelfth, less than nine lengths off the lead . . . then it's Exterminator, followed by Forego, Secretariat, John Henry, Nashua, Seabiscuit, Spectacular Bid, then a gap of three, and Whirlaway, as is his wont, is twentieth and last . . . maybe eighteen lengths from the front . . . and they've got a mile to run as Swaps, Bold Ruler, and Count Fleet lead the pack into the clubhouse turn. . . .

"Now Man o'War asserts himself . . . boldly he sweeps three wide to take command . . . Swaps takes up the chase second . . . Bold Ruler skims the rail third . . . Affirmed mounts an early challenge . . . he's four deep, and right with him goes Seattle Slew . . . Kelso also joins the fray . . . Citation losing ground slightly, he's still right there in seventh . . . Count

Fleet forced back eighth . . . right behind him, there goes Phar Lap, surging earlier than expected . . . Secretariat also is on a power-sweep to the middle of the track . . . yet to be heard from are Seabiscuit, Nashua, Forego, and John Henry . . . and shuffled further back are Buckpasser, Exterminator, Round Table, Native Dancer . . . and Spectacular Bid and Whirlaway are going to have to do it—if they can?—from last and next-to-last.

"Now they swing around the far turn, less than a half mile to run in the race . . . and Man o'War's in full command . . . he dares 'em all 'to catch if catch can.'

"There goes Kelso with a flourish . . . Count Fleet's also charging . . . as is Nashua . . . Citation shakes loose from between horses . . . Seattle Slew's on a tear . . . and here comes Secretariat, he's for real . . . hey, we've got horses coming from everywhere!

"Here they come, spinning out of the turn . . . Man o'War cuts the corner a length and half in front . . . Kelso driving between horses second . . . Secretariat's flying third . . . Citation boils inexorably between horses fourth . . . Count Fleet's charging fifth . . . and Nashua, Forego, Seattle Slew, Round Table, and Whirlaway—they're all coming like gangbusters. . . .

"They're at the eighth pole . . . and they're ganging up on Man o'War . . . he digs in bravely . . . Kelso's running at him . . . Secretariat is on a roll third . . . Citation's mowing 'em down fourth . . . Count Fleet hangs tough along with Seattle Slew, Nashua, Swaps, and Spectacular Bid . . . and out in the middle of the track Round Table and Whirlaway are flying, but it might be too late!

"A hundred yards to come . . . it's Kelso clinging to the rail, Secretariat between horses, and, on the outside, three deep, here's Citation . . . he means business . . . and he's not to be denied.

"Here comes the wire . . . put a ring around Citation! Cy wins it a long neck . . . Secretariat is right there second . . . with Kelso nosing out Man o'War for third . . . and right behind this classy quartet come Count Fleet, Nashua, Seattle Slew, Spectacular Bid, Swaps, Round Table, Whirlaway, Native Dancer, Phar Lap, Forego, Affirmed, Buckpasser, John Henry, Exterminator, Seabiscuit, and Bold Ruler."

Citation, the winner! You expected less?

What a race! Excitement, action aplenty, from start to finish, only fifteen lengths separating first from last.

The official Fantasy Race chart follows:

All-Time Thoroughbred Great Fantasy Race
Eighth Race, Dreamtime Downs, Twenty-First Century
1¼ Miles Inaugural Running Phil Georgeff's Fantasy Race
Matching Twenty of the Greatest Thoroughbreds of All Time

P.P.	Horse	Start	½	¾	Stretch	Finish
4	Citation	2	5	7	4	1 nk
17	Secretariat	14	14	9	3	2
9	Kelso	11	10	6	2	3 ns
10	Man o'War	6	3	1	1	4¾
5	Count Fleet	5	4	8	5	5 hd
11	Nashua	18	16	11	7	6
16	Seattle Slew	4	7	5	6	7¾
18	Spectacular Bid	19	19	13	9	8
19	Swaps	3	1	2	8	9 ns
14	Round Table	12	11	12	14	10
20	Whirlaway	20	20	19	15	11 1
12	Native Dancer	9	8	10	11	12 1
13	Phar Lap	8	12	14	12	13¾
7	Forego	17	14	15	17	14¾
1	Affirmed	7	6	4	13	15 nk
3	Buckpasser	10	15	17	16	16¾
8	John Henry	15	17	18	18	17¾
6	Exterminator	16	13	20	19	18½
15	Seabiscuit	13	18	16	20	19 2
2	Bold Ruler	1	2	3	10	20

Trackman's Comment: Citation was away alertly, and, confidently ridden, threaded his way between and around rivals, collared the leaders in the final seventy yards, then determinedly outgamed Secretariat in a historic finish. The latter, unhurried early, uncorked an eye-popping surge in mid-stretch, only to succumb to the winner in the final yards. Kelso unleashed a powerful charge leaving the half, grabbed command between calls, strove mightily, simply could not withstand the top pair. Man o'War, as always the personification of speed and class, looked home free turning into the stretch, tried gamely, was simply outrun as the finish loomed. Count Fleet raced bravely and evenly throughout. Nashua, Spectacular Bid, Round Table, and Whirlaway finished courageously. Seattle Slew turned in an heroic effort. Swaps was burned by his early duel with Bold Ruler.

Citation was in a class by himself. All the others were valiant.

References

ESPN. *Citation*. Sports Century telecast, December 2000.

Glass, Margaret. The Calumet Story (updated 1999). Unpublished manuscript.

Hirsch, Joe. *Daily Racing Form*, July 4, 1997. "Racing Greats of all Time."

Hollingsworth, Kent. "Citation," *The Blood-Horse*, June 2, 1984.

Milbert, Neil. *Arlington Park* (Chicago: Arlington Park Race Track, 1986).

Polzin, Elmer. Personal memoirs, 1990.

Robertson, William H. P. *The History of Thoroughbred Racing in America* (New York: Bonanza Books, 1963).

Smith, Pohla. *Citation*. Thoroughbred Legends, no. 3 (Lexington, Ky.: Eclipse Press, Division of *The Blood-Horse*, Inc., 2000).

Stone Reeves, Richard, and Patrick Robinson. *Decade of Champions* (New York: Fine Arts Enterprises, Ltd., 1980).

Winants, Peter. *Racing Review*, January 5, 1973. "Citation"

Personal conversations since the early 1940s with Ben and Jimmy Jones; jockeys Eddie Arcaro, Steve Brooks, Doug Dodson, N. L. Pierson, Robert "Bobby" Baird, Johnny Longden; race track officials Benjamin F. Lindheimer, Bob Henderson, Tommy Trotter; sportscaster Jack Drees; and aforementioned journalists.

Index